Praise for **NECROPOLITICS**

"Before Covid-19, Mbembe's picture of a world enchanted by its own practice of mass murder-suicide in the name of democracy and liberal values seemed accurate enough. After, or during, or whenever we are, Mbembe's prescience is horrifying, comforting, and absolutely necessary."
—Aria Dean, *Artforum*

"The appearance of Achille Mbembe's *Necropolitics* will change the terms of debate within the English-speaking world. Trenchant in his critique of racism and its relation to the precepts of liberal democracy, Mbembe continues where Foucault left off, tracking the lethal afterlife of sovereign power as it subjects whole populations to what Fanon called 'the zone of non-being.' Mbembe not only engages with biopolitics, the politics of enmity, and the state of exception; he also opens up the possibility of a global ethic, one that relies less on sovereign power than on the transnational resistance to the spread of the death-world."   —Judith Butler

"This book establishes Achille Mbembe as the leading humanistic voice in the study of sovereignty, democracy, migration, and war in the contemporary world. Mbembe accomplishes the nearly impossible task of finding a radical path through the darkness of our times and seizes hope from the jaws of what he calls 'the deadlocks of humanism.' It is not a comforting book to read, but it is an impossible book to put down."
—Arjun Appadurai

Praise for **CRITIQUE OF BLACK REASON**

"With *Critique of Black Reason*, Achille Mbembe reaffirms his position as one of the most original and significant thinkers of our times working out of Francophone traditions of anti-imperial and postcolonial criticism.

His voyages in this book through a painstakingly assembled archive of empire, race, slavery, blackness, and liberation—an archive that Mbembe both reconfigures and interrogates at the same time—produce profound moments of reflection on the origin and nature of modernity and its mutations in the contemporary phase of global capital. A tour de force that will renew debates on capital, race, and freedom in today's world."

—Dipesh Chakrabarty

"Achille Mbembe speaks authoritatively for black life, addressing the whole world in an increasingly distinctive tone of voice. This long-anticipated book resounds with the embattled, southern predicament from which its precious shards of wisdom originate. There is nothing provincial about the philosopher's history it articulates. Mbembe sketches the entangled genealogies of racism and black thought on their worldly travels from the barracoons and the slave ships, through countless insurgencies, into the vexed mechanisms of decolonization and then beyond them, into our own bleak and desperate circumstances."   —Paul Gilroy

"Achille Mbembe has placed the discourse of 'Africa' squarely in the center of both postmodernism and continental philosophy. Every page of this signifying riff on Kant's *Critique of Pure Reason* is a delight to read. African philosophy is currently enjoying a renaissance, and Mbembe is to its continental pole what Kwame Anthony Appiah is to its analytical pole. Every student of postmodernist theory should read this book."

—Henry Louis Gates Jr.

BRUTALISM

THEORY IN FORMS

A series edited by Nancy Rose Hunt, Achille Mbembe, and Todd Meyers

BRUTALISM

ACHILLE MBEMBE

Translated by

STEVEN CORCORAN

Duke University Press

Durham and London

2024

Brutalisme © Éditions La Découverte, 2020

English translation © 2024 Duke University Press

All rights reserved

Printed in the United States of America on acid-free paper ∞

Project Editor: Ihsan Taylor

Typeset in Arno Pro by Westchester Publishing Services

Library of Congress Cataloging-in-Publication Data

Names: Mbembe, Achille, [date] author.

Title: Brutalism / Achille Mbembe.

Other titles: Brutalisme. English | Theory in forms.

Description: Durham : Duke University Press, 2024. |
    Series: Theory in forms | Includes index.

Identifiers: LCCN 2023022615 (print)

LCCN 2023022616 (ebook)

ISBN 9781478025580 (paperback)

ISBN 9781478020875 (hardcover)

ISBN 9781478027720 (ebook)

Subjects: LCSH: Social evolution—Philosophy. | Civilization,
    Modern—21st century. | Civilization—Philosophy.

Classification: LCC HM626 .M42 2024 (print) | LCC HM626
    (ebook) | DDC 303.4—dc23/eng/20230612

LC record available at https://lccn.loc.gov/2023022615

LC ebook record available at https://lccn.loc.gov/2023022616

This book received a publication subsidy from Duke University Press's Translation Fund, a fund established by Press authors who donated their book royalties to support the translation of scholarly books.

To my three countries, in equal measure

CONTENTS

PREFACE

I have borrowed the concept of brutalism from architectural thought, though in my view, the category is an eminently political one. How could it be otherwise, for there is in architecture an element that is political from the outset—the politics of materials, inert or otherwise, that are sometimes presumed to be indestructible. Conversely, what is politics if not a capture performed on elements of all orders, to which one strives to give a form, if needed through the use of force, an exercise in torsion and re-structuring if ever there was one?

Second, architecture is political insofar as it inevitably sets into motion a tension, or, as it were, a redistribution of the force factor between acts of demolition and acts of construction, often from what one might call build-ing blocks. Politics is, in turn, an instrumented practice, a work of assem-bling and organizing, forming and redistributing, including spatially, of living bodily—but for the most part immaterial—ensembles. Indeed, it is at the point of juncture of materials, the immaterial, and corporeality that we ought to locate brutalism.

Situated at the point of articulation between materials, corporeality, and the immaterial, architecture and politics are not only part of the world of symbols and language. They are also constitutive of the technical world, the world of objects and bodies, and above all, of divisions (*découpages*), of that which must be cut into or out, weakened and molded, forged and erected, in short, verticalized and thereby set going. Their point of inter-vention is the material zone as a region of the living, this incandescent crossroads of intensities whose raw materiality, in the figure of fire, concrete, lead, or steel, is the fillip that immediately dismisses the old oppositions between, on the one hand, a world of the spirit and the soul and, on the other hand, a world of objects. It is this raw material that is subjected to the metamorphic processes of forcing and crushing, ransacking, incision, dissection, and if necessary, mutilation.

Architecture and politics thus concern the orderly arranging of materials and bodies. They deal in quantities, volumes, expanses, and measures as well as in distributing and modulating force and energy. One of brutalism's concrete traces is the erection of the vertical into a privileged position, whether this case is carried out on bodies or on materials. But architecture and politics are mostly about working with, against, on, over, and through elements.

In this book, I invoke the notion of brutalism to describe an age gripped by the planetary-scale pathos of demolition and production of stocks of darkness, in addition to all sorts of waste, leftovers, traces of a gigantic demiurgy. It is not a matter of writing the sociology or political economy of brutalization, and even less so of outlining a historical picture of it. Nor is it a matter of looking into the violence, or forms of cruelty and sadism, in general, that tyranny has produced. Making use of the extraordinary wealth of already available socio-ethnographic material (to which I shall refer liberally in the reference notes), the objective is to make *cross sections*, thus enabling a *fresco* to be painted, so that questions can be raised differently and, above all, to say a word on what is specific to this age, which has been given many names, and in which three central lines of questioning dominate: calculation in its computational form; the economy in its neurobiological form; and the living beset by a process of carbonization.

At the core of these questions are transformations of the human body and, more generally, the future of "populations" and the technological mutation of species, human or otherwise. Yet the harm and injuries that these shifts cause are not accidental or simply collateral damage. If, in fact, humanity has been transformed into a geological force, then we cannot speak of history as such. All history, including the history of power, is now, by definition, geo-history. By brutalism, I thus refer to the process through which power as a geomorphic force is constituted, expressed, reconfigured, and reproduced through acts of *fracturing* and *fissuring*. I also have in mind the molecular and chemical dimension of this process. Is toxicity, or the multiplication of chemical substances and dangerous waste, not a structural dimension of the present? These substances and types of waste (including electronic waste) attack not only nature and the environment (air, soils, water, food chains) but also bodies that are thereby exposed to lead, phosphorous, mercury, beryllium, liquid refrigerants.

By means of these political techniques of fracturing and fissuring, power is re-creating not only the human but the species. The matter to which it endeavors to give form (anew) to, or to transform into new species, is treated similarly to that which one utilizes when attacking rocks and schists, dynamiting them for the purposes of gas and energy extraction. Thus seen, contemporary powers more than ever have the function of making extraction possible. For this to occur, an intensification of repression is required. Part of it involves boring bodies and minds. The law—as the state of exception becomes the norm and the state of emergency, permanent—is being maximally used to multiply states of lawlessness and to dismantle all forms of resistance.

We ought to add to the logics of fracturing and fissuring those of exhaustion and depletion. Once again, fracturing, fissuring, and depletion concern not only resources but also living bodies that are exposed to physical exhaustion and to all sorts of sometimes invisible biological risks (acute poisoning, cancers, congenital anomalies, neurological disturbances, hormonal disruptions). The living in its entirety is, reduced to a layer and a surface, undergoing seismic threats. The reflections that follow aim precisely at this dialectic of demolition and "destructive creation," insofar as it targets human bodies, nerves, blood, and brains, just as it does the entrails of time and the Earth. Brutalism is the name given to this gigantic process of eviction and evacuation as well as to the draining of vessels and emptying of organic substances.

Through this name (brutalism), the effort is to provide what might be called a thought-image. The aim is to paint the contours of a primordial (matrix) scene, or at least a backdrop against which a myriad of situations, histories, and actors stand out. Yet regardless of these differences, and beyond particular identities, fracturing, and fissuring, processes of draining and depletion obey the same master code: the universalization of the black condition, the becoming-black of a very large swathe of humanity a humanity that henceforth faces excessive losses and a profound syndrome of exhaustion of its organic capacities.

This question of reserves of darkness and, consequently, of figures of time and power has haunted me since at least the last quarter of the twentieth century. In my thinking, it has always been bound up with the question of what we have become, what we might have been able to accomplish, and what we might have been—whether Africa, the planet, humanity, or the living, more generally. Far from yielding to melancholy, it is a matter of laying the foundations for a critique of the relationship between memory, potentiality, and *futurity*.

The issue has been to understand why all that which circulates, all that which goes by, beginning with time's passing, remains the ultimate stake for all power. All power indeed dreams, if not to make itself time, at least to annex it and colonize its intrinsic properties. In its abstraction, is the specificity of time not its being inexhaustible, objectively incalculable and, above all, inappropriable? Further still, it is indestructible. It is perhaps this last property—indestructibility—that fascinates power in the last instance. This is why all power, in its essence, aspires to make itself time or, at least, to ingest its qualities. At the same time, power is, from beginning to end, a technique of instrumentation and construction. It needs putty, concrete, cement, mortar, beams or girders, stones to crush, lead, steel—and bodies made of bones, flesh, blood, muscles, and nerves. Demolition is truly a gigantic task.

These practices of demolition, breaking, stone throwing, ransacking, and crushing lie at the core of brutalism in its political meaning. They are not the exact equivalents of devoration, autophagy, or cannibalism (regardless of the definition given to these terms) that are habitually located in ancient or primitive societies. Driven simultaneously by old machines and by the most advanced computational technologies, they are profoundly futurist and have come to bear a singular weight on the Earth's future. They have a geological, molecular, and neurological dimension.

I became aware of this as I was writing the present book: some of my reflections over the last quarter of the twentieth century have focused on the practice and experience of power as an exercise in the demolition of beings, things, dreams, and life in the modern African context. I was struck by the amount of energy devoted, especially at the bottom of the social ladder, to interminable acts of patching up, or even repairing of that which has been broken, or simply engulfed by rust, left in a state of prolonged abandonment.

It slowly dawned on me that many practices of demolition had nothing accidental about them. In many cases, we were coming up against modes of regulating living things that functioned by increasing the number of apparently intolerable situations, sometimes absurd and inextricable, often unbearable. This was because such contexts were ruled by the law of impossibility and demolition. As my work became subject to multiple reappropriations in various contexts, what at first appeared to me as a feature of what I was calling the postcolony began to lose its singularity. I understood that this plot had a scope far broader than the African continent. The latter was, in truth, only a laboratory of mutations of a planetary order. Since then, I, along with others, have set down to work on this planetary turn of the African predicate and its counterpart, the African future of the world.

The age truly is one of the forge and the hammer, ember and anvil, the blacksmith being perhaps the last avatar of the great historical subjects. A vast enterprise of occupying territories, of seizing hold of bodies and imaginaries, and of disassembly, unlinking, and demolition is underway. It is leading, pretty much everywhere, to "states of emergency" or "exception" that are expeditiously extended and made permanent. Contemporary modalities of demolition are crystallizing, profoundly putting into question the classic dichotomies form/matter, matter/materials, material/immaterial, natural/artificial, and end/means. A logic of permutations, convergences, and multiple conversions has replaced that of oppositions. Matter is no longer fundamentally available and docile. It is there only as co-constituted on the basis of a heterogeneity of matrixes and connections.

A change of age is unquestionably underway, as well as a change of condition engendered through transformations to the biosphere and technosphere. This process, unprecedented in the shocks it is triggering, is planetary. Its goal is to precipitate the mutation of the human species and accelerate its transition to a new condition, at once plastic and synthetic, and consequently also pliable and extensible. To arrange the transition toward a new earthly dispensation (a new nomos of the Earth), society must indeed be abolished, or at least sculpted and eventually replaced by a nanoworld whose devices are cellular, neuronal, and computational. As a world of plastic tissues and synthetic blood, it will be peopled with half-natural, half-artificial bodies and entities. In a final gesture of hybridization of matter and mind, the human must then be repatriated to the junction point of the material, the immaterial, and the incorporeal, as it effaces, once and for all, the trace of clay that has been inscribed on humanity's forehead and face ever since the Earth welcomed it on its surface and in its entrails.

Brutalism's ultimate project is to transform humanity into matter and energy. The focal point of the book bears singularly on the monumentality of this project. The undertaking is vast, since it is not only the architecture of the world that must be remodeled but the tissue of the living itself and its diverse membranes. It is clear, then, that the reflections contained in this book essentially make up a long argument for a new planetary consciousness and the refounding of a community of humans in solidarity with the living in its entirety. Without a struggle, no belonging to a common soil, tangible, palpable, and visible, will occur. But, as Frantz Fanon sensed, authentic struggle is, in its primacy, a matter of reparation, beginning with the repairing of that which has been broken.

ACKNOWLEDGMENTS

If this argument for a new politics of reparation has any merit at all, I owe it to the solicitude of many friends and institutions, beginning with the Witwatersrand Institute for Social and Economic Research (WISER) in Johannesburg, where I have benefited from extraordinary freedom and incomparable working conditions since 2001. I express my gratitude to the Institute's director, Professor Sarah Nuttall, and to my colleagues Keith Breckenridge, Isabel Hoffmeyr, Sherine Hassim, Pamila Gupta, Jonathan Klaaren, Hlonipha Mokoena, Richard Rottenburg, Adila Deshmukh, and Najibha Deshmukh.

The Ateliers de la pensée held in Dakar have been a bona fide laboratory, the site of sustained dialogues with Felwine Sarr, Elsa Dorlin, Nadia Yala Kisukidi, Françoise Vergès, Abdurahmane Seck, and Bado Ndoye. I have benefited from the hospitality of many institutions and circles abroad. In particular, from the Jakob-Fugger Zentrum at the University of Augsburg, the Chair Albertus Magnus at the University of Cologne, the Institute for the Analysis of Change in Contemporary and Historical Societies at the Catholic University of Leuven, the Litteraturhuset in Oslo, the Franklin Humanities Institute at Duke University, the Whitney Humanities Center at Yale University, the Gerda Henkel Stiftung in Düsseldorf, the Ernst Bloch-Zentrum in Mannheim, Thalia Theater in Hamburg, the Düsseldorfer Schauspielhaus, the Maison du banquet et des générations in Lagrasse, the research unit LLCP (contemporary logics of philosophy) and the UMR LEGS (research unit in gender and sexuality studies) at the University of Paris 8–Vincennes-Saint-Denis, and the Forum Philo Le Monde Le Mans at Le Mans University.

As in the past, I have been able to count on the loyal friendship and unfailing support of David Goldberg, Paul Gilroy, Jean and John Comaroff, Charlie Piot, Ian Baucom, and Éric Fassin. Les Éditions La Découverte, Stéphanie Chevrier, Pascale Iltis, Delphine Ribouchon, and Bruno Auerbach afforded me great encouragement.

Fragments of chapters have been published in various formats in *Le Débat, Esprit, Le Monde,* and AOC.

INTRODUCTION

No matter how much we pretend that technological acceleration and transitioning to a computational civilization can pave the way to salvation anew, in truth, it is as if the short history of humanity on Earth has already been consummated.[1] Time itself might have lost all potentiality. With the system of nature now so out of kilter, it might be left to us merely to contemplate the world's end.[2] The task of thought then consists simply in announcing it. Hence the current rise to power of all sorts of eschatological narratives and the discourse of collapsology.

Combustion of the World

Collapsology truly risks dominating the decades ahead. Multiple anxieties backdrop its spread. On the one hand, the predatory reflexes that marked the first phases of capitalism's development are being honed everywhere, as the machine wrests free from all moorings or arbitration and seizes the living itself as its raw material.[3] On the other hand, from the point of view of the production of signs that speak to the future, we keep going round in circles. In the North in particular, old imperialist impulses now combine with nostalgia and melancholy.[4] This is because, stricken with moral lassitude and boredom, the center is now being irremediably gnawed at by the aggravated desire for a border and the fear of collapse. For this reason, we see barely disguised calls not for conquest as such, but for secession.[5]

If the mood is one of withdrawal and closure, it is partly because we no longer believe in the future.[6] With time having exploded, and duration having been evacuated, all that counts now is emergency.[7] The Earth is held to be irremediably contaminated.[8] We no longer expect anything, except the end itself. Besides, the norm, our common condition is more and more one of the living of life at the extremes. The concentration of capital in the hands of the few has never before attained the astronomical levels that it has today.[9] On a planetary scale, a devouring plutocracy has never stopped playing here and elsewhere at capturing and sequestering humanity's goods and, soon, all living resources.[10]

At the same time, the heightened risk of a dizzying loss of social condition affects entire strata of society.[11] Until quite recently, such strata had had the possibility of changing status and experiencing upward mobility. Now that the race to the bottom runs at full tilt, however, they are confined to a struggle to hold on to, and possibly to secure, what little is left to them. Yet, instead of blaming their setbacks on the system that causes them, they shift the threat of impoverishment wielded against them onto others more unfortunate than they, others who have already been denuded of their material existence, and they call for those who have already been stripped of almost everything to have even greater brutality meted out on them.[12]

This desire for violence and endogamy, together with the rise in forms of anxiety, takes place against the background of the awareness of our spatial finitude, which is much keener than ever before. The Earth is indeed contracting continually. In itself a finite system, it has reached its limits. The division between life and nonlife is all the more telling. Living bodies exist only in relation to the biosphere, of which they are an integral component. The biosphere is not only a physical, organic, geological, vegetal, or atmospheric reality. As many scientists are rediscovering, it is also interwoven with noumenal realities that lie at the source of existential meaning.[13] Some will come up against this experience of limits before others do. As a matter of fact, for many regions of the South, *having to re-create the living from the unlivable* is already a centuries-long condition.[14] What is new is that the ordeal is one these regions now share with many others, others that no wall, border, bubble, or enclave will be able to protect in the future.

The experience of the world's combustion and the headlong rush toward extremes is manifest not only in the vertiginous depletion of natural resources, fossil energies, or metals that support the material infrastructure of our existence.[15] It is also manifest, and in toxic form, in the water we drink, in the food we eat, in the technosphere, and even in the air we breathe.[16] It occurs in the transformations undergone by the biosphere, as evidenced by phenomena such as ocean acidification, rising water levels, the destruction of complex ecosystems—in short, climate change—and the flight reflex and hastened path to exodus of those whose living environments have been wrecked. In fact, the very food system of the Earth is impacted, and perhaps thus also is the ability of humans to make history with other species.

Even our conception of time is called into question.[17] While speeds continue to explode, and distances to be conquered, the concrete time of the flesh and breath of the world, and that of the aging Sun, is no longer infinitely extensible.[18] The countdown has begun.[19] Ours is an age of planetary combustion. An emergency is thus upon us. Yet many peoples of this Earth have already known the reality of this emergency, fragility, and vulnerability—of the ordeal facing us—peoples who have had diverse disasters inflicted on them, disasters that have marked their histories with exterminations and other genocides, with massacres and dispossession, with slave raids, forced displacements, confinement in reserves, carceral landscapes, colonial ravages, and skeletal remainders along mined frontiers.[20]

The possibility of a generic rupture thus hovers over the membrane of the world, subjected as it is to corrosive radioactivity.[21] This possibility is fostered, on the one hand, by today's technological escalation and the intensification of what I am here calling *brutalism*, and on the other, by logics of combustion and the slow, indefinite production of all kinds of ash clouds, acid rains, and so on—in short, of all the ruins among which those whose worlds have collapsed are forced to live.[22] Strictly speaking, the age of the world's combustion is a posthistorical age.[23] The prospect of this event has seen reruns of old races, starting with that to redistribute the Earth, to partition it anew. Old nightmares have also resurfaced, above all the human race's division into different species and varieties, each marked by their supposedly irreconcilable specificities.[24]

This is perhaps what explains the revival, on a planetary scale, of the desire for endogamy and of the kind of selection and sorting practices that stamped the history of slavery and colonization—two moments of rupture borne by the storm of steel and fed by the fuel that racism has been for modernity.[25] Unlike in those times, the selection drive is now based on manifold forms of nanotechnology.[26] It is no longer simply about machines.

This time it concerns something even more gigantic, something apparently limitless, that stands at the juncture of computation, cells, and neurons, and which seems to defy the very experience of thought.[27] Technology has become biology and neurology. It has become a figurative reality, shaking up all humans' fundamental relations with the world.

Everything is converging on an unprecedented unification of the planet. The old world of bodies and distances, of matter and expanses, of spaces and borders still persists, but through its metamorphosis. Further still, the now transformed horizon of calculation continues to see a spectacular return of animism, a cult of the self and of objects, while the almost indefinite extension of logics of quantification is leading to an unexpected acceleration of humanity's becoming artificial. This becoming-artificial of humanity and its counterpart, the becoming-human of objects and machines, may well constitute the real substance of what some today call the "great replacement."

Brutalism is the proper name for this apotheosis of a form of power without external limits or an outside, which dismisses both the myth of exit and that of *another world to come*. In concrete terms, what characterizes brutalism is the tight interweaving of several figures of reason: economic and instrumental reason; electronic and digital reason; and neurological and biological reason. Brutalism is based on the deep conviction that the distinction between the living and machines no longer exists. Matter, in the last instance, is the machine, which today means the computer taken broadly—the nerves, the brain, and all numinous reality. The spark of the living lies in it. The worlds of matter, machine, and life are henceforth one. As privileged vectors of the neovitalism that fuels neoliberalism, animism and brutalism accompany our transition to a new technical system, one more reticular, more automated, more concrete, and more abstract all at once. Under these conditions, can the Earth and the living be places not only of intellectual provocation, can they also be properly political concepts and *events for thought*?

The idea of a generic rupture, at once telluric, geological, and almost techno-phenomenal, can be found at the basis of modern Afro-diasporic thought. The idea is particularly manifest in the three currents of Afropessimism, Afrofuturism, and Afropolitanism. A theme impels each of these currents, namely that of the fallen seed that, landing on barren soil, struggles to survive by catching light rays in a hostile environment. Thrown into an unknown world and confronted with extremes, how can this seed germinate in a place that is so poor and where everything tends to desiccate? What root systems must be developed and what subterranean parts maintained? In each of these three currents of thought, and particularly in Afrofuturism, the invention of a new world is a vibratory act. This act proceeds from what we could call radical imagination.[28] The vibratory act is characterized by its straddling and going beyond the given and its constraints. This is how it participates in technical activity, where such activity is understood as the capacity to actualize, deploy, and manifest a reserve of power.[29]

In these three currents, Africa, beyond all its wounds, is that which will have paradoxically represented this reserve of power, or this *power in reserve*, as the sole power able to repatriate the human being not to Earth, but to the Cosmos. It is a potentially constitutive power, in its reality as well its form, in its vibrations as well as its matter, since it is liable to open onto an unlimited field of permutations and new structurations. In this essay, then, we set out from the hypothesis that *it is on the African continent, the birthplace of humanity, that the question of the Earth is now posed, and is posed in the most unexpected, complex, and paradoxical manner.*

In Africa, indeed, the prospects of decline are the most glaring. But it is also where we find the ripest chances for *creative metastasis*. Many planetary issues related to the question of reparations manifest themselves with the greatest acuity in Africa, starting with the reparation of the living, the persistence and durability of circulating human bodies in movement, of our accompanying objects but also of the *part of the object* now inseparable from what humanity has become. Africa is, as the Earth's *vibranium* (in the sense that others speak about a *sensorium*), also the place where all the categories that have served to envisage what art, politics, need, ethics, technology, and language are, face the most radical challenge, and where, simultaneously, paradoxical forms of the living emerge ceaselessly.

Moreover, this planetary turn of the African condition and the Africanization of the planetary condition will perhaps constitute the two major philosophical, cultural, and artistic events of the twenty-first century. It is indeed here, in Africa, that the great questions of the century, those that challenge the human race most immediately, are posed with the utmost urgency and acuteness—whether concerning the ongoing planetary repopulation, significant population movements and the imperative to deborderize, the future of life and reason, or further, the need to decarbonize the economy. Thanks to Africa's gigantic animistic reserves, all truly planetary thinking will inevitably have to confront the African sign.

The *Pharmakon* of the Earth

This is why the expression "African sign" ought to be understood as that which always exceeds what is given to be seen. As it happens, contemporary Afro-diasporic creation is engaged precisely in an attempt to show this excess and this beyond of appearances. It strives to imbue it with a particular energy. On the world stage, Africa is once again an object of intense psychic and oneiric activity, just as it was at the beginning of the twentieth century. From within and among its various diasporas, there is renewed interest in the dream of a nation that stands on its own feet, powerful, and unique among humanity, or of a civilization (the word is not out of place) capable of grafting a futuristic technological core onto thousand-year-old indigenous traditions.

In cinematographic productions, Africa is portrayed as a land that harbors unfathomable riches, an abundance of minerals and *raw materials* that undoubtedly make it the *pharmakon of the Earth*. In science fiction, dance, music, and novels, Africa evokes almost telluric rituals of resurrection, as when, on clay or buried under the red ocher soil, the king's body undertakes its journey to the ancestors, carried by the shadow of Osiris, and begins dialoguing with the dead. In fashion and photography, Africa seizes upon costumes of solar beauty, depicted in a deluge of colors and a tornado of forms.

In gleaming colors, bodies are making their appearance everywhere—from dark blue black to sun black, fire black, brown and yellowish black, clay black, copper and silver black, lunar black, volcanic black, and crater black. These are true hymns to multiplicity, proliferation, and dissemination. And what can we say about matter at the level of dreams and machines that are themselves sculpted in the image of the world of animals, birds, flora, fauna, and an ancient aquatic environment? And, above all, how can we not evoke woman? Is she not ultimately, when it comes to the world's duration and rebirth, the enigma and the secret alike?

Here in Africa, everything has always been plurally combined. Life itself has always been about learning to put together composite, disparate, and in a pinch, incompatible elements, then establishing equivalences between them, transforming the one into the other. In addition to this social polytheism, we must also add movement, *circulations*. Its apparently immobile expanses are actually worked by extensive movement, on the surface as well as subterraneanly.[30] Even duration is a mobile cut. There is thus a planetary becoming of Africa that forms the counterpart of the planet's becoming-African. The task of critique is to take this planetarity on board.

But, apart from this, every project to do with repairing the Earth will have to take into account what we, in this essay, call *humanity's becoming-artificial*. The twenty-first century has indeed begun with a spectacular return to animism.[31] This is no longer the nineteenth-century's animism, whose expression is modeled on the worship of ancestors; this new form is based instead on the cult of the self and of objects as our multiple doubles. More than ever, these latter constitute the sign par excellence of the unconscious states of our psychic life.

It is through their mediation that experiences of strong emotional intensity are increasingly felt, and what is not directly symbolizable now tends to be expressed. Humanity no longer stands and looks down from above on a system of objects. Humans are now traversed, from one side to the other, by objects that work us as much as we work them. There is a becoming-object of humanity that is the counterpart of the becoming-human of objects. We are the ore that our objects are tasked with extracting. The objects act with us, make us act and, especially, animate us.

Digital technologies have above all made possible the rediscovery of this power of animation as well as this psycho-prosthetic function. As a result, the new animism merges with electronic and algorithmic reason, which is its medium and its envelope, and even its motor. On the political level, this new animism is a knot of paradoxes. Virtualities of emancipation are to be found in its deepest core. It announces—perhaps—the end of dichotomies. But it is also able to serve as a privileged vector of the neovitalism that feeds neoliberalism. The new animist spirit must therefore be critiqued. The aim of this critique would then be to contribute to *protecting the living against the forces of desiccation* Therein lies the signifying force of the African object in the contemporary world.

This critique, undertaken on the basis of precolonial artifacts, also bears on matter and the mechanical principle itself. To this mechanical principle, the African object opposes that of breathing, as that which is specific to all forms of life. In fact, African objects have always been the manifestation of what lies beyond matter. While made of matter, they are actually a strident call to overcome and transfigure it. In African systems of thought, the object is a discourse on the beyond of the object. It acts, with other animated forces, within the framework of a regenerative and symbiotic economy. An uncompromising critique of this civilization in the process of immaterialization in which we bathe would gain inspiration from this history and this epistemology.[32] What do these latter teach us if not that life is not sufficient to itself? It is not inexhaustible. Neovitalism asserts that life will always survive all sorts of extreme and even catastrophic situations. We can thus, according to this logic, destroy life as much as we want.[33]

But neovitalism does not know how to live with loss. Within humanity's ongoing and frantic race to extremes, our shared lot is dispossession and deprivation. It is increasingly likely that that which is being taken is both invaluable and unable ever to be returned. The absence of any possibility of restitution or restoration will perhaps mark the end of the museum, understood not as the extension of a cabinet of curiosities but as the figure par excellence of humanity's past, one to which it would be a sort of silent witness. The antimuseum alone would remain—not the museum without objects or the fugitive residence of objects without museum, but a kind of attic of the future, whose function would be to welcome what must be born but is not yet there.

To anticipate a potential, as yet unaverred, presence, one that has not yet assumed a stable form, should perhaps be the starting point of any future critique whose horizon is to forge a common ground. It would be a question of starting not from absence, not from what is vacant, but from an *anticipatory presence*. For, it will be impossible, without this common ground and thus without deborderization, to repair the Earth or set the living back in circulation.

ONE
UNIVERSAL
DOMINATION

Over the last four centuries, the human species has embarked on a gigantic race, both irresistible and vertiginous, whose almost cosmic character is now being measured. Where to? We will have to wait until the end to answer this question with certainty. This race will have required the production of innumerable tools and pieces of machinery and the capture of the force inherent in matter in general as well as its transformation into energy and movement. At the confluence of body and movement, matter and energy, combustion, for example, made its appearance, as did foundry metals, and the world of motors, roaring parts, artificial organs, and moving machines, to which we must add imaginary activity—in short, that which André Leroi-Gourhan calls "series of gestures."[1]

Series of Gestures

In so doing, the human species has undergone decisive mutations, which, we may well suspect, have not stopped. The Cartesian fable of hydraulic man, made of bones, nerves, arteries, tendons, and veins, similar to the pipes of machines, has perhaps not materialized.[2] But the machine itself is not far from being endowed, if not with a consciousness, then at least with a nervous system. Superimposed on man-muscle we find the man-brain, the man-in-the-machine, the machine-in-the man, a volcanic burst at the point of convergence between organic creation and artificial creation.[3]

The goal of this race has been the conquest of the universe, the deployment of power, its forward thrust and unleashing for ends of universal supremacy. By "force" and "power," we ought to understand not only the spurting explosion of bodies and muscles, of fire, machines, electricity, rolling mills, gases, or even what have been new materials, or even the kind of "storm of steel" most effectively summed up by the idea of the bomb.[4] We must finally understand the term "force" as the *appropriation of the inappropriable*. Ultimately, is the appropriation of the inappropriable not modern technology's very object, its glowing sun? Further, is this not exactly why a tenacious tradition of Western metaphysics has made the inappropriable man's Other, that with regard to which there is no limit?[5]

It is significant that this tradition opposes "force" not to "weakness" but to language, the endowment that is presumed to make each human being a subject of speech. This tradition has long pursued the belief that language constitutes the specificity of the human species, that it is one of those singular traits that confers humanity with not only its uniqueness but also its genius. This genius seems attested by the exercise of reason but also by its corollary, the capacity for free renunciation. For, while possibilities for doing seemed limitless, the human being alone was deemed capable of self-limitation. Technology was *man's Other* because it was incapable of self-limitation. Thanks to and through language, humanity was alleged to have ascended to the summit of the living. Life itself was confounded with the capacity to perform salient acts, speech being first and foremost among them.

Further still, language is that which has enabled humanity to engage in the uniquely human pursuit of symbolic activity, that is, the production of meaning through ways of arranging signs. By mastering the knowledge of signs, humanity gave itself the means to give an account of itself and of reality, to inhabit space and time and, above all, to participate in the unveiling and manifestation of truth. It is thus through language that humanity had succeeded in lodging itself firmly in the universe and in obtaining its right to dwell there. That being so, language became its dwelling place, its fundamental shelter, or to put it in another way, its key to accessing being, meaning, and truth. But language was not everything.

Added to this power of symbolization was the ability to make all sorts of tools and instruments, as if the symbolic gesture had to respond to the technical gesture at all costs. Very early on, one variant of Western metaphysics established a distinction between these two gestures, as if they referred to two different empires, albeit ones that maintained complex relations between themselves.[6] Hence the division between, on the one hand, the regime of signs, meaning, ends, and value (language, culture, speech, and civilization) and, on the other hand, the realm of doing, the prosaic reign of tools and artifacts, of instruments, machines, and organs (technique). Humanity became convinced that one was at the service of the other. In its eyes, technology's reign could be justified only insofar as it was arranged to fulfill humanity's own destiny, namely, the unveiling and manifestation of truth. The symbolic order became the privileged site of this unveiling. Assuming it has been valid everywhere and for everyone, this great division now seems to be obsolete.

But what are we to make of one of Western metaphysics' central pillars, namely, the idea that humanity is not given but incessantly summoned to reactualize itself? For this is the other dogma that seems to have lost all credence. According to the hypostatized representation of humanity inherited from Greek idealism, the true destiny of the human species was the exercise of truth. The history of humanity itself would then consist in expanding the field of truth and its manifestation. Humanity's sojourn in the world had this meaning, it was that which made it the *last species*. As the ultimate frontier of biophysical evolution, there was nothing of the kind that could go beyond it. Being fundamentally ordained to produce symbols and distribute meaning thanks to language would distinguish it from all other beings as well as from other animate and inanimate entities. Its will to power was justified, then, and with it, its project to master the universe. It was alone regarded as capable of self-objectification, that is, of being simultaneously in and outside itself.[7] It alone generated life. Such was the myth, and it was dazzling.

More than any other, speculative Western thought maintained this myth in a maniacal way. It claimed that man had an *essence*. The ultimate end of our sojourn in the world was thus to coincide with this so-called essence. What depended on man's coinciding with his essence was the ultimate advent of the symbolic reign—that of truth. To be prevented from coinciding with its *essence*—and thus to experience scission indefinitely—represented the summum of man's tragedy. The design of universal mastery, by which freedom would be called to manifest itself, and truth to reveal itself, was thus thwarted. To remain master of the universe, to continue to sojourn in it, could have no other meaning, and technology was cast as a mere means to service this desire for accomplishment and plenitude.

So, if humanity made tools, it was not only to improve its material conditions or to satisfy its vital needs. Nor was this done only for humanity to then lose control of the tools themselves, or in an unheard-of reversal, to find itself under the influence of its own productions. From the point of view of humanity's sojourn in the universe, technology's function was eminently eschatological. By removing every impediment that stood between humanity and its essence, technology was meant to return humanity to itself. Technology would thus contribute to the ultimate and brilliant manifestation of the truth. History, so it was believed, had an end.

This end would be marked by the overcoming of alienation and the accomplishment of humanity. The "suppression of alienation" would pave "man's return to himself." The future itself, then, consisted in nothing other than this great "movement back to the origins," a prelude to "universal reconciliation," including the human being's reconciliation with nature.[8] Technology's eschatological function has misfired.

Pace an often-repeated claim, the unhindered and unrestrained deployment of an almost limitless power of manufacture has not led to a demythologizing of the world. Further, and despite what might be otherwise said, it is far from clear whether the human species has entirely detached itself from any connection with the rest of the living. The human has surely equipped itself with an externalized apparatus, but this has not led to a complete "deanimation" of the universe as such, if, indeed, this was ever the goal. It may be that some mysteries have been annexed and come to terms with. But there is still a way to go. Paradoxically, and perhaps unexpectedly, technology has reinscribed humanity in a movement of cosmic speed. It has precipitated the advent not so much of a sanitized universe incapable of accommodating different forms of life, but of a world in which no outside can exist any longer that is not calculable and therefore appropriable.

Capitalism has been one of the spurs to realizing this project of a *world without an inappropriable outside*. This enterprise has, strictly speaking, not been about separating the human from other forms of life—a claim that is repeated all too often. Nature's apprehension as an essentially animated and autonomous totality ought certainly to have subsided. To be sure, man did set himself the task of subjugating it and leaving his traces and imprints on it. But, further still, his placement thus at the center of the universe *and* the world was the outcome of a process of *calculating manufacture*. The fundamental structure of matter was finally to be penetrated and unveiled, the division between the human and the nonhuman abolished, and the radical vulnerability of the human replaced by the powers of the nonhuman. Technoscience and capitalism are this work's very demiurges.

As the twenty-first century has opened, the road to this *world of manufactured nature and manufacturable being* is largely marked out. Technology has finally succeeded in erecting itself as the ontological destiny of all living things.[9] The question is no longer whether irrationalism can go hand in hand with *technolatry*.[10] It is no longer whether to advocate technology or oppose it. That "anthropophagous technology" "violates" nature, debases or strips it, that it "devours men and everything human," that it uses their bodies as fuel and their blood as "coolant," or "murders life" (Ernst Niekisch)—we know all this; but there is more.

For many of our contemporaries, the reality of technology is now material *and* immaterial, psychological, personal, and internal. It no longer belongs only to the external world, as a membrane delimiting the border between an inside (humanity) and an outside (nature). It is our clinic, the place where the three constituent realities of the living world are manifested in their somber clarity, namely: the biological, organic, vegetable, and mineral reality of bodies of all kinds; the psychic reality of affects; and the social reality of exchanges, language, and interactions.[11] Today technology is that through which the activity of thinking and the work of representation, symbolization, and memorization are carried out. It also harbors a reserve of dreams. What account can we give of the hallucinatory experiences proper to the time and, as far as humans in particular are concerned, about the figurative activity, the mass of paranoid projections, or the preformed psychic material we so avidly consume?[12]

No one doubts that time is running out for us. Yet the human adventure on Earth, not to mention species mutations, are far from over. But the perspectives that they outline start from a point where the work of manufacturing a world without an incalculable and inappropriable outside is now real. Almost no split exists any longer between the human being and matter, the human and the machine, or the human and the technical object—the thing. Henceforth, the human being is not only coupled to the machine, to matter, and to the object. It is not only lodged in the folds and refolds of these latter. It has literally found in them the privileged places of its embodiment, and in return, they are in the process of taking on, if not the face of the human, then at least its mask. There is no longer technology, on the one hand, and what Western philosophy has called the "truth of being," on the other.[13] The two are now one and the same, one and the same dwelling. At least such is the new belief.

It might thus be said that the age of alienation, like the age of secularization, has come to a close. Technology is no longer simply a means, a tool, or even an end. It has become word and flesh. It is the epiphanic figure of the living—henceforth economy, biology, and eschatology all at once.[14] It has not only become religion in the sense of an unexpected marriage between the world of mysteries, the immaterial world, and the world of rationality.[15] You have only to see how, in the United States for example, the possibility of a technological sublime is reproduced in science fiction stories as well as in transhumanist prophecies. Very few people now doubt the New Age roots of digital society or the new forms of spirituality typical of informational neognosticism.[16] Discourses on nanotechnologies, biotechnologies, information technologies, or cognitive sciences all meet the conditions for a re-enchantment of the world.[17] The boundaries between religion, science, and mythology are not even clear-cut in contemporary engineering systems and techno-shamanism.[18]

After undergoing this mutation, another kind of existential test arises. Being comes to experience itself as an assembly indissociably human and nonhuman.[19] The transformation of force into the last word on the truth of being signals the entry in the last age of man, the historial age, that of fabricable being in a fabricated world. For this age, we have a name: brutalism, the big iron burden of our time, the weight of raw materials.[20]

It might be believed that brutalism is a moment of temporary intoxication. Completely unbounded, power would thus be provisionally free to indulge in bloodshed and carnage.[21] It would kill while also enduring, from time to time, the anger and rage of its targets in the form of riots or uprisings without tomorrow.[22] It would give itself over to waging expensive wars during which extreme violence is subject to trivialization. "Brutalization" ought thus to be understood as a "making savage," as the process of internalizing the violence of war that permits an acceptance of all its dimensions, including the most paroxysmal.[23]

But brutalism cannot simply be reduced to the horrors of war and other atrocities. It is, to a certain extent, the way in which the intoxication that carries power translates horror and extreme situations into the interstices of everyday life and, in particular, into the bodies and nerves of those it brutalizes. This process of miniaturization and molecularization is at the origin of a social metabolism. In such contexts, demolishing, killing, or being killed do not necessarily illustrate the return to some state of nature. The act of killing is not only done with rifles, guns, revolvers, or cutlasses. Little matter the weapon used—the one on whom death is inflicted, and who thus suffers it, falls in a heap, not without uttering a strangled cry. Seen from this angle, brutalism consists in the production of a sequence of things that, at a given moment, leads to a series of fatal outcomes.

Brutalism is also a way of administering force. It is based on the production of multiple and complex sequences, which almost inevitably result in an injury, a fatality, a strangled cry, the collapse of some human, or more generally, some being, and then everything revives, starts up again. This permanent recommencement or routinization is where, perhaps, its specificity lies. Still, we must add exultation and delight to the act of killing, that is, the pleasure of killing, of executing summarily, and sometimes en masse.[24] Or, simply, ice coldness.[25]

Murder, under the regime of brutalism, ceases to be an exception. The transposition of the state of war into a civil state leads to the normalization of extreme situations. The state itself proceeds to commit common-law crimes against civilians. The figure of the murderer, the gang leader, or the hired assassin is metamorphosed because instincts of cruelty are released, and fear seeps out of the bowels. The combat is carried out hand to hand, but it can also take place at a distance or at altitude. In all cases, bodies, or fragments of bodies, are made to explode into the air. And, always, screams, the power to take life or to blow it to smithereens.[26]

Brutalism is recognizable through the transfer of battlefield techniques to the civilian sphere.[27] By way of example, the police are happy to surround a crowd and use Flash-Balls against unarmed demonstrators. They are happy to use 44 mm rubber-bullet launchers and other "defensive" bullet launchers as well as so-called crowd dispersal grenades, blast grenades, and despite a prohibition on using them, they do not hesitate to employ GLI-F4 explosive tear gas grenades. In most cases, these devices are used as weapons of war.[28] Some of those who carry these weapons dress as civilians and hide in the crowd. Others are hooded, and still others wear motorcycle or skateboard helmets. They have no badges or armbands. They wound many demonstrators in the process. Were they aiming at the lower limbs, the upper limbs, or the torso? They happen to hit some demonstrators in the head. Other demonstrators will lose an eye. Still others will have their hands blown off.[29]

The aim is to blunt feelings of revulsion at killing, to break the prohibition on murder.[30] Previously censored, the instincts are now freed. War conducts become a value in themselves and are transferred to the civilian sphere. Dehumanization becomes standard practice, outbursts of violent impulses become legitimate and are even encouraged, the quest for the dissimilar reigns, and exculpatory techniques proliferate. Civilian life comes to be regulated by special units. "Cleansing" becomes a program. To eliminate individuals, or even finish off the wounded and kill prisoners becomes the norm, without so much as anyone speaking up to demand accountability.[31] But brutalism also functions on the basis of a derealization of both its facts and its effects. Derealization consists in hiding the hideousness of violence and especially of mass but molecular death.[32]

There is also the myth of male virility, of the Christ figure as a symbol of the new civic religion that, while functioning only through injury and even mass death, unceasingly and permanently shrouds such injury and death.[33] This is quite apart from the sexual dimension.[34]

Brutalism, considered from this angle, is not situated at the limit of the political. It is not merely an event that can be reduced to momentary circumstances. It is simultaneously political and aesthetic. As a politics, it sets in motion a social metabolism whose purpose is the annihilation or incapacitation of distinct population cohorts; and in the era of the Anthropocene, it accomplishes this annihilation or incapacitation in the mode of managing the most diverse kinds of waste.[35] Thus seen, brutalism is about naturalizing social war. War in general is presented not only as the expression of life itself but also as human existence's highest manifestation. The truth of life, according to this line of thinking, resides in its destructive force.[36] Destruction reveals its ultimate truth, is its main source of energy. It is simultaneously inexhaustible and uncontainable.

Brutalism, an age of unleashing of forces and propulsion, coincides with multiple forms of destruction of the living and habitats, but also of humanity's reinsertion into first nature. It also marks the entry into an age of depredation.

In his discussion of depredation, Friedrich Georg Jünger speaks, rather significantly, of hunger. The machine, he thinks, creates an impression of hunger that is acute, growing, unbearable. As a force that engages itself without consideration, it is sustained by the spectacle of hunger. What characterizes the machine in Jünger's eyes is not only its ugliness and its gigantism. It is also its insatiable hunger. Hunger sets it in motion, pushes it to destroy, devour, and swallow without respite or remainder. Besides, the machine can scarcely eliminate hunger, let alone get free of it or reach satiety. This is one reason why what characterizes technology is blind depredation, constantly amplified. But depredation also means extraction. This can be the extraction of coal, oil, and minerals. But irrespective of the object, depredation necessarily leads to devastation.

We see this explicitly at those sites where, once the ore has been extracted, the production process begins. A case in point is the plutonium production site in Hanford, Washington. As Jünger says, where uranium ore is processed into plutonium "you can only enter with rubber shoes and gloves, masks, ionization chambers and radiation-sensitive films, Geiger counters and alpha radiation counters; microphones, loudspeakers and alarm signals must mark the way. Radioactivity pollutes everything," not only for today and tomorrow but for millennia. Wherever there is radioactive waste, the Earth becomes uninhabitable for man. The air is darkened with smoke, and, he adds, "the rivers are contaminated, the forests, animals and plants are destroyed." As he advocates, nature can be protected from exploitation not by returning it to life, but by "setting apart large tracts of land, fencing them off, and placing them under a taboo, like museum pieces."[37]

In any event, the hour of the great linkup has sounded. On all sides, beings appear who can adapt to increasingly singular and unexpected hybridizations, without apparent biological coherence. They defy the limits of the natural. Almost everything has become duplication, grafting, and superposition. To all appearances, most uprisings no longer aim at overthrowing and dismantling the global apparatus of capture that capitalism has become. Instead, they are motivated by a complete liberation of flows of desire, in particular, the irrepressible desire to sell to buy and to buy to resell. The preference here is one for being captured, rather than simply bypassed and pushed aside.

Has the communism of affects—in the era of mass individualism and nanotechnologies—not replaced the community of interests and, in the process, led to the dilation of the self and an "infantile regression towards the origin," a senilization of minds?[38] Far from jamming the overall functioning of machines and other devices of subjection, this concertinaing and interlocking of childhood and old age has only accentuated the hold of these machines and devices. Escape seems possible no longer.

Extractions

In today's capitalism, we see this replacement, notably, with the manufacture of superfluous lives. Indeed, the proletarian reference is no longer sufficient. Work—and consequently the wage—no longer determines either questions of income and purchasing power or the living conditions of the various fractions of the masses. In other words, the masses are no longer structured by the centrality that the working class once occupied. For the racialized fractions of postindustrial societies, this fact is especially true. Mobility choices in these groups are often limited either to residing in the ghetto or to incarceration.[39] Today, the institution of the prison, like that of the border, plays a lead role in the global management of virulent and "excess" bodies.

The targets of this management are identified early on. Simply being a minor is enough. No other sleight of hand is needed than a law that reduces otherwise precocious lives to a stigma: murderer, rapist, aggressor, and predator. Thus is the door closed and one's destiny decided. Among the racialized fractions of industrial societies, laws against minors are based on the simple theory of moral poverty. As Jacky Wang explains, you have only to grow up "surrounded by deviant, delinquent and criminal adults, in a vulgar, violent, Godless, fatherless, and unemployed environment" to be suspected of "moral poverty," and, in the case of crime, to be liable to life imprisonment without the possibility of parole.[40]

The shift can therefore occur very quickly and over something trifling, such as shoplifting a can of beer from a storefront.[41] After such a microevent charged with significance (trespassing on private property), everything goes into overdrive: arrest, detention, court appearance, fine with a probationary period, including the wearing of a bracelet that one must rent or otherwise risk going to jail. This fake object of decoration is not free. It costs money, on top of which there is a monthly service fee and also a daily usage fee. Around the minor, criminalized body, a sovereign chain now links law and justice to a structure of depredation and systemic withdrawal.

The state and the market share the spoils. Is the fine paid to the municipality? Is a private company pocketing the other fees?

This is how brutalism works: according to a mode of extractions and subtractions from bodies. And because they are considered potentially virulent (and virulent because they are racialized), racialized bodies are targets of abduction and capture, apt for being ensnared by the law. In actuality, the law's function is not to render justice. It is to disarm these bodies and make them easy prey.[42] Brutalism does not function without a political economy of bodies. It is like a huge pyre. Racialized and stigmatized bodies constitute both its wood and its coal—its raw materials. Spaces of relegation and confinement, such as ghettos, have a rich endowment of bodily resources. These are quantitatively reliable, available, and accessible. You have only to know how to use them. As degraded as these energies may indeed be, such bodily resources and flows are like a freely available energy source that, left to its own devices, would anyhow dissipate. Instead of being entirely abandoned to entropy, the heat this energy produces and releases is thus captured, contained, and transformed into "work" through various extraction mechanisms. This is what defines brutalism as a form of *thermopolitics*. It subjects the debased bodies, energies, and lives of certain kinds of being to the work of fire—to slow combustion.

From the perspective of racialized bodies, what is called neoliberalism is in fact a gigantic device for pumping out and carbonizing. Like the minor who shoplifts a can of beer from a store, many have only their bodies as their sole source of income.[43] A syringe in the arm sucks out their blood, extracting a yellow liquid rich in protein, namely plasma, which the pharmaceutical industry puts to use. At the center of this system stands the prison. It then needs all the other mini devices to reproduce itself: the police, the municipality, the county, finances, taxes, fines. In short, it requires countless chains of subtraction. On top of this we should add all the equipment and interlinked activities required for the operation of places of detention: surveillance, probation services, monitoring equipment, and algorithmic devices. Taken together, these chains form an iron circle with neither outside nor inside. In circumstances where the outside becomes the inside and *vice versa*, what meanings could politics possibly take on?

Politics, we should recall, consists in the interminable effort to imagine and to create a common world and future. The starting point of the construction of this common world is the sharing, or distribution, of speech.

Like movement, speech is the expression of the living. Formal rules, institutions, and norms derive in part from a primary gesture, the gesture of speech in the form of address, a response to an address or, better still, deliberation. It is the distribution of speech that makes politics a force of exchange and connection. A sharing out, or distribution, certainly does not eliminate conflict. It does, however, make it possible to deal with disputes through something other than the sword: debate in the public sphere.

Liberal democracy, in today's world, is partly threatened by the growing number of men and women who no longer want to think and judge for themselves. As in previous times, many prefer to subcontract these faculties out, or delegate them, to authorities other than themselves, or even to machines. Paradoxically, the smaller the world becomes, the more the horizon of a common world recedes. And, in the absence of living speech, the idea that reason, law, or morality can open onto humanity's emancipation is constantly losing credibility. At the same time, everything seems to militate against even the slightest effort on the part of the subject to engage in self-limitation, and the utter renunciation of instinctual satisfaction almost never features on the agenda and is no longer among humanity's urgent tasks.[44]

Ideas of autonomy and critical reason are not only in retreat. They are losing their allure and their aura. Authority no longer invests one's ability to think and one's critical faculties. The fascination resides elsewhere. Many technological devices of our time arouse different sorts of desire. The need to believe in general, and especially in what we already believe in every way, does not cease to assert itself. Today's new technological devices not only contribute to accelerating fragmentation and to enclosing different parts of the social body. They complicate, more than ever before, this body's coalescing around anything other than the singular self.

The self is far more split than psychoanalysis considered it to be at the turn of the nineteenth and beginning of the twentieth centuries. This internal splitting has become more pronounced with the complexification of the logics of individuation and the appearance of multiple selves made possible by digital devices.[45] This fracturing of the individual subject is no longer considered to be part of its structural or even ontological fragility. That diverse figures can cohabit in the same individual, either simultaneously or successively, is now an obvious fact, and this constitutive fragmentation needs no psychological apparatus to disclose it. By contrast, the subject's uncertainty and versatility are now taken on board, along with idea that impulsive and involuntary acts are acceptable and that, eventually, it might be desirable to function using someone else's brain or a machine.

The subject may be multiple, but there is no need for endless labor to achieve its unity and synthesis. The technological devices of our time incite this at least. In fact, they work against all the great horizons that psychoanalysis, philosophy, and other systems of thought inherited from modernity delimited. These technological devices have taken control of both the clinical and political dimensions that were, until recently, in the hands of other bodies and authorities.

From this point of view, digital technologies have the peculiarity of liberating impulsive forces that at least a century of repression had helped to contain. Basically, the quest for unity and synthesis has given way to the quest for multiplication, which is perceived as creating surplus value. The physical person is not bound to correspond to the digital person. The key thing is the passage from one to the other.[46]

An unbridled desire for sensation has replaced repression. The focus is squarely on a rather spectacular renovating of the power of passions and the tumult of instincts. Religious and nationalistic passions are cases in point. The split in consciousness is no longer operative. Instead, this new cultural program involves interrogations into identity, the self, race, gender, and the nation. The program's aim is not to renounce the drives, but to re-anchor them in a self without outside mediation. From this viewpoint, identity comes to be perceived not as a never-ending construction to be constantly reinvented but as a fixed custom established once and for all. This new cultural state is the source of some of our time's most intractable dilemmas. That is how it goes with identity.

Identity Troubles

For, when it comes to identity and difference, it is one thing to be able to say freely who you are, to spell your own name, to say yourself where you come from, and where you are going. It is quite another to see yourself dressed in a mask that you are obliged to wear and that functions, from then on, as the double of the person who you really are.[47] But do we ever know who we really are? Does this not bear on the mystery that human beings will always remain and on the opacity that, ineluctably, makes us fugitives by definition?

The fact remains that, throughout the modern period, most identity struggles among subjugated peoples have sought to dispense with the ontological veil with which they were covered, thanks to the work of racism.[48] They were struggles for recognition and for self-affirmation, even self-determination. By presenting eminently progressive characters, these struggles participated in the great narrative of human emancipation. This was the case in the great struggles for the abolition of slavery; for women's rights, decolonization, and civil rights; or for the dismantling of apartheid.

Today, a deep malaise engulfs us. First, we still struggle to understand that there is no such thing as a history of man in general. Were it to exist, this history would be more than a long series of abstractions. It could only be written in blood. The reason is that, all told, such a history could only be that of a dominant subject, of a subject-master who in recent history has, as if by chance, often been white and male.[49] There is no history of the future except where human beings in situ set themselves in motion.[50]

Moreover, it is significant that many movements call for a continued proliferation of difference. Abstract universalism, steeped in colonialism and blended with racism, has fizzled out. It has ended up adopting the form of this master-subject who, in his rage to pass as man tout court, must define himself first in and through what he includes and disqualifies, in and through what he authorizes and devalues, and in and through the borders he erects between himself and his others. As a result, these movements play on difference, not to exclude themselves from the in-common, but as a lever to renegotiate the terms of belonging and recognition.

This sort of struggle should not be confused with the demand for secession that gnaws at many of the dominant classes in today's world. Instead of lifeless and energyless bodies, it aims to bring forth speaking bodies, members of a real community of those with rights. These movements also show that, to arrive at the similar, the sharing of differences must be the starting point. For, when an encounter occurs within a situation of violence, recognizing difference is always going to be the starting point for any politics of a shared humanity, of the similar, or better, of the in-common.

At bottom, wherever the idea has long prevailed that the hierarchy of races is a natural fact, the claim to difference often appears as the substratum of the claim to humanity. Proclaiming oneself to be different then becomes a way of escaping the imposition of a negation. The same is true with claiming the right to memory. The existence of this historical legacy is what pushes us to say that there is no politics of the similar, or of the in-common, without an ethics of otherness. There are indeed situations where difference is not, a priori, a refusal of similarity. Insofar as the possession of a memory functions as a dividing line between humans and "others," the right to memory is inseparable from identity struggles.

That said, we can hardly remain in denial about the dangers that the desire for difference could conceal, especially when difference is conceived politically and culturally as the place, by nature, of an unfathomable specificity. The desire for difference can, in fact, be constituted as a desire that is entirely turned toward the bad object. Nowadays, identity has tended to become the new opium of the masses. This is because reason as a universal human faculty is under siege, and the model of liberal democracy, which is supposed to be one of its manifestations, is under attack from all quarters. Most political antagonisms are increasingly expressed in a visceral form. Identity-based tensions are symptoms of this entry into the era of viscerality. Viralized by the new communications technologies, these symptoms have led to the release of negative energies that seek scapegoats to explain the misfortunes of the times.[51]

On another level, the desire for difference is not always a spontaneous one. The slaveholding and colonial regimes were, for example, in addition to being economic systems, enormous machines for fabricating racial and cultural difference.[52] The regime of integral capitalism in which we live is, among other things, a regime of proliferation of differences. Difference, under globalization, is produced and circulated as a medium of exchange and an object of consumption. In many ways, the contemporary political economy has made difference not only its raw material but also its currency.

Classical humanism, which lies at the foundation of liberal democracy and republicanism, is too compromised to attract lasting and unconditional support. It must be amended and returned to an integral conception of the world or, indeed, the Earth. In addition to belonging to us equally, the Earth is inhabited by several species, human and nonhuman, with whom we must negotiate new forms of complicity, coexistence, and conviviality. In relation to the immediate future, the question is therefore no longer so much that of the nation-state, ethnicity, or individual identities as that of the planet. But the planet itself has little meaning outside its cosmic dimension. The in-common will result from the recognition of our world's entanglement. This is why, in a redefined politics of the good of the world beyond the human, thinking and healing are inseparable.

Not long ago, people used to try to delimit more or less precisely the border between "here" and "elsewhere." The exercise has become entirely futile. The border has distended, if not dissolved, despite all the attempts made to externalize, miniaturize, or militarize it. Indeed, nationalisms and ethno-nationalisms notwithstanding, there has never been more than one world. We are all entitled to it, whether we like it or not. The time has never been so ripe to redefine the parameters of what is common to us in this planetary age.

Despite what you may think, the world is not infinitely expandable. Humans are neither its only inhabitants nor the only ones entitled to it. They are therefore unable to exercise unlimited sovereignty over it. This being the case, true democracy can only be that of the living as a whole. This democracy of the living calls for a deepening not in the sense of the universal but in the sense of the in-common; it thus calls for a pact of care, the care of the planet, the care given to all the world's inhabitants, human and other-than-human.

As the first steps toward a true planetary justice, the duties of restitution and of reparation figure at the heart of this pact of care. In ancient African thought, acts of reparation encompass the whole of the living world. The latter is seen as a fabric in becoming and therefore as open to the work of mending. These acts do not only concern wounds and the ensuing traumas. The clinic is not really about recovering lost properties. It aims, above all, to recompose relations. And this is of a cosmic order in the sense that it has to deal with all the bodies in the world. The clinic necessarily covers what Kant called "universal hospitality." This hospitality "is not a philanthropic (ethical) question, but rather a principle of right." As such, what does hospitality mean in the context of Kantian right? In Kant's eyes, it meant the right of a stranger not to be treated in a hostile manner by another upon his arrival on the other's territory. If it can be done without causing his death, the stranger can be turned away, yet as long as the stranger behaves peacefully where he happens to be, his host may not treat him with hostility. It is not the right of a guest that the stranger has a claim to (which would require a special, charitable contract stipulating that he be made a member of the household for a certain period of time), but rather a right to visit, to which all human beings have a claim, to present oneself to society by virtue of the right of common possession of the surface of the earth. Since it is the surface of a sphere, they cannot scatter themselves on it without limit, but they must rather ultimately tolerate one another as neighbors, and originally no one has more of a right to be at a given place on earth than anyone else.[53]

To the extent that "originally no one has more of a right to be at a given place on earth than anyone else," the border as such can no longer be an object of sacralization. It can no longer be transformed into a heavy prohibition. "Crossing the border is a privilege that no one, for whatever reason, should be deprived of," claims Édouard Glissant in response, adding that: "There is no frontier except for this fullness finally of going beyond it, and through it to share differences in breath's fullness. The obligation to have to force any border whatsoever, under the pressure of misery, is as scandalous as the foundations of this misery."[54]

As Glissant never stopped reiterating, "each of us needs the memory of the other, because it is not about a virtue of compassion or charity, but of a new lucidity in a process of Relation."[55] If we want to share the world's beauty, he added, we will have to learn to show solidarity with all its suffering. We will have to learn ourselves how to remember together and thus to repair together the fabric and the visage of the world. It is therefore not a question of closing in on yourself, of allowing yourself to be haunted by the obsession of a home, of an in-itself, of a transcendental in-itself, but of contributing to the emergence, upon an open sea, of this new region of the world where all of us will be able to enter unconditionally, in order to embrace, eyes wide open, the inextricable nature of the world, its untangleable structure, and its composite character.

And the project of the in-common makes room for the passer-by. The passer-by refers in the last instance to that which constitutes our common condition, that of being mortal, as mortals, on the way to a future, which is open by definition. The earthly human condition is, ultimately, to be passing through. The task of democracy in this new planetary era, then, is to ensure, organize, and govern the passage and not to develop new closures.

TWO
FRACTURING

What was called "universal history" until recently is far from concluded, and things are far from being set once and for all, forever petrified. Openness and movement remain two of the eminent hallmarks of the age, indeed of the living. Carl Schmitt, cognizant of this fact, affirmed that "as long as men and peoples have a future and not only a past, a new nomos will be born" in "ever new forms." For, he added, each new era of the coexistence of peoples, empires, and countries almost inevitably calls for "new spatial divisions, new enclosures, and new spatial orders of the earth."[1]

Body of the Earth

Before going further, we must go back over what Schmitt understands by the "Earth" and by the term *nomos*. Ordinarily, the term *Earth* evokes a spatial category, an expanse. Comprising more or less firm ground, it features landscapes, reliefs, depths, bedrock, traces, enclosures, reserves of wilderness, sanctuaries. It is believed to be inscribed within a set of directions (east, west, south, north). Made of mineral or vegetable matter, indeed of glebe, it is round and thus circumscribed. Above all, it is inhabited. By inhabiting it, humans, in particular, exercise their hold on it, consigning it to the land register and to development. They cultivate it and may take care of it. Their lives and destinies play out on a ground. As a common home, the Earth is the dwelling place of humans and other species, the object of a primitive sharing between all beings and, from this point of view, both their common name and their maternal body.[2]

Behind the "Earth" as generic image, there is thus something of the order of a particular power—the power of bedrock, of that on which work, regardless of the forms it takes and whoever its author is, finds its support. But there is also something that belongs to expanse, depths, and root—the root, if not the place of origin of all things, then—that whose limits escape the gaze, that which one digs, and which serves as a fundamental shelter to all those who inhabit it. Although round, the Earth is in fact a sign of the unlimited. No single individual or state can claim legitimate ownership of the Earth as a whole. Humans might leave some mark on it, but deep down, surrounded by a dark night, the Earth always remains distinct from its inhabitants. Few of them have witnessed its first beginnings, and it will never be for all to know its end. In one way or another, something in its substance and materiality therefore makes it fundamentally inappropriable. This is why it occupies such a central position in the "ages of the world."[3]

The Earth is therefore not merely matter, some geological formation, or compact mass made of multiple and stratified layers. Nor is it a silent entity. Beyond its multiple visages, it is also caught in an endless network of symbolic functions. A veritable "belly of the world," it ensures the equilibrium of the cosmos and, so doing, is the place par excellence of the in-common and of distribution.

It is also, however, that which always remains *in reserve*, that is, it is inappropriable. By inappropriable, we must understand not only that which is in principle refractory to procedures of alienation but also that of which no one can be deprived, or the use of which no one can be legitimately denied. In this sense, the Earth is the ultimate verifying instance of what the ancient Greeks called *isonomia*, that is, law not as it applies to all but as it is *equal for all*. It is also the appropriate name to give to the *homoios*, that is, the *like of all others*.[4]

In his *Nomos of the Earth*, Carl Schmitt is, it seems, entirely inattentive to the multiple ways that other cultures have made property and established relationships between the soil and the Earth as such. In his view, humans' relationship to the land is to be primarily considered in terms of law. The earth "is bound to law in three ways," he affirms. "It contains law within itself, as a reward of labor; it manifests law upon itself, as fixed boundaries; and it sustains law above itself, as a public sign of order." And he concludes: "Law is bound to the earth and related to the earth."[5] The

Earth is thus not considered in itself, but from the point of view of what it bears, from the point of view of its capacity to equitably reward those who plow it (fatigue, labor, and sowing in exchange for harvests), and from the point of view of its ability to figure, in this way, the idea of an almost immanent justice.

In the Schmittian schema, soil constitutes one of the Earth's intrinsic components. What characterizes soil, in turn, is its firmness. To inhabit the land is partly to clear the ground, to mark out and delimit fields, meadows, and woods. It also means planting and sowing, leaving some areas fallow and clearing others. Upon completion of this work, the ground is spiked with hedges and fences, boundary markers and walls. It is dotted with houses, buildings, and other infrastructures. In other words, land becomes meaningful only through the mediation of human labor. Left to itself, it produces no society at all. However, this labor consists essentially in a series of acts of partition and appropriation, or what Schmitt calls "seizures."[6] Such acts of acquisition, which he says are the foundation of law, take various forms. It does not matter if they are devoted to building cities and fortifying them, to colonization, wars, invasions or treaties, occupations, or forming barriers or blockades. Always, they create the "first order of all relations of possession and property."[7] In other words, these acquisitive acts are the original founding acts of law. To "seize" land, to delimit the soil, thus consists in creating legal titles and manufacturing property. It is to distinguish yours from mine.

Schmitt speaks of the "land grabs" as eminently political events, as the "origin of all subsequent concrete order[s] and of all subsequent law[s],"[8] the effective core of all history with a planetary dimension, that is, of a history that confronts everything that happens in the world. Such a history does not embrace only the entire earthly globe. As others have observed, it is also likely to give rise to all kinds of cycles, to set in motion world history, the human totality.[9] Even more, this historial character becomes apparent when the "land grabs" give rise to the emergence of a new "stage of human consciousness of space and global order."[10]

Seen from this angle, planetarity thus has a double dimension. On the one hand, there is no planetarity in the absence of a capacity for global representation of the Earth. On the other hand, there is no planetarity without the consciousness of a common belonging to a spatial order embracing all humanity. A planetary consciousness consequently supposes the representation of a world common "to all men and to all peoples," a common star.[11] It is the equivalent of a consciousness that is not of the world, or global, but truly astral, the inscription in a universe that, while signaling an earthly existence, extends it toward the cosmos as a whole. One of the great moments of such an emergent consciousness took place in the period known as the Age of Discovery during the fifteenth and seventeenth centuries, in reality, a moment of sharing and division of the Earth that led not only to a new spatial order, but also to a colliding of imaginaries.[12]

For the first time, the land as a whole was "seized and measured by the global consciousness of the European peoples."[13] We then moved from a land-based existence to a maritime existence. The Industrial Revolution allowed a further step forward with the advent of a technicized world. In the nineteenth century, this process of division and distribution of the globe continued with the conquest of Africa, the annexation of whole sections of its territory, colonial occupation, and the series of cessions that completely overturned Africa's previous spatial order, completing thus the *nomos* inaugurated by the land grabs of the fifteenth through seventeenth centuries. A structural reorganization of the planet ensued, with a new set of limits and a reorganizing of relations of violence and power. This new planetary spatial awareness in turn revived new struggles aimed at drawing lines, new confines, new enclosures.

Escalation

Indeed, since the middle of the twentieth century, the Earth has been undergoing rapid and multiform mutations with paradoxical results.[14] Its own borders are becoming less and less clear. The same is true for that which distinguishes it, for example, from vast maritime spaces, the riches they contain, and the conditions of their appropriation.[15] Whether it is new forms of conflict, the life of currencies, investments and exchanges, or even of spheres of cultural and artistic creativity, including urban forms and religious regimes, everything is being recomposed in conditions of sometimes radical uncertainty. Things that we had become accustomed to are dying. Others that we believed had disappeared for good are returning under new names, with new masks and sometimes on the same stages as yesterday, but with a different cast. Phenomena of mobility outline a multiply mapped world, crisscrossed with places of destination and transit; with crossroads, junctions, unsuspected forks and dead ends, walls and protean barriers; with enclaves, camps, and prisons. What new confines, enclosures, borders are there? Where are the new sanctuaries and reserves?[16]

Are the new spatial orders only terrestrial? Where do they begin and where do they end?[17] This world of interfaces and multiple interweavings also announces inevitable secessions. Contemporary logics of secession, segmentation, and expulsion are driven by various planetary technologies. The production of undocumented populations on a larger scale, and thus of populations without any protection, is going ahead apace. This phenomenon concerns not only migrants, refugees, and asylum seekers. It goes hand in hand with the monopolization of the planet's wealth by rich people who today hasten to exercise their *right to flee* and *to disassociate*.

Moreover, this world is not based on one soil but on a plurality of soils.[18] Its ontology is not only physical, geological, hydraulic, or mineral but also vegetal and synthetic. For its functioning and that of the infrastructures of planetary computation that are its prostheses, it requires an energy-consuming extraction of all kinds of resources and minerals, an acceleration of the processes of combustion of various orders, new imaginary, and linguistic mediations.[19]

Describing and analyzing the birth of this multiply mapped world requires knowing that the human race's present and future are inseparable from those of all other living species. To achieve this, we must decompartmentalize, deterritorialize, and open ourselves to questions that are not international or even transversal, but planetary; we must embrace the humanities and the natural sciences, deepen philosophical and historical questioning, and make room for disciplines of the imagination. We are further required to depart from established academic territories, and from disciplinary and institutional calculations, whose only function is to reproduce well-ordered pressures. We are also required to go via oblique or transversal paths in order to get domains to communicate that we normally tend to separate.[20]

In other respects, escalation is an indisputable phenomenon. There is no remaining sphere of contemporary existence that capital has not penetrated. This penetration is naturally uneven. Many parts of the world experience it mainly by proxy. Put in a stupor by poverty, indigence, and destitution, entire classes of populations experience firsthand the dissociation between the world as actually lived (that of bodily life at a particular point on the Earth's surface) and the blissful, ubiquitous world of screens, which is certainly within reach of their eyes but remains so far from their hands, their voices, and their means.

Whether we are talking about affects, emotions or feelings, linguistic skills or manifestations of desire, dreaming or thinking, in sum, life itself—nothing seems any longer to escape capital's grip. It has captured the world's very depths, often leaving behind vast fields of debris and toxins, wasted humans afflicted with sores, cankers, and boils. As everything has become a potential source of capitalization, capital has become—a hallucinatory fact of planetary dimensions—a world; it is the producer, on an enlarged scale, of subjects that are at once calculating, fictional, and frenzied.

Capital has become flesh, and everything has become a function of capital, including interiority. The processes that have led to this integral extension are erratic. They create randomness and uncertainty everywhere. That they institutionalize risk and precariousness everywhere is cast as the tough luck that reality dishes out.[21] Sometimes, they get targeted for embezzlement and solicitation. No matter, capital has become our common infrastructure, our nervous system, the transcendental jaw that now maps out our world and its psycho-physical limits.

This world creation is occurring at a time when the ordering of societies is being carried out under a single sign: digital computation. By digital computation, we must understand three things. First, a technical system or even a mechanical device specialized in the work of abstraction and, therefore, in capturing and automatically processing data (material and mental), which must be identified, selected, sorted, classified, recombined, and actioned. If, from this point of view, digitization is a work of abstraction, it is barely separable from another process, namely, calculation—at once of the livable and the thinkable. But whether it is supported by technical architectures, calculation is, in principle, a game of probabilities. Given the matter is ultimately about calculating chance, indeterminacy thus remains the rule.[22]

The computational, second, is an instance of production and the serial constitution of subjects, objects, and phenomena but also of codable and storable consciousnesses, memories, and traces that are, moreover, endowed with circulatory abilities. Third, the computational is the institution through which a common world, a new common sense, and new ordinations of reality and power are created and shaped. This common world and this common sense result from the fusion of three types of *ratio*, each subject to a dynamic of extension and increase: economic reason, biological reason, and algorithmic reason. All three forms are haunted by the metaphysical fantasy of technolatry.

Computational mechanisms, algorithmic modeling, and capital's subsumption of life in its entirety have become one and the same process. Whether we are talking about bodies, nerves, matter, blood, cellular tissues, brain, or energy, the project remains the same: on the one hand, the conversion of every substance into quantities, the preemptive calculation of potentialities, risks, and hazards with a view to their financialization and, on the other hand, the conversion of organic and vital ends into technical means. The aim is thus to loosen everything from an underlying substratum, corporeality, or materiality; it is to *artificialize* everything, and to *automate* and *autonomize* it. It is a question of submitting everything to effects of quantification and abstraction. Digitalization is nothing else than this capture of forces and potentialities and their annexation by the language of a machine-brain transformed into an autonomous and automated system.

Borderization

Humanity is indeed on the verge of being reborn to a second nature, thanks to an intrinsic transformation of the horizon of calculation and an almost indefinite extension of quantifying logic. It may seem paradoxical, counterintuitive even, to describe this technological moment as entropic. Yet in many respects it is. Indeed, capturing, identifying, dividing, sorting, selecting, and classifying are not activities specific to artificial machines. They are also characteristic of borders, of those places where, for many of our contemporaries, the world is undone and globalization hits its limits.

The border is no longer just a demarcation line that separates distinct sovereign entities. As an ontological device, it now functions by itself and in itself, anonymously and impersonally, with its own laws. To an increasing extent, the border is becoming the proper name of the organized violence that underlies contemporary capitalism and the order of our world in general: children are ripped from their parents and locked in a cage;[23] women and men are disregarded as superfluous and left for dead; shipwrecks and drownings occur by the hundreds, nay, thousands, per week;[24]

there are the interminable waits and the humiliation endured in consulates, so much suspended time; there is the enduring of days of adversity and drifting in airports, police stations, parks, train stations, and even on big-city sidewalks, where as soon as night falls, blankets and rags are torn from the very human beings who are already stripped and deprived of almost everything, including water, hygiene, and sleep—debased bodies—in short, humanity in distress.[25]

Everything, in fact, returns us to "the border," this zero-site of nonrelation and effective denial of the very idea of a common humanity, or of a planet—the only one that we might have, that we would seem to share, and to which our common condition as passers-by would bind us. To be fully exact, however, it might be necessary to speak not about borders but about *borderization*.[26]

What is *borderization*, if not the process by which this world's powers permanently transform certain spaces into places impassable for certain population classes? What is it if not the conscious multiplication of spaces of loss and mourning at which the lives of so many purportedly undesirable people are shattered?[27] And so what is it, if not a way of waging war against enemies whose living environments and conditions of survival have been destroyed in advance—ruined by the use of armor-piercing uranium ammunition and banned weapons such as white phosphorus; by the high-altitude bombing of basic infrastructures; by the cocktails of carcinogenic and radioactive chemicals that saturate the soil and fill the air; by the toxic dust that rises from the rubble of razed cities; and by the pollution caused by hydrocarbon fires?[28]

Let's turn to the matter of bombs. What kinds of bombs have civilian populations, habitats and environments not had to suffer over the last quarter of the twentieth century? They have endured conventional blind bombs converted by installing inertial navigation systems in their tails; cruise missiles with infrared homing heads; microwave bombs designed to paralyze the enemy's electronic nerve centers; bombs that explode in cities, emitting lightning-like beams of energy as they pass; other microwave bombs that do not kill but burn people and increase skin temperature; thermobaric bombs that trigger walls of fire, absorbing the oxygen of more or less enclosed spaces, killing by shock waves and asphyxiating almost everything that breathes; fragmentation bombs, whose effects on civilian populations are devastating, since they open above the ground and scatter, without precision and over large areas, minimal munitions designed to explode on contact with the target—all these bombs demonstrate *ad absurdum* an unheard-of power of destruction.[29]

How, under these conditions, can we really be surprised that survivors of a living hell take flight to, or seek for refuge in, whatever corner of the Earth their lives might be spared? This form of deadening war—calculated and programmed, carried out with new means—is a war against the very idea of mobility, circulation, and speed, whereas the age is precisely about velocity, about acceleration, and about ever more abstraction, ever more algorithms.[30]

Moreover, *borderization* does not target singular bodies but certain human masses deemed vile and superfluous. Their every organ must be the object of a specific incapacitation, inheritable from generation to generation—eyes, nose, mouth, ears, tongue, skin, bones, lungs, intestines, blood, hands, legs. Attesting to this are the maimed individuals, paralytics, and survivors of all the pulmonary diseases like pneumoconiosis, those with traces of uranium in the hair, the thousands of cases of cancers, abortions, infant malformations, congenital deformations, damaged thoraxes, dysfunctions of the nervous system—the great fissuring.

This war on bodies of abjection, piles of human meat, is taking place on a planetary scale. It is becoming the characteristic of our time. Often it precedes, accompanies, or completes that which is going on in our midst or at our doors, the tracking down of bodies that have made the mistake of moving (a notable characteristic of any human body), of bodies that are considered to have forced their way into places and spaces that they should not be, places that they now clutter by their mere presence, and from which they must be forced out.[31]

As the philosopher Elsa Dorlin suggests, this form of violence targets prey.[32] It resembles the great hunts of yesteryear. First of all, it resembles hunting with hounds and traps and their respective techniques—searching for, pursuing, trapping, and flushing out hunted animals, until they are surrounded, captured, or slaughtered with the help of foxhounds and other scent hounds. But it is also part of a long history of manhunting. Grégoire Chamayou has studied the modalities of this in *Manhunts*.[33] It is almost always the same ones who are targeted—runaway slaves, redskins, black skins, Jews, stateless people, the poor and, closer to us, undocumented migrants.[34] These hunts attack live, moving bodies that, while endowed with a force of traction, with an intensity, with capacities for flight and mobility, are deemed not to be flesh-and-blood bodies like ours, given how singled out and ostracized they are. This hunt is also taking place at a time when proliferating technologies of acceleration are creating a segmented, multi-speed planet.[35]

The technologization of borders is now running at full tilt. Physical and virtual separation barriers—the digitization of databases and filing systems; the development of new tracking devices such as sensors, drones, satellites, and sentry robots; infrared sensors and cameras of various kinds; biometric controls; and smart cards containing personal data—everything is being implemented to transform the very nature of the border phenomenon and to precipitate the advent of mobile, portable, and ubiquitous borders.[36]

Confinement and Purgation

Migrants and refugees are therefore not, as such, the primary object of the dispute. Moreover, they have neither proper names, nor singular faces, nor identity cards. They are only crypts, sort of ambulant vaults on the surface of multiple organs, empty but threatening forms in which one seeks to bury the fantasies of an era terrified by itself and its own excesses. The dream of flawless security, which requires not only systematic and total surveillance but also purgation, is symptomatic of the structural tensions that, for decades, have accompanied our passage into a new technical system that is increasingly automated, reticular, and simultaneously increasingly abstract, made of multiple screens—digital, algorithmic, numinous.

The world has ceased to manifest itself to us in the old terms. We bear witness to the birth of a new form of the human (the subject/object) and other types of spatialities. The phenomenological experience that we had of the world has been profoundly weakened. Reason and perception no longer coincide. Hence the panic. We see less and less what is given to us to see, and more and more what we want to see at all costs, even if what we want to see at all costs does not correspond to any originary reality. Perhaps more than before, others can give themselves to us in a concrete physical and tactile presence while remaining in a spectral absence and an equally concrete, almost phenomenal void. This occurs with migrants, refugees, and asylum seekers. It is not only their mode of appearance among us that besets us with historical and existential anxiety. It is also the ontophanic matrix of which we assume them to be a mere mask (what is actually there, behind what appears?) that plunges us into a state of radical agitation and uncertainty.

In an increasingly balkanized and enclaved world, where do we find the deadliest migration routes? Europe! Where, at the beginning of this century, do we find skeletons at sea in the world's largest marine cemetery? Europe! Where do we find all those deserts, territorial and international waters, inlets, islands, straits, enclaves, canals, rivers, ports and airports that are being transformed into technological iron curtains? Europe! And to top it all off, in these times of permanent escalation, Europe is also where we find camps. The return of camps.[37] The Europe of camps. Samos, Chios, Lesbos, Idomeni, Lampedusa, Ventimiglia, Sicily, Subotica—the rosary-beads of camps.[38]

Refugee camps? Displaced persons camps? Migrant camps? People held in waiting zones at transport hubs? Transit zones? Detention centers? Emergency accommodations? Jungles? A composite and heterogeneous landscape, to be sure. But let's sum it all up in one term, the only one that truthfully describes what is going on here: *foreigners' camps*. In the final analysis, it is not about anything else. They are foreigners' camps, and they can be found in Europe's core and on its peripheries. This term is the only fitting one for these devices and the kind of carceral geography they plot.[39]

A few years ago, the European Union had nearly four hundred of them. That was prior to the great influx of 2015. Ever since, Europe has created new camps, including triage camps, inside and on its borders, and it has had them built in third-party countries. In 2011, these various detention facilities were holding as many as 32,000 people. By 2016, the number had risen to 47,000. The detainees are mainly people without visas or residence permits, those deemed ineligible for international protection. These facilities are essentially places of internment, spaces of banishment, devices for segregating people considered to be intruders, unentitled, without rights, and thus devoid of dignity. These people flee from worlds and places that have been made uninhabitable by a twofold predation, both exogenous and endogenous, and then introduce themselves where they should not have, without being invited or wanted. The ultimate goal of regrouping and excluding them can thus hardly be their rescue. By arresting them in camps, the intention is also—after having placed them in a position of waiting that first strips them of any common-law status—to make them the sorts of subjects who can be deported, repressed, and even destroyed.[40]

This war, which consists of hunting down, capturing, regrouping, sorting, separating, and expelling has only one goal. It is not so much about cutting Europe off from the world, or making it an impregnable fortress, as it is about consecrating, as the European's exclusive privilege, the right to possess and move freely across the entirety of a planet to which we are all entitled.

Will the twenty-first century be about devising security technologies to sort and select? From the borders of the Sahara to the Mediterranean, is the camp on the way to becoming, once again, the terminus of a certain European project, of a certain idea of Europe in the world, its fatal mark, as Aimé Césaire intuited not long ago?[41]

One of the liberal order's major contradictions has always been the tension between freedom and security.[42] But this issue seems to have been resolved. Today security prevails over freedom. Yet a society of security is not necessarily a society of freedom.

A society of security is a society dominated by an irrepressible need to subscribe to a set of certainties. It is a society afraid of the kind of questioning that opens onto the unknown and therewith onto the risk that must be contained.

That is why the priority of a society of security is to identify at all costs what lurks behind every appearance—it wants to know who is who; who lives where, with whom, and since when; who is doing what; who has come from where; who is going where, when, by which route, and why; and so on and so forth. And, further still, who is planning to commit what acts, whether consciously or unconsciously. The project of the security society is not about affirming freedom but about controlling and governing modes of appearance.

Today's myth is that technology is the best tool for governing modes of appearance, that technology alone can solve this problem, which is one of order but also of knowledge, of reference points, anticipation, and forecasting. We may fear that the dream of a humanity transparent to itself, devoid of mystery, is only a catastrophic illusion. At the present moment, migrants and refugees are the ones paying the price for it. In the long run, they are sure not to be the only ones.

How can we, under these conditions, resist this claim by one of the world's provinces to have a universal right of predation unless we dare to imagine the impossible: namely, the abolition of borders, that is, the restoration to all the inhabitants of the Earth, human and nonhuman, the inalienable right to move about freely on this planet?

THREE
ANIMISM AND
VISCERALITY

The world has never produced as many kinds of knowledge as it has today. Most of them are about life processes and mechanical and physicochemical procedures. Others are in themselves unique acts of creation and imagination. Many have as their function the invention of mobile forces, situated at the interface between bodies and machines. Such forces are expected to be able to kill as quickly, as efficiently, and as "cleanly" as possible, all in the name of security.[1] Yet at issue is also the transformation of the entire real into a technical product, and of the human being, in particular, into a synthetic being, if necessary, by new methods of fertilizing, manuring, and animation.[2]

Humanity has never had so much information and data on hand about almost everything, indeed about all that which lives (*le vivant*). Never has that which exists been so accessible, even if, in the main, the most decisive discoveries and innovations in the military-technical, scientific, and commercial fields remain secret and patent-protected. All this is true. And yet, ignorance and indifference, induced or cultivated, have never been so widespread. This is because, like knowledge, ignorance is a form of power.[3] Knowing does not automatically lead to freedom, while not knowing frees one from almost any responsibility while allowing, where necessary, an increase in control and in power.[4]

On Demonic Life

The idea of progress has long been subject to criticism, so much so that there is almost nothing to add. As a concept, progress was based on the belief in a continuous movement not susceptible to being interrupted.

Movement itself was justified solely through its utilitarian and functionalist goals. According to the paradigm of progress, continuous movement and functionalism were confounded with vitalism. Progress stood fundamentally opposed to everything that presented the appearance of something dead. It could not tolerate ruin, decay, old age, or inanition. Every dead zone, every dead part, and every dead point contradicted its principle.

Despite criticism of the idea of progress, the desire to perpetually transform the human subject and the world has not let up, nor has the will to integrally master nature and life. This desire and this will to power basically remain the horizon to which humanity has never stopped aspiring. Today, this aspiration has been reduced to a simple matter of quantifying and draining the world. The world has, so to speak, become a curve, a circle, a diagram, an algorithm.[5] As numbers take precedence over words, numbers become the ultimate guarantor rather than simple indicators of reality.[6]

In fact, what the modern period called the project of rationalization became possible only thanks to a multiplicity of material, technological, and practical innovations. From then on, deciphering the universe, notably thanks to the sciences and mathematics, has presumed an integral and infinitely expansive knowledge of the universe and the phenomena that disrupt it.[7] We have become bound to this trajectory more than ever before, borne along by all sorts of mega- and nanostructures and, above all, by a new type of intelligibility or faculty that, for want of a better word, must surely be called digital.[8]

The advent of digital reason has given an old fantasy, the fantasy of integral knowledge, a new lease on life. Digital reason views the world as an immense reservoir from which to draw. It is mercilessly subject to man's desire for power, and its elementary forces are arrested in the mechanics of a regime of knowledge from which nothing should escape. Once again, to know, in these conditions, has meaning only insofar as it permits draining, drilling, and extracting.[9] Points of extraction alone count. And they count only because, at the end of the line, what has been extracted can be transformed into something else before being made available for consumption. In this process of extortion, machines play an invaluable role.

Similar to the way that, in our times, the world appears transformed into the image of an immense forge—given the increasingly intimate connection of the economy and neurological phenomena, or of technology and biology—so, too, did it strike the imagination of the first critics of the machine age. Movements of monstrous elemental forces, whirling speeds, vibrations and quiverings, explosive power, all this evoked the furnace at the very beginning of the combustion of the world. "This," Friedrich Georg Jünger recalls, "is the workshop of the Cyclops." Jünger specifies that the industrial landscape "has something of the volcanic about it, and we find in it all those phenomena visible during and after volcanic eruptions: lava, ash, fumaroles, smoke, gases, fire-lit night clouds, and devastation on a grand scale." And, turning to the "powerful elemental forces invading to the breaking point the ingeniously conceived machines," which automatically perform their uniform working operation, he adds:

> They spread in the pipes, the tanks, the gears, the conduits, the blast furnaces, they surge in the dungeon of the apparatus which, like all prisons, is full of iron and grids supposed to prevent the prisoners from escaping. But who does not hear these prisoners moaning and complaining, shaking the bars and vociferating in a senseless rage, when he lends his ear to this profusion of new and strange noises generated by technology?

These noises result from the connection of the mechanical and the elemental. They are, moreover, noxious, strident, piercing, tearing, howling. They are what manage to grant to technique the face and features of a "demon endowed with an independent will."[10]

All these features make up the subsoil of the project for integral knowledge in the algorithmic era.[11] Like the technical *ratio*, the digital and algorithmic *ratio* can truly be considered as the conjunction of causal thinking and teleological thinking, and necessarily also of predictive thinking.

In both cases, knowledge gets reduced to an apparatus. It consists in a form of constraining organization.[12] In the case of the digital and algorithmic ratio, we are dealing with knowledge for which the object is the totality of current and imaginable phenomena. Its field is unlimited insofar as, were it to exist, such a regime would cover not only phenomena in their abstraction, but also human intentions and behaviors, habits, desires, needs, and even people's most hidden aspirations.[13]

This new type of integral knowledge is the product of extraction procedures that work from the raw material of data and information, which are massively collected and analyzed in real or delayed time, and from which significant correlations are extracted and given automated interpretations. Automated machines increasingly carry out these procedures of extraction, analysis, and arrangement of relations with the ultimate ambition to displace sites of sovereignty and, ultimately, to strip the real forever of its fundamental shadow.[14] All mystery would thus be abolished. Nothing would be inconceivable anymore. The human subject, in the full clarity of itself, would finally face itself upright, in the full transparency of things and the brightness of its destiny. But is this even actually possible?

Moreover, in contemporary conditions, knowledge for knowledge's sake, gratuitous knowledge, is considered valueless. Knowledge is valid only insofar as it may have industrial application and thus be monetizable.[15] A priori, monetizable value is the only criterion of the truth of knowledge. Accordingly, it entertains no direct relationship either with morality or with wisdom.

If knowledge and truth alone rendered one truly free, humanity would have already found the key to happiness and peace—to an era of universal understanding—long ago having emancipated itself from ignorance and prejudice, fear, and superstition. And yet, despite today's unprecedented accumulation of knowledge, ideas that are simplistic, limited, and just very poor have never been so popular. For ours is a time of fragmentation, of small stories, of identity's spells, and its corollary, the desire for incest. We want to remain among ourselves, to tell ourselves stories that very few still believe—but little matter.

A key demand of our time is that of optimal performance and efficiency. Optimal performance and efficiency can allegedly be achieved only through an expansion of technology. And yet, the more that reason, science, and technology dominate our lives, the more the formative force of these seems to decline in the public mind. Indeed, contrary to the myth of Enlightenment, reason is very possibly not humankind's driving force. Life's technicization does not mechanically make us more rational, let alone reasonable, beings. In fact, the more that scientific and technological progress pushes back the frontiers of ignorance, the more the empire of prejudice, credulity, and silliness expands, as though humanity requires a dark and obscure background—the immense reserve of night with which psychoanalysis has tried to reconcile us. This phenomenon is similar to the consumption of signs of whose origins we have no idea. Technophilia and hatred of reason, we must fully understand, can happily cohabitate. And each time that this threshold of collusion has been reached, the resulting violence has been explosive and visceral.

Ideas may not be dead. But the trend is decidedly toward small stories, on the one hand, and technolatry, on the other. As Pierre Lévy puts it, "The proponents of Big Data maintain the epistemological illusion that they could do without theory and that it is possible for them to generate knowledge from a 'simple' statistical data analysis."[16] A false trial, perhaps. For behind each statistic, each piece of data, and each algorithm lies a hypothesis, implicitly or explicitly, a theory that does not say its name.

In the end, humanity has not given up on the production and manipulation of symbols. The desire for mythology remains intact. There is no—and there will never be any—real without a symbol. What is new, perhaps, is the accelerated production of symbols without any real, which are sufficient in themselves and now tend to occupy the entire surface of the real. Assisted by the digital age, humanity has thus entered new regimes of symbolic production and manipulation. Behind each statistic, each code, and each algorithm lies hidden a division of the world and the real, an idea and a theory, that is, an idiom capable of generating the reality that it claims to describe or encapsulate.

There is no human activity that is not exclusively conditioned by tools, techniques, and technologies. This is true for practical activities as well as for institutions and the spaces we inhabit. Technology is one of the mediations par excellence of the living. The same is true for humanity's mental creations, and even for democracy itself. Today, the essentials of human activities have moved into digital worlds. The public sphere itself has mostly become a digital sphere. It now has a name—the World Wide Web.

And as for the public itself, it is largely embodied in the digital, but in a novel manner and without either body or flesh. The relationship not only to the world but also to others, things, and ideas is henceforth conditioned by silicon technologies. This is the condition of the new century. One property of digital technologies is, if not to eliminate any idea of substance, then at least to desubstantivize substance all the better to return it to the only thing that really counts—speed.[17] The substance of things is no longer separated from their surface. Everything plays out in interfaces, as places of privileged imbrication between the real and the virtual.

The era is thus characterized by the uninterrupted generation of all kinds of flows. Each individual, taken separately, has become both a transmitter and a potential consumer of flows. These flows now constitute us and give substance and form to social life.[18] In a sense, then, the public sphere is now confounded with an economy of uninterrupted flows, which arise, swell, and fall in the manner of waves. Within the contemporary technological condition, this is a significant feature. The electronics industries have, in fact, made possible not only the expansive generation of data of all kinds on just about everything; they have also extracted unprecedented capacities to store such data. Material things are not the only target of digitization. Digitization also affects images, and indeed all human faculties, including those of calculation, understanding, perception, and representation and especially affects, feelings, and emotions.[19]

The Dark Zone

How else are we to explain the proliferation of small stories, tiny stories, which all boil down to stories about the self, about one's own ego? This contraction of history and its reduction to the ego-domain contribute to making the public sphere one of public expression of the private. In the era of mass narcissism, the public is reduced to the screen, to screens of all kinds.[20] The absence of connection is thus what henceforth links everyone to each other, that by which everyone recognizes themself, that which paradoxically holds them all together. But how do things stand with language?

The image has become the subject's privileged language. This holds for the body image in particular, the body of enjoyment, but also the suffering and victimized self, preferably when on screen. Surrounded by images, the subject has turned itself into image. The image now takes pride of place right where the Eucharistic act had as its crux the body and blood that one offered to be taken, drunk, and eaten.

The image's Eucharistic and sacramental dimension is such that we no longer see the—now veiled—subject. We are no more than a series of body images. "One of the fundamental properties of the image is indeed," affirms Éric Laurent, "that it puts causalities of potentially great diversity on the same plane."[21] Nowadays, he adds, to exist, to be seen and known, everything must be put into images. The most fundamental and hidden processes, whether of the body itself or of the brain, must be put into images. Seeing, understanding, and thinking all go through the image. Cognitive circuits, too. Certainty itself. Not even modalities of proof fail to yield to the image.

This being so, the function of the image is no longer to represent anything whatsoever. The new technologies of the image make possible the elision of place. Having done away with the very principle of representation, the image is left with only one function: to bear witness to the being-there of the id, or, if you like, of *the* "that," *of the hole that from now on has taken the place of that which has been, but is no longer, unless in the mode of the id.* The id, here, refers to impulses freed from all censorship. Superegoic censorship made it possible to structure the division between the subject and its image, and to regulate this division. Now the subject has become image, the division has collapsed and censorship is no longer necessary. There is only a huge hole that henceforth serves as a receptacle for absolutely any kind of desire.

It is no longer possible to ignore the relationship between the political and the drives. Today, the public sphere has become the place where the subject strives to make his or her self-portrait. But there can be no self-portrait in the absence of a body image. Self-portraiture is possible only if the body is caught in a social link with other bodies; if one agrees to make room for the marks of time on the flesh. But, in the new regime of existence that is ours, identity does not at all stand as something primary and stable.

Identity is rather a matter of composition and is constantly being made and unmade. It is something ultimately ungraspable. Identity is like a trace that speech or meaning tries in vain to recapture and register. This is why it is falsifiable. To make possible various modes of self-enjoyment, starting with the enjoyment of oneself through self-portraiture, is one of the new stakes of the political.

Further still, new technologies free the drives from all sorts of fetters. They force open most of the locks that authorized superegoic censorship. One might have thought that images' saturation of our lives would lead to a more logical fusion of the subject and its image. The paradox is that, underhandedly, the division between the subject and its image continues to haunt both. The living force of the raw body has not been extinguished.

The image did not manage to surmount it. Despite its dissolving power, it is obliged to return to the body, which is increasingly grasped as the result of an arrangement of heterogeneous components.[22] On the contrary, the subject conceives itself as a surface where an image or images come to be inscribed, and such images do not have to be consistent.

Narcissistic passion is key to the new imaginary. The subject is a se ries of partial assemblies lying in a field that is refractory to unification. The age, obviously, seeks to free itself from the unconscious. Its erogenous edges, drive circuits, and signifying matter indicate that the age cannot stand knowing anything about loss, debt, or even authority. To enjoy is to accumulate, certainly, but it is also crucially to expend, void, and squander. But the era is also characterized by a refusal of the last word. The public sphere is reduced to this impossible place, a receptacle of impossible self-portraits. A new psychology of the masses is thus taking shape, and with it a new political form, that of affects. To govern is, in complicity with capital, to produce structures of desire and modes of enjoyment. If there is projection, it is now egocentric, self-directed. One tries to project onto external things, but it is oneself onto other people taken as screens. At first sight, everything seems to boil down to self-presentation and self-nomination. But perhaps we are witnessing something that is both more obscure and more elastic, new *forms* for which contemporary nanotechnologies serve as a mold.

The cell phone is an example of these "little machines" and "nano-objects"; its introduction on the African continent was a considerably unique technological event.[23] The cell phone is not simply an everyday object. It has become a veritable storehouse of knowledge and a crucial assemblage that has changed the way people speak, act, write, communicate, and imagine who they are and their relationships to themselves, others, and the world at large.

Along with the development of other computer media, the introduction of the cell phone has also been a major aesthetic event. In Africa, this device is not a mere means of communication but also allows one to distinguish oneself, to forge one's own style, in short, to invent one's own signature. The cell phone is an object with which people spend a lot of time. More than a simple companion, it has become more an extension of being, a container for the lives to which it gives a shape, even a meaning. The way it is treated and cared for indicates in itself how many would like to be cared for and, ultimately, how they would wish to be treated.

But its impact has perhaps been most explosive at the philosophical, cultural, and imaginary levels. The obsession of precolonial African cultures with all sorts of ontological and metaphysical questions is rarely taken into proper consideration. These questions concerned the limits of the Earth; the boundaries of life, the body, and the self; the theme of being and relation, of the human subject as an assemblage of multiple entities, the arranging of which was a task that had to be taken up ever anew. As their myths, oral literatures, and cosmogonies attest, among the great human questions African cultures pondered were those about the world beyond the perceptible, the bodily, the visible, and the conscious.

They depicted the cosmos itself in the form of an uninterrupted journey toward the unknown and the unexpected. Everything played out at the interface, right at the place where, it was believed, reality's surplus lay. The time of objects was not foreign to the time of humans. Objects were not seen as static entities but rather as supple and living beings, endowed with magical, original, and sometimes occult properties. They were repositories of all kinds of energies, vitality, and virtualities, and as such, they constantly called for transmutation, and even for transfiguration.

Certain tools, technical objects, and artifacts belonged to this world of interfaces and apparatuses. In this way, they served as thresholds from which it was possible to measure the degree of transgression of existing limits. Successfully crossing such limits made it possible to access the universe's infinite horizons. "Cosmos-making" meant trading continuously on processes of reversibility, reticularity, and fluidity. With human beings and other living entities, objects maintained a relationship of reciprocal causality. "Animism" is the name that the first anthropologists gave to this relationship.

Today, everything transpires as if digital worlds were speaking, almost without mediation, to this archaic unconscious, or to the deepest technical memory of these societies. The age of the digital, or of computer media (the cell phone being one of its expressions), is that in which the Earth's limits are exploded and imaginaries of circulation—veritable cornerstones of societal production in precolonial Africa—are liberated. Subjects are now able to move, even if, objectively speaking, they are in an immobile situation.

The old layers of connection that existed before the radio, television, video, and even cinema have received the addition of a new layer. Today, it is possible to move almost seamlessly from the stone to the digital age. As a result, there is an enrichment of the very concept of relation. The relation now prevails over ontology, or, to put it differently, ontology and relation have merged.

What gives digital technologies their power is their plasticity, that is, their ability to be loosed from their original ecology and grafted onto other cultural matrixes. Technology means nothing without the capacity to act as a relay for something that already exists within a receiving culture, without its ability to allow its users to dream. A technical object is well received in a new space only if it is efficient and forthwith bears promises, driven by a utopian core.

Due partly to their plasticity, digital technologies have necessarily democratized the capacity to dream. They have already become the main containers for the great narratives of emancipation that were, not so long ago, invested in all sorts of revolutionary utopias. At the beginning of the twenty-first century, these great narratives of emancipation may well increasingly take shelter in the religious, the commodity, and technology. Animism's astounding return has been paved by this potential fusion of commodities, technology, and religion. On this ice floe that our world is becoming, new technologies have become tremendous resources for an economy of enchantment.

Moreover, the digital world is a world deeply underpinned by the oneiric structures of the religious, a privileged place in which the ontophanic face of reality is most strikingly manifest, a world whose extraordinary porosity favors the proliferation of all sorts of regimes of belief and affect. Religion itself is increasingly digital. Most contemporary religious forms and forms of belief are now electronic, or in any case are relayed by electronic media. The religious is nowadays the place par excellence of production of hybrid experiences.

Both religion and electronic objects can increasingly be bought as commodities, that is, produced, sold, and consumed on a marketplace that is itself planetary. The opposition between regimes of belief and technical systems and ensembles has basically collapsed. There is not even any aesthetics that has not, and more intensely than ever, become a site for the reconciliation of old antagonisms between the technical, the magical, and the rational.

This notwithstanding, there is no need to stick to a blissful conception of the political potential of digital technologies. Among other things, their popularization has allowed for a relative democratization of speech. Today, so long as you have a computer or cell phone and are connected, you can express yourself more or less freely, say something about almost anything, create a story or images without any prior authorization, and most importantly, have them circulate. In fact, there is not a single area of social or private life that now escapes this hold, and there is clearly nothing we can do about it.

But this completely novel situation of the contemporary condition does have its drawbacks, indeed, quite apart from the invasive dimension of these technologies. The point here concerns digital technology's capacity to erase the very idea of limit or truth, notions that are nevertheless crucial for the formation of democratic subjects as well as for the vitality itself of a public sphere and a civic space. For if practically anything can be said (and disseminated) about almost anything and everything, at any time, and under any pretext, then the way is opened to a cannibalism of a rather unusual kind.

Needless to say, in some circumstances these technologies can be used as powerful instruments for convening and mobilizing, for circulating all kinds of messages. From this point of view, the key thing is to produce content and to know how to disseminate it or how to set up platforms and networks. This aside, we will not be able to completely avoid face-to-face encounters. Indeed, as Judith Butler has shown, constituting spaces of the political and confronting power necessarily require face-to-face encounters, real bodies occupying public spaces, and real assemblies.[24]

The public space that the internet helps to create can be ephemeral. It is sometimes also hostile to the idea of civility. Reason by no means reigns supreme within it. The space thrives mostly on affect and emotion, excess and immoderation. Within it, the simple raising of indignation would seem enough of an act to obtain assent. The new digital world has led to a profound dislocation of language, at least to an extent. While the possibility of saying everything and its opposite has been present since the birth of language, today the confusion between what is true and what is false has reached new thresholds.

The confusion of ends and means is typical of an era in which fascination with power has reached unlimited proportions among the powerful as well as among the subordinate. People no longer cultivate any distance from power but rather seek to be incorporated into it. According to this logic, right necessarily goes to the victors. A political critique of the internet and of all forms of digital reason must begin with this imperious fact of our time, namely, the dissemination of microfascism in the interstices of reality.

The digital world is, moreover, a numinous world, that is, a gigantic reserve of data that countless machines strive continuously to extract. But this world also fulfills some of the modern human being's most primordial fantasies, beginning with that of self-observation, which was first experienced with the invention of the mirror. Before the mirror was invented, the individual subject had no image of themselves. You could be seen by others, but could not look at your own face. Your face escaped your own gaze. You could scarcely take yourself, then, as the main object of your own visual contemplation. You could see only your own shadow or the refraction of your double on the water's surface.

The digital world takes the mirror to its ultimate degree of efficiency. Bringing the history of shadow to its knees, it would have us believe that there can be a world without opacity, a world translucent and transparent to itself, devoid of nocturnal attributes. We can now become our own show, our own stage, our own theater, and even our own audience. In this age of endless exhibition, we can draw our self-portrait endlessly.

The digital age, the age of new media forms, is structured by the idea that the unconscious is a blank slate, that it harbors no opacity, no secret. To some extent new forms of media serve as new infrastructures of the unconscious. They lift the veil that previous eras had cast over it. Human sociability used to consist in keeping a lid on the unconscious. It was about maintaining vigilance over ourselves or conceding to particular authorities the right to exercise this vigilance. The phenomenon was one of suppression, or repression, as conditions of sublimation.

Thanks partly to the new media forms, the unconscious is now able to express itself freely. Sublimation is seemingly no longer needed. Language itself has been dislocated. Content lies in the form and form lies beyond, or in excess of, content. The real, it seems, can now be accessed without mediation. The new norm is direct, original experience. From the heart of this event of liberation from the burden of the unconscious, a new figure of the human subject is emerging.

For the rest, the technological tools that permeate our lives become extensions of ourselves, and through this process, other relationships between humans and objects are created, relationships that African traditions have long anticipated. Indeed, in ancient African traditions, human beings were never satisfied merely with being human. They were always seeking out a supplement to their humanity, often adding to it attributes of animals, plants, and various other beings. Modernity disqualified such ways of being, relegating them to the childhood of mankind.

The time is coming to an end when distinctions are made between ourselves and the objects with which we share our existence. Not so long ago, at least in the modern West, a human being was not a thing or an object. Nor was the human being an animal or a machine. Human emancipation was founded precisely on such a separation. Today, many want to appropriate for themselves the forces, energies, and vitality of the objects that surround us and that we have, for the most part, invented.

Societies in Africa are constituted, first, through circulation and mobility, through movement. Examining African myths about origin, one can only be struck by the central role that phenomena of migration and connection play. There is not a single ethnic group in Africa that can seriously claim never to have moved. Their stories are always stories of migration, about peoples who move from one place to another, and in the process, mix with other populations. In the stories, circulation and mobility are constitutive of space. These societies are—second—of an extraordinary plasticity. Plasticity implies a predisposition to welcome that which is new, unexpected, and unprecedented. It implies that one plays with that which had not been known but that is likely to open onto entirely new worlds, new possibilities of power, onto the marvelous.

This plasticity is also found in all areas of cognition and calculation. Certainly, African mythology does not involve any mechanized calculation. But the imaginary of numbers, the organization in networks, the ways of cutting up reality, the perceptual culture, the types of spatial consciousness—all these phenomenological structures were, contrary to what has been said, extremely conducive to innovation. These structures were also localizable at the heart of artistic practice. This flexibility, adaptability, and aptitude for constant innovation, for the extension of the possible, is also the spirit of the digital. This is why we can say that Africa was digital before the digital.

Miseries of the Times

Let's put aside the return of animism and the rise of new forms of idolatry, whether digital idolatry, the cult of neuroscience, or more prosaically, the religion of matter and objects spread by the neo-Pentecostal churches. We clearly live in a time of political and cultural pessimism. But it is also a time of sensations, in the context of the contemporary subject's extraordinary fragility. Aided and abetted by mass narcissism, the confrontation with the real now takes place not through language but through enjoyment and the body.

Despite the denials, the contemporary subject is anguished, torn between several bodies: the body-machine, the body-apparatus, and especially the body-image manufactured by the new technologies. All these bodies, taken one by one, are bodies of enjoyment, an enjoyment that we want to be immediate, instantaneous. In concrete experience, this desire for enjoyment inevitably leads to disappointment. Such disappointment is all the more traumatic as the numerous bodies that make up the subject are not, strictly speaking, organisms. They are essentially various kinds of devices and instruments whose primary function is to transform everything into images.

The upshot is that the speaking being no longer identifies itself with its organism. It identifies itself with the multiplicity of images through which it is born, no longer with a flesh-and-bone body, but with incessant reflections. This explains, at least in part, the proliferation of discourses about conspiracy and collapse, about resentment and identity, in short, the angry and conspiratorial temperament of our age.

It is in the bowels of identity that we notably find lurking all today's fears, obscure impulses, anxieties, most acute sufferings, and opaquest desires, starting with the desire to enjoy—and to enjoy always once more and right now. But there is also the desire for endogamy, to which we must add the muted will for sometimes gratuitous, sometimes vengeful, violence. In the age of algorithmic capitalism, such are the aspirations and the supreme injunctions.

Indeed, to many, the appeal to soil and blood and the recourse to identity appear increasingly as the last dikes capable of withstanding the miseries of the times. Brandishing their identitarian demand, such individuals ultimately seek simply to secure a spot at the table. Or, failing that, to have privileged access to the crumbs for which, in the absence of impenetrable borders, they believe nationals are increasingly forced to compete with various categories of intruders.

The multitudes therefore want to fight back— but with those weaker than they are and not with the increasingly abstract, reticular, and invisible forces that, in the North and the South alike, are crushing so many lives and shattering so many hopes. A great many people want nothing but to live among their own kind.

They call openly for the othered to be ill-treated, to rough up all those who seem already robbed of life but who still cling to it by any means available, including the riskiest and most illegal.

In this climate of rage and confinement to one's own kind, the future is no longer understood as the promise of some possible progress. It now appears as a force of dislocation and dissolution, as a truly negative experience. It is true that people are rising up in several countries of the world, and in the process, they are enduring ferocious forms of repression. At the same time, many have stopped believing in the possibility of genuinely transformative action. They struggle to imagine any break with the existing frameworks of thought and action. They have actually thrown in the towel and turned against the project of human emancipation.

How can we be surprised? At the end of the Cold War, were we not willing to believe that market democracy was history's last word? What can we say about the many measures of capitulation that were put in place in the wake of the war and that led to a vast resignation of the intellect to the existing order? In the meantime, capitalism seems to be undergoing new kinds of convulsions, all of them inflicting increasingly unprecedented violence against people, matter, and the biosphere. And as far as liberal democracy is concerned, it has been emptied of all content other than formal; it is teetering, even crumbling.

Unable to hide the fact that liberal democracy has become a mere adjunct to neoliberalism, supposedly liberal governments encourage the most gullible among us to think that their future can be guaranteed only by withdrawing into some evanescent national identity. Let us, comes the general cry, return everyone to their homes and build walls everywhere, while a global-scale war is waged against migrants.

Everything transpires, then, as if the inextricable questions of the living and of decarbonizing the economy will be resolved by forced planetary sedentarization, starting with that of populations deemed superfluous or in excess. To these masses tempted by exodus, we have, until recently, never stopped promising development. The facts on the ground, however, continually refute the fiction of a modernity on the march toward the realization of its normative principles. The neoliberal revolution has resulted in the slow dismantling of the social compromise forged in the immediate postwar period, and the terrain of struggle has shifted to questions of identity.

But how are we to interpret the strident demand for a return to a soil, a region, and a locality when everything advances toward the indisputable planetarization of the problems facing humanity? Is it true, as many observers suggest, that identitarianism is a language opposite to the desire of those who, having been stripped of it, want to regain a voice? Or is it a muted attempt to wrest the control of one's destiny back from the policies that neoliberal states seek to shield from all debate? Rather, is identity politics not perhaps, far from being the new opiate of the masses, a name for various populations' rejection of policies that are effectively responsible for destroying and atrophying their living environment?

When all is said and done, what ought we to understand by identity?

Western philosophies of the subject, dominant the world over for many centuries, have now fizzled out. They take for granted the idea that we have something intrinsic, fixed, stable, and therefore invariant in us. They teach us that the individual is the principle of their own being. As its own creator, it receives its identity from itself, and because it is endowed with a reflexive consciousness and an interiority, it is presumed to be distinct from all other living species.

Anti-Identity

This belief, supposing it to be true, is far from universal.

Certainly, as the citizen of a state, each one of us is subject to procedures of identification. Each one of us, for example, has a birth certificate. When we die, a death certificate is issued by the government. In the intervening period, we are given an identity card with our own number, and for those who travel abroad, a passport that indicates our gender, nationality, age, and profession. In the eyes of the state, all this data serves to say who we are and to attest our belonging, in return for which we enjoy a series of national rights and protections. In this sense, we are the products of state mechanisms of identification.

Furthermore, as human beings, we play a series of roles. Some are assigned to us as obligations. Others we create ourselves. But the roles we play are not sufficient to define who we are. In reality, we remain forever *undefinable* to ourselves and to others. And this property, which consists in never reaching a level of total transparency to ourselves and to others, is perhaps what are our identity ultimately is. All humans share it.

Other traditions of thought have understood this well. Ancient African thought is a case in point: in it, identity is never anything but fragmented, scattered, and in shreds.

Moreover, the crucial issue for it is the way that the self gets composed and recomposed, always in relation to other living entities. In other words, identity consists only in becoming, in the fabric of relations of which each condenses the living sum. Identity, in this sense, did not constitute an infinite substance. It was something that one entrusted to the care of others, in the experience of encounter and relationship, which always presupposed trial and error, movement, and above all, the unexpected—the surprise that one had to learn how to welcome. For, what is harbored in the unexpected, in the surprise, is the event.[25]

The event comes about because there is no world, society, or community that does not have its origin in some idea of debt. In ancient African thinking, the human person is a compound of multiple living entities.[26] It is not self-generating. Others are always responsible for its coming to life. It owes to these others not only its birth but also its language, its fundamental institutions, and the immaterial wealth, both incalculable and nonrepayable, that it inherits. This original form of debt, or the dowry that the generations owed to each other, stands opposed to the expropriating debt that, in its commercial form, today burdens the conditions of reproduction, and even of survival, of millions of women and men across the Earth's surface.

In these systems of thought, what we call identity leaves no room for self-enclosure, autarky, the face-to-face with oneself, the refusal to encounter the world, or mistrust, or a self that asserts itself in solitary fashion and, in so doing, sinks into the kind of repetition that ennui always produces. On the other hand, singularity and originality were socially valued individual attributes, and a point was made of cultivating, caring for and, when necessary, fully highlighting them.[27]

The important thing here is not identity, but the energy that is supposed to govern vital phenomena and guide conducts. The human person was defined essentially by its wealth of vital energy and its capacity to resonate with the multiplicity of living species that populated the universe, including plants, animals, and minerals. Neither fixed nor immutable, it was characterized by its plasticity.

Truly singular people, it was considered, were those with a recognized ability to produce various assorted arrangements of forces, to capture and reconfigure life's flows. In this sense, ancient African metaphysics can be said to be about becoming and not about substance. At a time when computational technologies are perfecting their hold over the entire world, such metaphysics are more apt than Western philosophies of the subject to help us to grasp identity as something that is ever in motion, never the same, always open to that which arrives, and that never ceases to synthesize itself anew upon encountering different energy flows.

In this new age of the Earth, liberal democracy has hit a real impasse. It is in the process of being engulfed by many regressive forms of nationalism. Instead of promoting a planetary politics able to set the history of the world and the living in motion, these latter forces intend to work toward regenerating supposedly pure and organic communities under threat from all sorts of intruders.

The combustion of the world underway means that we have to break with the circular conception of identity that has characterized Western reason for so many centuries. The theme of identity must be replaced by that of the living, that is, the destiny of the biosphere, notably, in an era where everything indicates that a new technological genesis is in gestation. If, in fact, the Earth is a whole, then identity can arise only under the sign of the generalized circulation of life and the living. And the times urgently call on us to return to these kinds of circulation and to these flows of life. From this viewpoint, Africa represents an immense reserve of possibilities. The eldest daughter of the Earth and humanity's youngest member, it harbors inexhaustible energies under its crust and in its entrails, not only a wound-filled past but also the sorts of powerful treasures needed in times of extremes. Africa inhabits these memories of trial and healing as her radiant home.

FOUR
VIRILISM

We cannot take an interest in how power and the economy profoundly work bodies over and test the subject's nerves without also undertaking to criticize the phallus, understood as the emblem par excellence of patriarchy. The point here is not to reduce one to the other but rather to show that the phallus is not merely an abstract place, a simple signifier, or a differentiating sign—a detachable object, divisible, and given to symbolic retranscription. The phallus can assuredly not be reduced to the penis as such. But neither is it the bodiless organ so dear to a certain Western psychoanalytical tradition.

In this chapter, we discuss the phallus as *that* which has the peculiarity of manifesting itself, in the purest way, as turgidity, as thrust or eruption, and as intrusion. There can be no speaking about thrust, turgidity, and intrusion without restoring to the phallus if not its physicality, then at least its living flesh, its capacity to attest to domains of the sensible, to experience all kinds of sensations, vibrations, and quiverings (a color, a scent, a touch, a weight, a smell, and so on).

The phallus and patriarchy are, moreover, like two sides of the same mirror, that of a power that we ought to qualify as orgasmic. This power is inhabited by a dog-spirit, a pig-spirit, and a rogue-spirit. It always seeks to establish all kinds of tension-filled relationships between corporeality (the intensive fact of the body and nerves), sexuality, and matter.

Proslavery domination and colonial subjugation were both historical expressions of this power. From start to finish, these expressions concerned genital domination. They were driven by the desire for some absolute enjoyment in which the dominated subject, whatever its gender, had to be transformed into a sexual object. It was a question, in the exercise of such a power, of experiencing a certain type of orgasm that not only touched the body and its different organs but was equivalent to a trembling of the senses.

Trembling of the Senses

On the plantation, as in the colony, imaginaries and sex practices, essentially derived from the West, contributed to forging domination of a libidinal nature that took racialized human bodies as its privileged target. This form of exercise of a power without apparent control passed through a device, racialized sex, which it was occasionally necessary to reduce to its simplest expression, the genital relationship. In principle and in practice, orgasmic power was a technique of heterosexual management of subaltern bodies. These latter were considered sometimes as objects, sometimes as pathological. To accomplish this, power required a semiotic apparatus capable of producing representations and knowledge about its targets.[1]

For the purposes of legitimization, it also undertook a larger-scale manufacturing of all sorts of images and silhouettes whose generalized circulation made it possible to normalize the treatment of these bodies, and thus of these people.[2] What do these images tell us about the act of enslaving or colonizing in general, or about the links between colonial domination and male and genital domination in particular? What place does race occupy in the order of sex, thus understood as an instrument of the enjoyment and violation of bodies, and of that which they are the symbols? This chapter attempts to answer some of these questions.[3]

Indeed, during its long history, the West has, of its own admission, entertained with sex and sexuality an exceptionally complicated relationship, which, characterized by an original anxiety, has been the subject of countless scholarly studies and commentaries. On the one hand, the West, perhaps more than any other region of the world, has been haunted by the question of the origin of sexual enjoyment, its nature, and its relationship with virility, voluptuousness, and brutality, including delirium and death. On the other hand, the analysis of a number of its sexual customs and expressions—including pornography—shows that it has given a preeminent place to the genital embrace, which, incidentally, it has grasped as the manifestation of a gigantic energy that is both biological and cosmic, in addition to being the original frontier between nature and culture.

The orgasm, in particular, is seen in it as that which prevents the human being from detaching itself completely from nature and the world of instincts. As a cataclysmic moment and the pinnacle of enjoyment, the orgasm is deemed to be that which points to man's ultimate defeat, man who, for the space of an instant, is totally subjected to a singular power of annihilation, to the site of collision of contradictory forces of energy and entropy.[4] In a word, as a mixture of pleasure and anguish, sexual life is held to conceal, in its depths, something potentially foul or squalid, something pertaining at the same time to the quagmire and the dump. Left to themselves, sexual impulses are considered thus to bring to the surface all that is abject and swampy about sex. Hence the necessity to repress the instincts by civilizing them, to surround the uses of sex with multiple prohibitions and moral precepts. In short, without the repression of sexual impulses and their sublimation, humanity, blinded by its passions, would be condemned to live under the yoke of its desires and prevented from being born to reason and maturity.

It is against this relatively pessimistic account of sexual life and humanity's becoming free that most libertarian movements have risen up since at least the nineteenth century.[5] Whatever forms they have taken, their ultimate objective has been more or less the same, namely, to cut the link between sexuality and the imaginary of sin and guilt so deeply registered in the unconscious of Western societies. This is why the sexual revolution would essentially consist in breaking with the circle that turns sexuality into a kind of cesspool, while sexual enjoyment never appears to consciousness except under the form of ecstasy, or of death itself, an ecstatic death.

Armed with this narrative, the "white man"—by which we must understand a fiction of limitless power in a conquered and occupied land—will come up against foreign bodies. Accustomed to winning without being right and thanks to the hold he has on spaces, territories, and objects, he discovers that it is indeed possible to enjoy remorselessly, to satisfy whims through exactions and depredations of all sorts, including on bodies transformed into objects, without having the slightest feeling of anguish or guilt.

"White man" begins to realize that he can literally empty the Other of its content and inscribe his own truth in this vacant place, inscribe it in the form of an image or a silhouette. He begins to see that he can effectively force this conquered humanity from the status of an imagined thing to that of an accomplished thing, as colonizing becomes, by the very fact, about subjugating foreign organs and bodies to the will of a conqueror. The plantocracy, and also the colony, were, from this point of view, privileged laboratories not only of sexual life but also of the libidinal character of any power. In them, many forms of enjoyment, sadistic games, and various figures of "reverse liberation," that is, at the expense of those weaker than oneself, were experimented with. Sexual freedom here consisted above all in the right to dispose of Others as if they were objects.

In the colony, it was actually possible to break with the idea that repressing sexual impulses in the unconscious was one condition for attaining substitute satisfactions. Experience tended to show that the subject was not necessarily structured at the meeting-point between desire and the law, experienced as one modality among others of repression. It was possible to live in the absence of prohibitions and other restrictions, or even to satisfy impulses with little regard for taboos. On a purely phenomenological level, colonial forms of brutalization (during the phases of conquest, pacification, and possession proper) involved something like an unleashed libido, a combinatorial of drives (sexual, sadistic) the very nature of which was to constantly turn back upon themselves.

The colonies thus served as a serendipitous terrain for all those for whom experimenting with pleasure was part of the great dream of complete genital satisfaction. Many were out for power of an orgasmic nature, of the kind that required no symbolic base and that could thus survive short-circuiting since it excluded a priori any possibility of debt or guilt. It is in these areas that it is important to look for the decisive springs of contemporary forms of *orgastic power*, those which, feeding on the sources of neovitalism, constitute neoliberalism's raw material.

In the plantation and the colony alike, the copulatory function—a physical and phantasmatic activity, if ever there was—would ultimately lead always to the same thing—the impossibility of absolute, fiery, and fusional enjoyment. Should we deduce from this that the sexual scene is by nature unrepresentable, a simple name on the tip of a tongue, or even on the tip of a lip? Or that there is never really any going back to any source or origin, since, in the end, going to meet *that* which encloses us so tightly and has conceived us pertains strictly to myth?

These questions arise for several reasons, the first having to do with the very nature of the colony. For what is the colony if not a strange hole, a paradoxical complex, one of whose characteristics is to provide, to those who desire it, an absolutely direct angle on sex, this great imaginary of objects whose specificity is to awaken desire? Indeed, one enters desire as one falls into a trap, between one body and another—brutal emergences, sometimes perverse and sometimes sadistic takings of control, forced movements, all kinds of ejaculations associated with aggressiveness, racism, and hatred, including self-hatred.

Colonizing indeed means brutalizing. In a colony, brutalizing means systematically introducing difference not only into the body's adornment but also into its cosmetics, its flesh, its nerves, its organs and, by extension, into the very structure of fantasy. It means splitting everything, including the gaze. It means, lastly, establishing a cut between what can be seen in itself and for itself, and what must only appear in the field of vision under the figure of the Other, that is, of a body called upon to support an enjoyment that overflows it and that is not necessarily its own. Because, as a deep hole around which everything seems to have been built, the colony is, moreover, traversed by the obsession for a particular knowledge—to know at any moment which sex belongs to whom, among the inexhaustible variety of the sexes.

As regards the sexual, the colony consequently differs from other scenes on several levels. On the one hand, it is a place where sex is not solely found in the sexual act. It is in the atmosphere, as it were, an inflammable material and a factory of possibilities. Man's sex? Woman's sex? Or sex beyond the two, as with the ancient Dogons, sometimes suspended in indeterminacy and sometimes drawing on the sources of twinness? In reality, sex-salmon, sex-with-hair, sex-fisher of shells, schizo-paranoid, anal and sadistic, if need be, polyvalent, belonging to nobody in particular. In both its genital and symbolic aspects, the sexual is not only transformed, it is in principle divided in the very act that constitutes it, in the desire, including in the love, that works it.

On the other hand, if, in the colony, sex is not encountered only in the sexual act, and if, to borrow from Jacques Lacan, there is strictly speaking no sexual relationship, then everything is sexual. In fact, the colony is far from being a desert of enjoyment.

In the colony and the plantation, it is indeed not uncommon to find seduction combined with perversion. As a traumatic force, the colonist can take his targets to his bed, smell their bodies and their odors, and then, as the undeflatable phallus, take advantage of them on sight, use them up, and wet them with his emissions. In his attempt to return to the body of enjoyment's first needs, situated somewhere between the lace diaper, pom-pom slippers, and the soft toy, try as he might to smother the "negress" or négrillon with so many nicknames—(ma pupuce [my doggy], mon cacalou [my little walnut], ma petite crevette rose [my rose shrimp], ma grenouille [my froggy], mon buffle [my buffalo], or mon crapaud [my toad])—many encounters are missed, retracted, and it is not necessarily because the Other carries a mask or participates, by essence, in an unfigurable void. It is also because, in both the colony and the plantation, the threat of the obsession for babies (bébéphilie), that is, the presence of the "child" in the colonial fantasy, is never far away.

Frantz Fanon may not be so wrong to suggest that the colonist can only enjoy as a pig, a fox, a wolf, a vicious dog, or a rat, if necessary, and have us believe that, owing to the perverse and racist structure of the colony, the Black is only a stallion's member that wails as it has lived, that is, as a castrated man. For the colony is also the land of incontinence. To not hold on, to lose control, to wet oneself, to soil oneself without pretext—all this is undoubtedly part of the will to pure enjoyment that authorizes one to "sadize" the colonized. To overcome his division, to suppress the point of anguish in the relationship with his mother or father, and to overcome his alienated childhood, doesn't the adult-sized-little-kid-colonist need to be bottle-fed, burped, wiped, scolded, that is, to find his own mirror image in the body of the child that he was, that he wishes to become again, and that the Black so profoundly figures?

We must, thus, necessarily turn our backs on certain myths. Concerning sexuality, the colony is the country of refused separations and disjunctive alliances, of the confusion of tongues and lips. There is no place for autoeroticism in it. The Other is a sex organ, the sight of which inevitably produces effects of excitement. One goes there to get oneself some enjoyment. Besides, to enjoy means to *enjoy oneself*. And enjoying necessarily passes through the Other. Little matter if the genital organs still bear this animal aspect or not, all the investments made concerning the Other's body often have no other goal than to touch oneself indefinitely.

For, ultimately, the colony does not precede anything. What precedes the colony is not part of some presexual stage. Sex (*du sexe*) had been there prior to the colony. The colony forced its way in on what was *already there*—a population of beings, the old anatomy with its belly, its breasts, its mouth, its jewels, its mechanisms of psychosexual structuring of the unconscious that came down neither to the fear of castration, nor penis envy, nor the Oedipus complex. Other signs and other prohibitions were there already also, beginning with the incest prohibition. A phantasmatic universe also, with its phallic vulvas and its vulval phalluses, twinness, the open and edgeless space of cloth, in short, the contents in the container, the dialectic of differentiation and complementarity.

With the advent of the colony, however, at least two events take place. First, the sites where the sexual is held—its perimeter and its objects—shift considerably, and its power emerges tenfold as a consequence of bourgeois neurosis and receding primitivism. Moreover, it is no longer possible to escape the Other's sex, its tongue, its lips, and its nuclei, the pearl. The modalities by which one lives sexuality change at the same time as the representations and fantasies that sustain sexual practices. More than ever, the subject has to face up to his lack.

From this viewpoint, colonization constitutes a great moment of intrusion and cleavage, of hold over the living. If this hold is apt to lead to loss, it is nevertheless not all and is not only that. This hold is also an occasion for the embroidering of myths, for inciting tales, for inscribing new signifiers on bodies, and for interweaving images that one hopes will open the window onto the Other beyond the screen that hides it. As a result, to attain the body and make it the fulcrum of libidinal fixations, it must necessarily be undressed. It will be necessary to pass directly to denudation, to confront nakedness, without which there is no presence, only lack.

That said, getting sexuality to function in the colonial situation is not only about object pleasure, and the *phallus* is not all of desire. Not all can be reduced to extraction and sexual sampling. The capacity to feel emotions, to have attachments, and to experience love remains, even if, owing to the racist structure of the colony, this capacity is clearly manifest in an opaque form. The risk of destitution, *of being only that*, nevertheless, remains omnipresent.

As a result, the question is to know how to traverse the fantasy but without staying in it. How can one escape the Other's lips and nuclei once they have become that through which the sexual subject henceforth becomes manifest, that with whose help the subject's enters life? By loosing oneself from oneself, beyond skin-to-skin contact. By finding a part of oneself in the Other—being in the Other; no being without Otherness.

As Frantz Fanon remarked, in a colonial situation, there is little real person-to-person contact. Yet, what prevails is contact between a person and his harem of objects. This applies to the level of sexual life. Constantly whipped by an insatiable phallus, the multitude of women who populate the images gathered in *Sexe, race et colonies* appear only as crossed-out subjects, in mirror image. They are each time summoned to appear as image only so that they can observe their own disappearance better, because what these images celebrate is the phallus in search of its epiphanic moment, the spectacle of colonial domination turned into genital domination and combining, by this very fact, masculinism and racism. These women have no sexuality as such. Most of the time, they are only gaping holes, beings of flesh at the service of someone else, bodies arranged in series, as genital combinatorials. They serve, above all, as proof that the "white man," as a fiction of power in a foreign territory, exists only through the devices of his sadism, which threaten him with madness and perversion each time he is exposed to the Other. Colonization was thus as much a visual event as a bacchanalia of the senses and sensations.

The Phallos

But in all other respects, the history of sexuality in Africa remains to be written.[6]

If it comes to be written, it will not be a history of repetition, nor even necessarily of difference, although this does exist, but rather a history of twinness and inversion, of joy and celebration.[7] It will be the history of what, necessarily, exceeds assignations of origin all the better to manifest the principle of ambivalence.[8] It will be a history of the struggle between the subject and its body—a struggle whose stake, each time, is to inaugurate new expressive possibilities, to make singularities suddenly appear through composition.[9]

Indeed, no matter how much we try to make an object of the human being, there is always something of his or her humanity that eludes this objectal reduction, this desire for objectification. Individuals can be reduced to silence, but they are still capable, through their gaze, of articulating a gesture, of sketching a mute word that nevertheless interpellates. Their bodies can be exhibited as trophies or as scenery, but their self can escape the spectacle. The body is there, but the self is elsewhere. The characteristic of colonial violence is to dissociate the self from its appearances, to force the dominated to appear only in the mode of absence, the hollow, and the void. Indeed, this void is where racism and its world of fantasies takes up its lodging.

It so happens that the status of the phallus in the African imaginary, or at least in the art and sculpture of African peoples, bears innumerable similarities to that of the Greek *phallos*. In all cases, as a sculpted subject, the phallus, here in Africa, is defined above all by its enormous power of affirmation. It is the name of a totally affirmative force.[10] From an anthropological and phenomenological point of view, this is what links it so closely to power, itself conceived as a trial, an arraignment.

Accordingly, power here is not only endowed with a phallus that functions as its emblem and ornament. Power *is* phallus. Power is possessed only by mounting it. And the phallus is the master agent of this straddling operation.[11] This master agent claims to act as a source of movement and energy. It functions in the manner of a subject that seeks to mount everything. This is why it engages in permanent gymnastics, in little games. Hence the mixture of violence and comedy that a share of contemporary literature is concerned with. Phallocracy, from this point of view, is a dimension of brutalism.[12] It is basically a power formation, a series of institutional, corporeal, and psychological devices that function on the basis of the belief that the phallus (and thus the masculine) is where things happen; that an *event* occurs in and through the phallus; that, in fact, the phallus is the event.

The foundation of brutalism is precisely this belief that power is ultimately the effort that the *phallos* exerts on itself to become a Figure. This belief continues to function as the unspoken, the underside, even the horizon of our modernity, although few want to hear it spoken about. The same is true of the belief that the phallus is phallus only in the movement by which it seeks to escape from the body and endow itself with an autonomy of its own. And it is this attempt at evasion, and this thrust or eruption, that produces spasms. Phallocracy varies its identity precisely through these spasmodic thrusts and violence.

Elsewhere, it has been demonstrated how, under postcolonial conditions, the spasms and violence through which power and its vibrations are recognized and identified only draw the hollow and flattened volume of that same power.[13] For the phallus may dilate, but this dilation is always followed by a contraction and a dissipation, a detumescence. Moreover, it has been argued that under postcolonial conditions, the power that makes the subject yell and that wrings incessant cries from his chest can be only a power coupled with his beast—his dog-spirit, his pig-spirit, his rogue-spirit. It can be only a power endowed with a bodily material, a carcass of which the phallus is the brightest manifestation as well as a darkened surface. A power that is *phallos* in the sense that we have just defined can present itself to its subjects clothed only with skull and crossbones. This is the skull that makes these subjects emit such screams and makes their life almost zoological.

We know, for example, how the lynching of black men in the American South during slavery and in the aftermath of the Emancipation Proclamation took its origins partly in the desire to castrate them. The racist "small white" and the planter, filled with anxiety about their own sexual potential, were gripped with terror at the thought of the "black sword," fearing its supposed volume but also its penetrative and assaulting essence. In the obscene act of lynching, they sought to protect the supposed purity of the white woman by keeping the black man level with his death.[14] They aimed to bring him to contemplate the extinction and the darkening of what, in the racist phantasmagoria, they held for his "sublime sun," his *phallos*. The shredding of his masculinity was wrought by transforming his genitals into a field of ruins—separating them from life's powers. This was because, as Fanon puts it so well, in this configuration, the Black does not exist. Or, rather, the Black is above all a *member*.

The overinvestment of virility as a symbolic and political resource is not only a historical effect of the techniques of dehumanization and devirilization that characterized the plantation regime under slavery or colonial governmentality. This overinvestment is part of the very life of any form of power, including in liberal democracies. This is indeed the pure activity of power in general, that which gives it its speed and, therefore, its violence. Virility represents the northern line of power in general, its frenzied zone.

In this regard, we have only to observe what is going on today. At a time when some would have us believe that "Islamo-fascism" is the danger of all dangers, are the wars being waged against Muslim countries not experienced as so many moments of "discharge," whose paradigmatic value results precisely from the fact that the model of this release is the erection of the male genital organ, with advanced technologies playing the role of assault objects that enable some kind of coitus—racial nationalism?

Is the object of these wars not, to a large extent, the stock market? Wars, which are to be understood here as logics of a struggle to the death (as war, precisely), through the logic of profit? Is each high-altitude bombing, each torture session in the secret prisons of Europe and elsewhere, each laser-guided discharge, not the manifestation of a virile orgasm, of the West discharging itself by making the destruction of states declared enemies the very beacon of pleasure in the age of advanced technology? How else can we understand this intoxication with destruction, the massive debauchery that accompanies it, its attendant booze-ups, rapes, and orgies, grimaces, and obscenities?[15]

It would be naive to question the functions of contemporary wars and their political economy while ignoring the racist and masculine eroticism that lubricates them and that is an essential constituent of them, or while concealing their theo-pornological essence. In the violence without rhyme or reason that marks our time, there is a kind of projection of the virile imagination and of perverse desire that we would be wrong to underestimate. The production of racial nationalism in the neoliberal era also depends on many female silhouettes. The "father" always underlies these silhouettes, that is, the one who alone enjoys the status of the primary "planter" (a begetting and fertilizing power). Moreover, contemporary neoliberal culture is haunted by the figure of the incestuous father, a father possessed by the desire to consume his virgin (or his boy), or to annex his daughters to his own body, with the aim of using them as a complement to his failing stature as man.

The extreme stylization of the phallic reference and the investment in femininity and maternity aim to situate sexual enjoyment in the wake of a secular politics of rapture. But the way in which power relentlessly solicits the body (those of men as well as those of women) and informs it, works it, crosses it, and delimits it as an extensive zone destined to satisfy and fill all kinds of drives is no less marked by brutality. It is obvious that this has nothing "African" about it, if by this polemical term one understands an obscure and psychotic force, walled in a time in some way preethical, prepolitical, and premodern, in short, in a world apart.

Moreover, in Africa, what is striking is the extraordinary symbolic richness of the relationship to the body and to sex. Body and sex are, by definition, plural. Like almost everything else, they are the result of operations of composition and assembly. Sexual difference fundamentally takes shape through all kinds of ambiguities, inversions, and metamorphoses. It means very little outside this field of ambivalences.

The body as well as sexuality outside power always opens onto a field of dispersion and therefore of ambivalence. In this field, as in art and especially music and dance, a logic of unexpected meanings prevails.

The body is not something we simply have. We live our bodies. And preferably as a symbol of absolute ambivalence—the ambivalence of the symbol as precisely that which frees desire, removes it from the nets of power that try to colonize it. This is why the body and sex as lived are body and sex only insofar as they open up to all sorts of expressive potentialities, to singularity. It is enough to see how Africans dress, use ornaments, and dance. How can we ensure that these expressive potentialities escape the language of induced needs and manipulated desires (the code of capital)? Or that they continue to manifest the certainty of life in the face of all sorts of threats that aim to destroy it after having devalued its meaning? These are fundamental questions.

They are far more important than the West's brandishing of the theme of respect for women to defend goodness-knows-what cultural superiority. As in the colonial era, the devaluing interpretation of how the black man or Muslim treats "his women" deals in a mixture of voyeurism, horror, and envy—a desire for the harem. The manipulation of gender issues for racist purposes, through the highlighting of male domination in the Other, is almost always aimed at obscuring the reality of phallocracy at home.

It remains to be seen how the successive crises of the last quarter of the twentieth century in Africa have variously affected relations between men and women and between social elders and minors. In some cases, they have contributed to deepening already existing gender inequalities. In other cases, they have brought about a profound change in the general terms in and through which male domination and femininity are now expressed.

Among the poorer segments of the population, the status of head of household, held usually by men, has seemingly been downgraded, especially where the ability to feed one's family can no longer be fully guaranteed for want of material means. The new cycle of subsistence struggles generated by the crisis and by austerity has, paradoxically, opened up opportunities for movement for a relatively small but influential number of women, particularly in certain informal spheres of material life. These increased opportunities for mobility have accompanied a renewed challenge to male prerogatives and an intensification of gender violence.

These shifts have, in turn, led to two major consequences. On the one hand, one of the pillars of male domination, namely the notion of family debt, has been strongly undermined and is now a point of contestation. Indeed, until recently, the relationship between men and women, and the relationship between men and children within the family, had been built around this notion. One of the cornerstones of African phallocratic systems was, in fact, the idea that sons owed a debt to their fathers and that the inequality between men and women had to do with their complementarity. The relationship between men and women within the family was based on a logic with two levers: that of appropriation and that of reciprocal instrumentality between unequals. The male prerogative with respect to women and children was to feed, protect, and guide, in return for which he exercised domination based on the discriminating factor of inheritance. However, to a large extent, political domination *stricto sensu* relies on extending these same ideological frameworks to the civilian and military domains, with those "above" playing the same functions and having the same attributes with respect to their subordinates as the father within the family unit. A process of demasculinization has affected all the dominated; the pleasure of male domination, properly speaking, has become the exclusive privilege of some, at least in the political field.

Whatever the case, during the last quarter of the twentieth century, the phallus as a central signifier of power and a privilege of male domination has been profoundly challenged. This contestation has been expressed through different figures. Some have taken the form of marital instability and the relatively chronic circulation of women. Others have been expressed in the form of urban panics, at the center of which stood the fear of castration. Certainly, the phallus continues to represent an essentially differentiating sign. However, its primordial functions have become increasingly blurred as we witness a devirilization of minors, itself an effect of diverse forces.

Onanist Societies and the Drive to Ejaculate

Patriarchy and coloniality form a single frame. Each is the condition of possibility of the other. Such is notably the case within societies that we must qualify as onanistic. Onanistic societies are organized around a central motive—the expending of seminal matter. They are preoccupied with the drive to ejaculate. Patriarchy, for its part, can be interpreted as the measure that grants semen its exceptional status and that defines the conditions of its expenditure: inside which reservoir it can legitimately be deposited, what sets it apart from the domain of simple refuse, and its ultimate goal.

From this point of view, as a measure of power and as the ideologeme par excellence of an onanistic society, patriarchy maintains a constitutive relationship with the economy of ejaculation. This latter is the outcome of an excitation. Ejaculating means spreading the seminal matter that results from excitation, friction, and combustion, without which the sensation is neither experienced nor the seminal liqueur secreted and released.[16] Seminal fluid is, for its part, treated as a precious good and collected as such, its primary function being to bring life, to ensure it for the long term through descent and the enabling of a genealogy. It is through the production of this supposedly vital source that patriarchy self-immunizes, seeks to escape profanation, and protects itself against defilement. Performed in the appropriate conditions, the extraction of seed by no means pertains to the sacrilegious.

In onanistic societies, moreover, patriarchy represents a form of—if not complete, then at least aggravated—narcissistic desire. Ejaculation in onanistic—and patriarchal—societies is one of these desires. This desire manifests itself in different forms. In all cases, this desire is the source of an intense phantasmatic activity. Consummated or not, it excites the imagination. Participation in fantasy is one of the reasons for the permanence of patriarchy as well as of capitalism, which is also structured around the ejaculation drive. In this latter case, ejaculation is of masturbatory doing.[17] New contemporary digital devices have paved the way for and facilitate an unprecedented convergence between ejaculatory and scopic impulses. It is no longer enough to "pleasure yourself" in secret. It must be seen, by you and by the spectator, preferably through a small hole, anyone will do. In the case of the spectator, this seeing does not at all require co-presence.

You can see while not being there at all. Only the hope of excitement counts. This is what makes self-excitement possible through imagination and fantasy. The mass production of readily excitable male bodies seeking ejaculation through masturbatory touch is undoubtedly one of the major transformations that patriarchy has undergone at the beginning of this century. For in its extensive reproduction, patriarchy can now largely do without women. All it needs is to touch and play with itself, to self-arouse. Imagination has become an institution in itself.

At the same time, heteronormativity is being radically challenged. We are irreversibly moving toward a new sexual era in which the binarization of the sexes (male and female) will be a distant memory. Indeed, the flexibility and diversity of genders are constantly gaining in intensity. The same is true of a panoply of sexual practices that resonate with the ongoing "hacking" of genders.[18] Once dominated by the classical family, the domestic environment has undergone deep reconfigurations. Besides father, mother, and children, we find in it a panoply of subjects inhabited by all kinds of desires: husbands at home, idle, and solitary; men and women who have transgender or homosexual tendencies, some of which have been explored, and others not. There are also "butches," male-identifying lesbians with or without partners, classic male-identifying wives, and other subjects who have left sexual activity for varying periods of time.

It is an age of trafficking in sexual signifiers. This trafficking is carried out through performances:

> He is on all fours, his hole open to the camera. A gloved and clean hand draws and engraves carefully a black sun around his hole with a tattoo machine. . . . He is naked. A very precise genitorture which consists in injecting a non-toxic liquid (a saline solution) has deformed his penis and his testicles. His genitals, which protrude and jiggle between his legs, look more like a kind of external uterus than a male sex organ. His penis is turgid without being erect. He is full but not of semen. Instead of ejaculating, he received the technical and calculated ejaculation from the syringe. His sex is contra-sexual. He has garter belts. He walks on high heels. He walks slowly, very slowly as if he is going to fall with every step. Two dildos have been attached to his heels like two spurs. He has attached them to his feet. They hang behind his shoes like flaccid, secondary heels.[19]

The trafficking of sexual signifiers also proceeds through sessions of tattooing around sexual organs. The sort of ejaculation impulse and masturbation proper to onanistic societies occupy no central place here. Neither does the erection. Sperm is put out of play, almost neutralized. There is no vulva in sight. Orgastic climax is reached thanks to a panoply of techniques and objects and thanks to a series of practices with varied names. One such is "self-dildoing" (or anal "self-fucking").[20] Self-dildoing requires equipment: an enema pump, a pair of high-heeled shoes, two dildos, one small and hard and the other larger and softer, two ties and a chair.

There is a dance practice, *butoh*, that originated in Japan in the early 1950s, in which the dancer learns to let go. Similar to most African ritual practices, the dance is about experiencing metamorphosis. *Butoh* is not a ritual of possession. The performance's goal is to let yourself go, to release your ego, to thrust yourself into a state of "perception that will make the dancer the stone or the tree, the fetus or the old man, the rod or the vulva, the black or the white."[21]

Emptying oneself, fragmenting oneself, multiplying oneself through metamorphosis—such is the goal. Similar to practices of self-dildoing, there is another imagination of the body at work here. Masculinity is symbolically deprived of its sovereignty. We are no longer up against ejaculatory bodies, those that have contributed to expropriating women's reproductive power. Nor are we dealing with the patriarchal-colonial body, as that which proceeded to transform the body of the Black and that of all the colonized, in general, into labor force. The disqualification of the patriarchal-colonial body, or its hypertrophy in the neoliberal and onanistic regime, does not mark the end of virilism nor the end of the "desire of the phallus" as such. But perhaps it prefigures its forthcoming minority status. The ensuing relative genital panic contributes, in return, to narratives of the end characteristic of our times.

Yet, in the same movement, we must take into account considerations of race and class and the virility rooted in certain traditions of white feminism.[22] How to account, for example, for white virile femininities in their relationship with men of other races?[23] A case in point is white female soldiers or women in positions of power who mistreat prisoners of color, subjecting them to acts of torture and degradation, including scenes with homosexual connotations, which prisoners are forced to perform against their will.[24] In these situations of racial violence, an erotology of cruelty is mobilized.[25] This sexualized violence is the work of a virility that is both masculine and feminine and that makes a pretense of being more civilized than that found elsewhere on the planet.[26] It not only reconveys relationships of domination beyond the male/female dichotomy but also necessarily channels hatred and contempt of representations of masculinity other than those that serve white supremacy.[27]

Genital Panic

In ancient African traditions, there was no such thing as the perfect body. In the absence of incarnation, there was no corporeality. The body did not exist as a unit with a unique sexual valence. The body was a semiotic field and, from this point of view, was permanently worked over by all kinds of narratives and open to be experienced in multiple ways. Certain organs, on the other hand, took part in the construction of singular identities, equally as revisable, unstable, and marked with ambivalence. The subject possessed a body just as he belonged to a body. The relationship between possession and belonging was such that the one was the condition of the other and vice versa, which contributed to making the human the prototype of opacity and sexuality an enigma. This enigmatic character of sexuality and the constitutive ambivalence of the bodies showed during the great rituals and performances, in particular dances, but also during festivals and other practices of possession and cure. They were based on the acceptance of the body's organic incoherence and the polymorphic character of the living.

Furthermore, the body was widely understood as borne by narratives, through which it was given life, since life itself proceeded from storytelling. In their multiplicity, the organs were relays, even specialized tools. They were detachable and could conflict with each other. Sometimes the body was too heavy to carry, and the carrier sought to free himself from it. Sometimes it was also cumbersome. Loaded with bones, nerves, fluids, and viscera, it was comparable to a burden.[28] Yet it had a plastic dimension that granted it an extraordinary capacity of metamorphosis. Sex organs, in particular, were more than an anatomical node. Just like the face, they were an essential pivot in the activity of fabulation. They were, to the point of confluence between sensoriality and interiority, the metaphor par excellence of chaotic multiplicity.

In the era of hormonal and surgical manipulations, the contemporary body is in the main "under permanent reconstruction." In the process, what strikes the eye is not only its intrinsic vulnerability but also its malleability, its capacity to receive and to be ground into different materials, from wax to bronze, from glass to terracotta.[29] Further still, it has become, in the words of Michaël La Chance, "an abstract algorithm, a biotechnological clone, or an avatar in the virtual." He adds,

> With the advent of technological images our ability to create images is akin to the construction of new bodies. Image processing serves as a model for the genetic manipulations of the future, the synthetic body is the most perfect, because it cannot be affected by age and disease. Photoshopping has become the equivalent of anti-wrinkle cream, 3D animations in the cinema guarantee us eternal youth.[30]

Neither sex nor gender escapes these transformations. Like the body, sex displays a dispersion at once ontological and organic. As a fundamental pulsation as well as an ancient principle of opening, multiplicity, and proliferation, sexuality in the ancient African corpus was that which no envelope could contain. It was a site at which the subject prepared itself for a permanent risk, the risk of its own negation. The body, rendered into pieces, escaped its own figuration. This granted sex all its power of irrigation, innervation, and gestation. This was so because in the space of an instant, the sudden possibility of going beyond the flesh, in its materiality, was suddenly open. This exceedance enabled the transition toward other bodies, beyond genders and senses. By liberating contemporary sexuality from the constraints of the patriarchal-colonial gaze, the door to all sorts of genital panic is flung open. It may be that, for the first time in the history of modernity, these sorts of panics prefigure the phallus's relegation to minority status.

This fall to minority status is partly driven by ongoing technological transformations. These transformations are not only at the origin of new sensory experiences. They also displace the terms in which the question of sexual desire as such and the modalities of its satisfaction was posed until now.[31] On the one hand, the human body is being rediscovered as a proliferating entity, open to the world, to all kinds of grafts and flows, and to the universe of sensations. On the other hand, the life of the human body is being reinvested at the intersection of three kinds of practices: practices of connection, of substitution, and of vibration. A fully alive and animated body is a moving, connected, vibrating, and potentially plural body, apt for metamorphosis. It is, potentially, an immense field of pleasures.

In order for the fields of pleasure to be expanded and to reach their maximum point of intensity, sexual potentials must necessarily be grafted onto one or another of these nodes of tension. The body alone, unable to achieve this, needs adjuvants or accessories. The development of robotics, computer science, cybernetics, and artificial intelligence has led to the invention of new generations of sexual accessories and other "naughty machines" (*machines coquines*). In most cases, these are connected and vibrating objects. They are designed to add to what exists, to increase the layers of pleasure. In this respect, they play the role of motors. The diverse sorts of "vibrators" available illustrate the point. Coming in various sizes and formats, they can be handled in a variety of different ways. Some of them are remotely controllable and thus operate at a distance. Others are real prostheses.

As the boundaries between the human and the machine free up, there is the emergence of a possible plurality of bodies, affects, and sexualities. Robophilia fosters this emergence. Alongside the multitude of vibrators, all sorts of ersatz humans are cropping up, such as the new generations of sex dolls and other anthropomorphic manifestations of technology, whether silicon sex dolls or other android forms. The appearance of new sexual machines constitutes a significant event in the transformations underway. It contributes to augmenting the masturbatory practices whose role we know in the production of the hedonistic bubbles that are neoliberal subjects. On another level, these new sexual machines make possible the development of experimental sexualities that are no longer limited to humans, or that no longer involve only men and women, but admit many other actors.

Thanks to technological transformations, the phallus is being progressively decentered. Desire is moving steadily in the direction of connected objects, vibrators, ersatz humans, and other anthropomorphic figures. But it is also moving toward more and more multiplied and abstract planes. There is thus a distension in the relation of desire to biological reality. The intimate extends henceforth to any zone or object charged with a coefficient of ambiguity. Furthermore, sexual activity is becoming an activity connected to interfaces, of which platforms constitute the privileged field of exercise. It is also supported by the miniaturization of components of all kinds; in this system, the body itself becomes the equivalent of a sensor, an assembly of chips connected to an enormous nervous system, the phantasmagorical system of techno-capital.

In the future, the phallus as such may well become effectively deposed. The time when sexuality's founding myths had man and woman at their center is over. There will be several sexualities connected with multiple plastic bodies. We will enjoy with the help of encoded signals. Sexuality will be as much the work of human subjects as of technological devices that function in the image of real forms. In the age of neurons, the phallus will be replaced by the libido's primary motor, the brain. The final objective will be to get as close as possible to it, to secure its instrumentation.

It will no longer be necessary to seek stimuli via the clitoris, anus, or phallus. Intensive bombarding of pleasure-related cerebral zones by waves of all kinds will do everything you need for you to become directly ensconced in the throes of ecstasy.[32] The era of sexuality free from contact with other humans will underwrite the end of the long-prevailing hegemony of sexual relations between genders. Techno-sexuality will come to be added to sapiosexuality among humans. This former will combine intimacy together with possibilities for the sexual release of the instincts with machines. We have only to see if this is enough to make the possibilities of a love without sexual desire flourish again, and if, with the phallus finally deposed, it will result in a greater equality among genders.

FIVE
BORDER-BODIES

Contemporary forms of brutalism are characterized not only by the dismantling of social safety nets and by risk-hedging mechanisms or, more generally, by the attempt to replace democracy with the market. These forms are also identifiable in the obsession with abolishing politics, a foremost feature of what is now called "authoritarian liberalism." Indeed, the most decisive changes in contemporary capitalism are not only about deregulating financial transactions, serving public services up to private-sector profiteering, reducing taxes for the rich, or contending for the good graces of liquidity providers. Above all else, one of the major anthropological transformations of our time is humanity's division into multiple *racially typed class* fractions. This involves a distinction, between solvent and insolvent human persons, on the one hand, and a planetary-scale division between what Étienne Balibar calls the "mobile part of humanity" and "wandering humanity," on the other.[1]

"Too Many" Humans

The border institution is the mechanism by which this new division becomes part of reality. Moreover, borders are no longer made of irreversible lines that only rarely cross. They are no longer exclusively physical. They are fundamentally hybrid and deliberately incomplete and segmented. If they are sites par excellence that manifest today's depredation, it is because they are the point of convergence formed by various measures that ensure the managing and regulation of the living as well as the unequal distribution of the perils we face. Sometimes they are combined with security measures, sometimes with humanitarian measures, and sometimes with identity measures.[2] Even the law of mortality now meshes with the border institution.[3] Whether physical, virtual, or dotted lines, all borders share the common feature of being tension-charged. Now that they operate toward the exterior as well as toward the interior, they have effectively become fish traps, apparatuses for capturing, immobilizing, and removing populations deemed undesirable, surplus, and even "excessive." But what do "surplus populations" name?

Answering this question requires that we return to two types of fears that have shaped Western discourse on "population mathematics" since at least the seventeenth century. These are the fear of overpopulation and its opposite, the fear of depopulation. The latter, that is, fear of the conditions that permit the extinction of the human species, resurfaced as of the seventeenth century, a time when the physiological subsistence of humans was at stake. The example of France was acute. Between 1565 and 1788, the kingdom was shaken by interminable subsistence crises. Sometimes they were the consequence of climatic reversals, or the rise in wheat prices and tax pressures, and sometimes they resulted from a combination of food shortages and epidemics. Fertility and mortality rates canceled each other out in successive phases.[4] During the last twenty years of the reign of Louis XIV, the great famines of 1693–1694 and 1709–1710 resulted in a population decrease.[5]

Of all the epidemics, the plague, but also cholera, smallpox, typhus, and measles were the most devastating.[6] Each of these epidemics always caused a sharp increase in deaths and had devastating effects both in the cities and in the countryside.[7] Additionally, epidemics and famines caused Balibar's "wandering humanity" to pour out onto the streets in search of food. While hunger does kill, epidemics have often led to a sudden multiplication and circulation of virulence. In these conditions, the word "population" referred to a mass reality, and more precisely to potentially virulent bodies.[8] This mass was at once physiological, organic, and biopolitical.

The issue concerned the mass of bodies and organisms potentially exposed to the risk of enfeeblement due to their contact with disease and misfortune. The issue of virulence appeared in different forms, in particular in the case of fevers. These fevers were given many names: putrid fever, malignant fever, pestilent fever, purple fever, or typhoid fever. In their various guises, fevers flagged an organism's putrescent part, that which was liable to host worms and have maggots eat into it.[9] In short, depopulation was interpreted as a real biological threat, situated at the meeting point of climatic accidents, crop and price regimes, and rates of natality, mortality, and mobility.

The fear of depopulation was matched by the fear of overpopulation. It was commonly believed, for examples, that states were put at risk by having "too large a number of people." Excessive and uncontrolled population growth was likened to a plague. If the multitude lacked for food and space, so the thinking went, people would readily start devouring each other. Population excess was, moreover, likely to prepare the ground for frightful riots, even revolutions.[10] The scarcity of births, combined with an increase in infant mortality, would likely wipe out certain social classes, especially with the addition of subsistence crises.[11] Death was not just a matter of singular destinies, and it was not distributed randomly. Mortality did not increase exclusively with age. Births and deaths obeyed laws that could be mathematized.[12] All things considered, population policy was for a long time subordinated to the question of subsistence.[13]

The idea that a country's population ought to be proportional to its means of subsistence was, for example, at the core of Malthusianism. "Subsistence" referred not only to economic resources but also to the basic nourishing capital without which life itself is threatened, starting with the body turned to waste and its multiple endowments. For example, crises related to hunger and food shortages, plagues, other epidemics, and wars were likely to affect subsistence. Major crises of high mortality and low natality rates usually coincided with these key moments. Medical advances (prophylaxis) were key to nipping them in the bud.

An increase in the number of people was considered legitimate only if there was a simultaneous increase in means of subsistence.[14] If, like the absolute sovereign of the seventeenth century, a feudal lord viewed "with a favorable eye the multiplication of his subjects," and if the nineteenth-century industrialist was sympathetic to a "vigorous birth rate among the working population," this did not hold for the castle owner. The latter, as Alfred Sauvy would later state, viewed with concern "the development of a population of vagabonds, who prowled around his estate. Are they not, one day, capable of resorting to a distribution of goods outside the usual law?"[15] The problem was therefore not the birth rate in general, but that of the popular classes. As we shall see, this concern was later directed toward "proletarian nations," leading Sauvy to say that the "fear of the multiplication of others," and of the proletarian races, in particular, led to "a fresh outbreak of Malthusianism in populations already undermined by demographic ageing."[16]

Amid this ebb and flow, the demographic regime was generally characterized by stagnation. Whatever the intensity of the fluctuations, both subsistence and demographic crises constantly called into question the political order itself. They dramatically raised the question of what to do with the poor in general and with errant poverty in particular: How to feed the poor? Who was in charge of them? Insofar as food shortages and epidemics had the consequence of throwing multitudes out onto the streets without a safety net, the number of errant populations, and mobile and weakened bodies increased each time. This being the case, population policy was, more than ever, couched in terms of surpluses; that is, the number of humans and bodies was deemed to be "in excess," and draconian rules were devised to regulate their mobility.

From that point on, some enduring questions were raised as a matter of course within each historical cycle and regime of domination, starting with the question of how to define who is part of the "too many," what to do with those who are part of those infected lives of the "too many," and how to deal with them with regard to the law of survival and mortality?[17] How do we stop the production of "too many" humans? How can we ensure that we have simply the right number of subjects, and what would be the "best means of euthanasia for an excessive population" and the cohort of "excess mouths"?[18] And, above all, how do we regiment the mobility of potentially virulent bodies, that is, human waste, those who are unexploitable as manpower, unable to be absorbed and, therefore, superfluous?

Up until the fourteenth century, it was the poor, wandering beggars who figured as the living expression of these "surplus" men. Being associated with Christlike figures, they received alms and were the target of charitable care. Then, from the sixteenth century onward, a phase of stigmatization began.[19] Having the specificity of living everywhere and nowhere, being without community or territorial attachment, didn't they question the values of sedentary life? As they barely worked, as their strength was already diminished and they were destined to a premature death, didn't they belong to the useless part of humanity? Attempts were consequently accelerated to control this supernumerary, disaffiliated, and mobile humanity, resulting, on the one hand, in the establishment of welfare systems, such as the General Hospital (1656) and the beggar's warehouses created in 1764, and, on the other hand, in the increasing penalization of illicit forms of migration, henceforth regarded as vagrancy.[20]

The repressive arsenal targeting poor and migrant populations were subsequently designed to partition them off, to confine and imprison them, and possibly also to deport them to the colonies.[21] The treatment of migrant bodies, which were likened to virulent bodies or to human waste, gradually came to appear as measures of social prophylaxis. The best way to deal with this human waste was to evacuate it from the ordinary spaces of life. This would not stop them moving about. But it would ensure they moved about simply as flows and rejects directed toward drainage points. The movement of such bodies would thus be limited. They would be subjected to sorting procedures, not because they were to be considered as resources to be tapped into, but with a view to their possible elimination, since they were potential sources of nuisance.

Virulent bodies would also become trapped in the mesh of several penalizing measures. Sometimes, during epidemics, the constabulary might be ordered to pursue vagrants and send them to the galleys or subject them to forced labor in fortifications. Migrancy was thus criminalized, and beggars and vagrants were transformed into convicts and forced to serve their sentences in the navy's prisons or in the ports and naval dockyards. Having escaped natural death, they were subsequently caught, sentenced to the galleys or to perpetual banishment, to a whipping, to making a public apology, or to undergoing a period of banishment.[22]

This preventative treatment of the issue of "excess" people and surplus populations came to be supplemented with practices of elimination. In terms of eliminating "surplus" people, the demographic consequences of mass wars and other military campaigns could be considerable. In the event that the troops were numerous and stationed in the territory they crossed through, they were able to decimate civilian populations, especially if they engaged in exactions or pillaging. War was therefore part of the panoply of devices available for regulating surplus populations.

The population also counted as ammunition for fighting against the enemy. Payment of the blood tax largely fell to surplus populations. Sometimes they were forcibly conscripted into militias formed through the introduction of compulsory service. The incorporation of large numbers of subjects into armies depended on the wealth of the state. After the French Revolution in particular, the idea prevailed that the state's military power was proportional to the extent of the population it could place under arms.

In itself, emigration to the colonies was not a practice of elimination, except when the colonists undertook to liquidate the indigenous populations living in the territories where they wished to settle.[23] This was sometimes the result of a multiform process, which the anthropologist Paul Broca described well to the Academy of Medicine in 1867. What happens, he asked, "wherever men multiply on an inextensible soil"? His reply:

> They begin by compressing somewhat, clearing the heaths, fertilizing the moors, drying out the marshes. Up to this point, then, it's wonderful; but there comes a time when the whole place is occupied. And afterwards? There remains the resource of emigration. Thus we will expatriate; we will go across the seas to expropriate and destroy little by little races weaker than ours: we will fill America, Oceania, southern Africa. But the planet on which we live is not elastic. So, what will happen in future generations when the temporary resource of emigration has been exhausted? There will be an aggravation of the struggle for existence that Darwin called the struggle for life, which is manifested in nature at every level of the chain of beings.[24]

Other practices of elimination relied on population transfers.[25]

The Mathematics of Populations

We have just shown that the notion of "surplus," or "excess," people, has been a core part of the European mathematics of populations since the beginning of the modern era. It served as the basis for many theories about "living space" and as a pretext for policies of extermination between the two World Wars.[26] It also played a crucial role in European emigration to the rest of the world because of colonization.[27]

Today, and for the rest of the twenty-first century, the Earth is and will be divided between "high-fertility countries" and countries suffering a "decline in fertility."[28] The question of population control is once again on the cultural and geopolitical agenda. Already many people, especially those in the world's North, are making a direct link between migration pressures and population pressures. The idea of sterilizing the dominated classes and nations has resurfaced in the imagination of the dominant. Fears about the spilling over of prolific populations have resurfaced. Why? Because the problem of the population is one of the Earth's distribution, namely "the fear, more or less declared, that one day there will have to be some sharing."[29] While in the countries of the South, extractive capitalism is reaching cruising speed, neo-Malthusianism is consolidating and is now considered the "ethical" counterpart of neoliberalism.

In practice, neo-Malthusianism is based on what the philosopher Elsa Dorlin calls the "colonial management of the human herd." This, she reminds us, "branches into different techniques of social sterilization."[30] This paradigm is what enables us to understand antimigration policies and the phenomena of detention, encampment, refoulement, and deportation of errant humanities. In the age of brutalism and ostentatious disregard for the rule of law, "surplus" humans now have many faces. Not all fit the portrait that Marx paints of them in his descriptions of the capitalist social relationship.

In Marx's time, "surplus" bodies were clearly part of what he called the "industrial reserve army." Generally speaking, surplus bodies were a reservoir of muscular force that was sometimes useful (especially when the capitalist system was expanding and needed to replenish its labor force), and sometimes useless (when an expansion phase was followed by a contraction phase). In contraction phases, such bodies were relegated to unemployment. With regard to capitalist logic, Marx also distinguished different scales of "overpopulation." Thus, he dealt with the "relative overpopulation" typical of the early phases of capitalism, in particular when it was a matter of destroying traditional ways of life and creating the objective conditions for proletarianization.

One was then faced with bodies from which one removed the material conditions of reproduction and existence. This removal was the prelude to their being thrown into a labor market in which they were subjected to new logics of exploitation. In this phase, these bodies were dispossessed and relatively expropriated, as dispossession and relative expropriation were both necessary conditions of entry into process of primitive accumulation.

But dispossession and expropriation could not be absolute. This held, in particular, in the case of the settler colonies. In South Africa, for example, the system of "reserves" and the later "Bantustans" worked to subsidize capital. Thanks to these "subsidies," a part of capital's operation costs was shifted onto traditional systems of reproduction, which figured women at their core. These systems were not totally dismantled. Instead, they came to be articulated in a relatively complex way to the machinery of exploitation itself.[31] To these categories, Marx added those of "floating overpopulation," which names the mass of potentially exploitable bodies; and "latent overpopulation," in which he included social minors such as women and children; and "stagnant overpopulation," which included peasants and craftsmen.

It is not clear that this taxonomy holds any longer, as the capitalist social relationship now largely operates by enforcing loans and debts, and as the price of labor power is falling.[32] Competition for credit allocation is now the keyword in the dispute. If, within capitalism's new orientation, profit is increasingly based on credit, then the rules of production of obsolete populations also necessarily change. Today's "surplus" people are those with neither the skills to make them employable nor the assets, titles, or property to guarantee their solvency.[33]

The age of *land grabs* has thus been superimposed upon by an age of relative disembodiment and the *setting in motion* of flows of all kinds. By no means is this about the abolishing of matter. The Earth itself continues to be targeted by all sorts of appropriation.[34] But, more than ever, matter is effective only in articulation with dematerialized movement. A case in point is credit and currencies. Their space of circulation is allegedly the "boundless space" of the globe as a whole. In this regime of dematerialized movement, no border is a priori impassable. Borders are fundamentally no longer effective. All that exists is the horizon and its beyond. In principle, then, movement is no longer restricted. Space is also returned to its zero degree insofar as it serves circulation alone. In return, circulation is not only a spur for technology; it is also a spur for movement—it is movement's substratum.

But how do human bodies fare in all this? And which bodies precisely? Patterns of exploitation have changed from those at whose center stood the Marxian bodies of the worker, the peasant, or the "excess" woman. Perhaps there has never been a time when belief in an integral body, a full member of a political community, was the norm. Perhaps in every community the sacrifice of bodies has always been at the foundation of the imaginaries of any community, understood as a vital hearth. Perhaps the taking of certain lives from time to time has always been the very condition of possibility of life in its generality.

In ancient African systems of thought, the human body was seen as a digest of energetic relationships, their clustering as well as their point of convergence and coagulation. In the context of the Black Trade, human bodies could be bought and sold. Slave bodies were captured and put to work as privileged sources of energy. The plantation system extracted this energy, exploited, and eventually depleted it. These bodies were occasionally subjected to various technologies of torment, mutilation, and torture (cf. the *Codes Noirs*). In effect, the point was to hollow out life as much as possible.

Much the same occurred with the transition from the workshop to the factory, with the exception of the salary (however modest). The submission of bodies to the machine and its rhythms was designed to produce consumable goods. This production involved machines in squandering the energy of bodies of workers and laborers. With the slave and the worker alike, the body was not only the object of an energy extraction. It was without integrity, pulverizable and dislocatable, both dispensable and indispensable, too much and too little. In the age of the machine, the body has been one of the machine's innumerable excreta. In the passage to the immaterial, other figures of the virulent body make their appearance.

Neo-Malthusianism

The border-body is a key example, insofar as—divisible, dismemberable, re-memberable, and decomposable—it is an assembly governed by the law of codes and space. The border-body is essentially a racial body, the body of a racial class subjected to a new kind of intensive calculation. It brings together externalization and internationalization. Always on the verge of falling onto the other side of the fence, it fundamentally lacks any safety membrane. A body torn to pieces, it is folded in several layers and carries the memory of partitions and subdivisions in its flesh. This body can be found on land, at sea, in abstract spaces, in transformations of the air into light and vapor, both solid and fluid, lurking under optical fibers.

To a great extent, the decisive paradox of African history within capitalism is the largely unresolved tension between movement and immobility. This is also its great enigma.[35] In other parts of the world, this tension received some resolution through the machine and that which made it possible, namely the automobile and road, the train and railway, the airplane and the ship, and today, the great material infrastructure that has enabled distances and speeds to be overcome. The machine has made it possible to tame natural environments, whether forests, deserts, rivers, oceans, or mountains. It has vastly increased the ability to set beings, things, and objects in motion. In this way, the machine can rightly be considered "materialized movement," or matter that has the specificity of appropriating movement. This appropriation is, as Yves Stourdze remarks, original and decisive, not only because it effectively revolutionizes the social order but also because it enables new chains of domination to be established.[36]

In Africa, humans, draining the vitality of other humans, damage the Earth in the process. But neither the Earth nor man have been entirely, at least not until now, subjected to mechanical movement. For the time being, this subjection is partial and relative. Extortion therefore takes singular forms. The privileged means used to extract riches are extraction and drilling. This space is composed of a multitude of points of drainage and evacuation that do not constitute an actual network. The great movement of elemental forces is far from reaching the explosive speed and swirling power of which it is capable, and which is typical of what we might call the *great forge*. In the absence of this experiment of the great forge, the body of race remains a soot-covered firebrand, subject to accident, even to planned calamity.

The border, however, is simply the visible part of larger measures and installations that have been constituted in response to the question of what to do with the flows of waste, that is, with the *surplus of humanity* of which the fleeing and stray fraction—which is undergoing accelerated growth—is only a tiny part. Borders and other facilities comprise so many platforms for oversorting. The border-bodies are part of these waste-filled worlds.[37] Unlike slaves, they have little added value. Their market value is limited. Some wastes travel long distances. Once captured, many border-bodies will end up in the same channels. The operations of capture are increasingly subcontracted to external or private service providers. Most of these providers are tasked with eliminating such bodies in remote areas. A case in point are the bodies buried and incinerated in the desert. Other forms of disposal without treatment or recycling characterize the maritime sectors.

The mass production of border-bodies has led to a reactivation of imaginaries concerning the population that were typical of the period that coincided with the emergence of capitalism and then colonialism.[38] This reactivation could be called *neonaturalism*, that is, the revived belief in a series of fundamental truths that nature as a system would supposedly legitimize. Such truths are seen not as social or historical constructions but instead as fundamental, self-justifying facts. It is similar with imaginaries concerning the species and the evolution of living beings. Our time is a time in search of new foundations on which to classify living beings. Once again, the limits of the species are being inquired into, since new forms do not cease to appear, notably given today's technological escalation. Among these "new" figures are what were formerly referred to as "aberrant forms," part of which is the wandering fraction of humanity.

The other imaginary that neonaturalism sets in motion concerns hybridity. Originally, hybridity was seen as the result of the sexual mating of two individuals of different species, "the fruit of which had to be necessarily and radically infertile."[39] Species could be distinguished from one another on two levels. First, on that of external dissimilarities; second, on that of fertility or, more precisely, the impossibility of mutual fertilization. The language of zoology has already done the work of overseeing the discourse on species.

Today, belief in the existence of distinct species has made a comeback, as have fears concerning infertile mating. The discourse on life and on the living has come once more to revolve around the theme of fertility and its other—heredity. The desire for endogamy comes as a response to hybridity insofar as hybridity is perceived as a threat to distinguishing species. The conviction here is that humanity comprises different kinds; and that, while there is no race as such, there are in fact different species. The possibility of fertilization or fertility is lost without the presence of a number of common characteristics. As such, fertility is regarded as possible only within the limits of one and the same natural kind, that is, within the confines of an *anatomical and epidermal community*. Such a community would be, moreover, the surest means by which to determine the individuals who compose it.

In the contemporary context, which is characterized by the growth of computer and computational systems, we are thus witnessing the establishment of another architecture and other ways of dividing the planet into sovereign spaces.[40] These sovereign spaces do not emerge through land grabs and control of the sea- and airways so much as through the extension of a hold on speed and on the living, understood in part as that which moves. Spatial machines are ever more calculating, abstract, and ubiquitous. They operate through the segmentation of spaces, and in the process produce places conducive to greater mobility for some and to more immobility for others. The dialectic of speed and immobility (or immobilization) has the effect of making life burdensome for "surplus" people. In its treatment of them, the state is no longer bound to repress its constitutive violence.

The treatment of border-bodies no longer takes place along the line separating inside from outside. Each now dissolves into the other. As a result, the mesh of ordinary repression and practices of immobilization operate on a different basis. They most often begin with generalizing practices of identity verification, which lead to possible police custody. It is increasingly the case that special police deployments are called upon to deal with civic demonstrations. They will effectively smother protest movements with tear gas. The police-justice chain, especially during protest events, increasingly involves searches, arrests, the obstruction of movement, placement in police custody, and if necessary, examinations and subsequent court referrals.

Nowadays social peace is secured through molecular forms of social warfare. This warfare centers on the body that is forced to turn around for handcuffing, not without having been subjected to searches beforehand. It is a matter of applying innumerable mechanisms that make it possible to exercise the power to punish and intimidate, the power to exact retribution, but within the margins of legal interpretation, that is, on its arbitrary edge.

The combination of police arbitrariness and judicial coercion indeed allows for the creation of zones of legal indeterminacy that, in turn, enable the preventive punishment of people who have been transformed into suspects, but who have not been formally judged or convicted.[41] The war against border-bodies also depends on an economy that it also has the function of feeding. This explains, for example, the uninterrupted manufacture and sale of equipment and software intended to track down or neutralize virulent bodies. We can find all kinds of instruments of brutality on these markets, and in these workshops. The most eye-opening are those that enable bodies to be torn apart, that can emit gas clouds over men and women down on the ground with a boot on the neck—instruments that make it possible to dent, break, and violently deform the body, thus returning it to bare existence. These instruments, torture equipment included, aim to terrify those who are already afraid, to break their power of endurance, to encircle bodies like rings of fire.

All these forces are about wearing bodes down. This is the case, for instance, with "electric ankle restraints" or "electric shock anti-riot forks," which are designed to impart "electric shocks to the thighs," or with tear gas launchers.[42] But we must also include facial recognition devices, identity management systems (which are supposed infallible and made of interoperable components), integral biometric modules able to bring together registers of civil and social security status, identity cards, passports, and geolocation and body-tracking technologies.

We know the significance of population issues in Hitlerian and fascist thinking. The destruction of peoples was its climactic dimension. But we must also bear in mind the mass deportations and other forms of elimination achieved through so-called natural death as well as through other forms of death caused by malnutrition, ill-treatment, lack of protection against epidemics, food shortages, and starvation.[43] Brutalism is a form of planetary social war. As molecular warfare, it is largely directed against those who, wishing to sell the only commodity they possess, namely their labor power, can no longer find any buyers. Their transformation into border-bodies is perhaps the greatest challenge to contemporary population policies.

SIX
CIRCULATIONS

Together with climate change, the governance of human mobility is set to be the major problem of the twenty-first century. On a planetary scale, the combined effects of "absolute capitalism" (Étienne Balibar), the intensification of speed, and the saturation of daily life by digital and computer technologies have led to the acceleration and densification of connections. Local, regional, and international circulation is increasing, and with it comes a complex network involving every sort of exchange. Large and small spaces are not only colliding. They are also becoming entangled, thus redrawing the maps to which we have become accustomed.

Caged Humanity

But not everything runs smoothly. Physical roughness persists. Many passageways are blocked. Controls and constraints are tightening, and periods of forced inactivity are increasing.[1] As are deportations.[2] The world's powers are increasingly outsourcing their borders. The markers of this hardening are not only the seas and oceans.[3] In the Anthropocene era, the deadliest factories include islands, mountains, and above all, deserts and other arid zones.[4] In many regions of the globe, systematic surveillance is already the rule. Time is being ceaselessly pulverized and a vast swath of humanity is reduced to leading its existence surrounded by barbed wire, as if in cages.[5] The camp, in particular, has come to take on the form of a huge hutch, where, like trapped animals, human beings run around in circles, a place where spaces collide, where lives are broken against large and small walls, barriers and checkpoints, leaving behind the debris of time and, often, bodies in shreds, thanks to their having to endure multiple states of siege, untimely border closures, repeated blockades, and cluster bombs—in short, devastation.[6]

Caged humanity—Palestine in general and Gaza in particular have become its emblems par excellence. Palestine and Gaza are the great laboratories of a regime of brutalization that is in the process of technological completion and is seeking to globalize itself. The aim is to generalize and extend, on a global scale, the methods that have been refined during the management of the "occupied territories" and other wars of predation. This regime of brutalization is based on the extreme fissuring of spaces deliberately made unlivable, on the intense cracking of bodies constantly threatened with amputation, forced to live in hollows, often under rubble, in the interstices and unstable cracks of environments subjected to all sorts of ravages, to abandonment, in short, to general dissection.[7] If we have indeed entered a reticular world, it is one made simultaneously of enclaves, zones of erasure—including erasure of memory—of dead ends and of shifting, mobile, and diffuse borders. It bears repeating: the dissection of spaces—of which it is the corollary—is itself a key element of the contemporary regime of universal predation.[8]

The excising of territories and the power to decide who can move where and under what conditions are being contested in struggles for sovereignty.[9] To be sure, the right of foreign nationals to cross the borders of another country and enter its territory has not yet been officially abolished. But, as the countless events typical of this period show, it is becoming increasingly procedural and can be suspended or revoked at any time and on any pretext.[10] This has partly to do with the new global security regime that is taking shape.

This regime is characterized by the outsourcing, militarization, digitalization, and miniaturization of borders, by an infinite segmentation and restriction of rights, and by the almost generalized deployment of tracking and surveillance techniques, which are seen as the ideal method for preventing every kind of risk, including clandestine immigration.[11] Their primary function is to facilitate the mobility for certain racial classes and either to prohibit it for others or else to grant it to them only under increasingly draconian conditions.[12] This security regime has paved the way for underhanded and sometimes overt forms of stigmatization and racialization, most often targeting individuals who are already either disenfranchised or particularly vulnerable. This violence is sustained by new logics of detention and imprisonment, deportation and refoulement, and sometimes inspired by the practices of erasure, sorting, enclosing, or zoning and invisibilization inherited from colonialism.[13] It has resulted in thousands of deaths, particularly at Europe's borders but also in transit zones.[14]

Mobility today is thus defined more in geopolitical, military, and security terms than in terms of human rights or even economics. In theory, individuals with a low-risk profile have all the latitude they want to move around. In practice, risk assessments are carried out to justify unequal and discriminatory treatment, often based on unstated criteria of skin color or religion. As the trend toward balkanization and inward-looking attitudes continues, the unequal redistribution of capacities to negotiate borders at the international level is becoming a dominant feature of our times. In the countries of the North, anti-immigrant racism is constantly gaining ground. "Non-Europeans" and "non-whites" are subjected to more or less blatant forms of police violence and discrimination and, sometimes, to executions performed by the book.[15] Racism has changed its rhetoric: added to the old discourse on the epidermis are concepts of difference and foreignness that get openly inflected in cultural or religious terms.[16]

On another level, forms of circulation are now a central stake of today's major social struggles. Obstructing the circulation of flows and operating blockades has become one of the most prominent methods of the new forms of mobilization whose final objective is to overturn the capitalist system. It is not only a question of blocking flows, roads, shopping centers, and nerve centers of the circulation of capital or goods, nor of occupying symbolic spaces, but also of blocking time itself, of decelerating speeds, as time and speed are part of contemporary capitalist infrastructures and logistics.[17] The blocking of time aims at changing both the terrain and the nature of struggles. To finish with the present and (re)conquer the future, it is no longer enough to rise up in protest. The masses must also be disenchanted. The new forms of uprising seemingly no longer need leaders or representatives. Verticality and delegation are widely seen as discredited. Other new forms have been added to (or substituted for) the form-assembly. The network-form is a case in point. This form mobilizes various digital supports, such as cell phones and other platforms. In these new political bodies, the immediacy of action takes precedence over all else. Priority is given to the local and to transversality, the objective being to multiply the fixation points within circumscribed spaces. Moreover, unpredictability is used as a resource. The occupation of spaces from which the multitudes have been excluded is crucial. In this process, blockade is a decisive weapon. It is a form of shutting down the machines of circulation—ports, airports, refineries, railway stations, and logistics centers. It brings the system to breaking point. It is then possible to initiate the process of taking back control of things, starting with the locality or, indeed, the land. For life can be materially and symbolically reorganized, in horizontal fashion, precisely from the locality or the land.[18]

In other contexts, it is more a question of intensifying mobility and circulation, or of transforming the relationship between the dynamics of mobility and the forces of immobilization. This is particularly the case in Africa, where these relationships are structurally precarious, unstable, and often ephemeral. This is not because practices of immobilization are necessarily opposed to those of circulation but because, if we want to account for the complex range of circulations, these fundamental categories require the addition of others, such as "passage" or "transit." Here, in fact, transitory presence on a territory is as decisive as setting up in a singular place. Indeed, periods of mobility, intensity, and frequency of movement can be followed by long periods of immobility.

It is not all about departure and arrival. The immobility of some is often an indispensable resource for the mobility of others.[19] Moreover, the link between that which moves and that which is fixed has become increasingly complex as temporary circulations have been joined by circular mobilities, both of which clearly play decisive roles in the social and economic reproduction of families, and even in their survival strategies. The circulation of some is not only the means to ensure the upkeep of others. Circulation and immobility "are negotiated, shared, and organized" between "members of a group, community, or family." Practices of circulation also occasion a splitting up of living spaces. The single, permanent residence is no longer the norm. The principle of sedentarity is being challenged more than ever by the so-called dispersed family and its multilocationality.[20] To all this, we should add not only the specific place that women occupy in processes of circulation and mobility but also the effects of spatial mobilities in the dynamics of change in gender relations.[21]

Forced Sedentarization

On a global scale, the aim is now to deprive as many people as possible of the right to mobility, or at least to attach draconian rules to it, so as to pin as many undesirables as possible to their residences.[22] When this right to mobility is recognized and granted, colossal efforts are made to make the right of residence uncertain and precarious. In this segregationist model of global circulation, Africa is doubly penalized, from the outside and from the inside. Many African states around the Sahara are under pressure to stem migrant flows. Yesterday, Europe and the United States needed African bodies to develop plantations, grow cotton, and harvest tobacco and sugar cane. They were slaves. They bought them for junk, or else they grabbed them after embarking on Homeric manhunts in the interior of the continent. Today, very few countries in the world want Africans on their territory. Neither as refugees nor as persecuted people fleeing uninhabitable environments and seeking asylum, and especially not as victims of the economic and environmental war that European and industrialized nations have been waging in Africa for several centuries.[23]

Europe has therefore decided to militarize its borders and to extend them to distant places. They no longer stop at the Mediterranean. They are now located along the fleeting paths and winding routes that would-be migrants take. If, for example, an African would-be migrant takes the route from Yola to Kaduna, and then from Kaduna to Agadez and on to Tripolitania, then Europe's new border will extend as far as Yola and will move as the migrant passes through places and spaces. In other words, the body of the African, of any individual African, and of all Africans as a racialized class, is what now constitutes Europe's border. Such a border is mobile, ambulant, and itinerant, borne not by fixed lines but by bodies in motion.[24]

This new type of human body is not only the "skin-body" of epidermal racism but above all the "border-body," one that it is forbidden to shelter or protect (hence the proliferation of laws against hospitality in Europe), to save from drowning in the middle of the sea, or from dehydrating in the middle of the desert. Europe has decided that it is not responsible for the lives of would-be migrants, nor for the suffering bodies that it keeps manufacturing. Having braved natural obstacles such as deserts and seas, these hopeful migrants must, according to Europe, assume their own peril, provided that this happens far away, out of sight, in third countries if necessary.[25] Not being an island, Europe seeks to achieve this objective by reanimating and redeploying, in unprecedented circumstances and on a much larger scale, a geo-racial and geo-carceral imaginary of the sort perfected, in its own time, by South Africa during the apartheid era, or that many colonial states attempted to put in place in the context of forced sedentarization policies.[26]

These polices were not only aimed at so-called nomadic peoples. Colonization in general was a form of government designed for sedentary peoples. It did not at all tolerate elusive forms of existence and was, from start to finish, driven by an obsession with fixity and with territorializing populations. But many of the territories captured by colonial states sheltered ways of life that depended heavily on the ability to move. In them, movement was the cornerstone of domestic life as well as of social and economic life. In addition, nomadism, seminomadism, and agropastoralism could coexist alongside sedentary lifestyles. In such contexts, the colonial state tried to absorb indigenous structures into its mesh. It co-opted the old elites to whom it granted fiscal, political, legal, and even real estate prerogatives. In so doing, it sought to influence forms of social stratification.[27]

Sedentarization required a census of individuals and new administrative divisions. The new territorial distribution aimed to make the administrative territory coincide with the kinship system. Lineage or tribal groups were thus assigned to specific territories and vice versa. The measures taken to assign each entity or kinship group to its territory were not all coercive. Some consisted of the creation of small urban areas around basic infrastructure and the provision of incentives to enter the wage system.[28] The objective was not to directly control the populations or the territory in question. This control was often placed under the responsibility of local chiefs who, acting through delegation, were in charge of managing the populations, and who, co-opted from among the local elites, owed allegiance to their new masters.

The project of forced sedentarization affected individuals taken in isolation, but above all, it affected social and *racial bodies*. It was not so much a question of conquering or exercising a direct hold on territories. It was not a question of *grabbing territories as such, but of seizing control over the racially circumscribed bodies of subjects (natives)*, against whom the real and effective prohibition on unauthorized movement was applied by delegation. In many cases, colonial policies of forced sedentarization paved the way for the confinement of so-called tribal populations to reservations. These were designed for populations deemed backward and were basically military territories. In fact, it was necessary not only to modify the relationship of the natives to space, but also to use the territory as a vehicle for capture, subjugation, and tribalization.[29]

Enclavement

Of all the major challenges facing Africa at the beginning of this century, none is as urgent and as far-reaching as the mobility of its population.[30] To a large extent, the immediate future of the continent will depend on its ability to free up forces of circulation, to set up territories and spaces in such a way that its people can move about as often as possible, as far as possible, as fast as possible and, ideally, unimpeded. Whether in the form of a generalized defection or through planning, this circulation of populations is ineluctable, if only because of the combined effects—and in any case predictable ones—of demographic growth, of the intensification of economic predation, and of the dynamics of climate change.

Indeed, the great social struggles in Africa this century will not only be about the transformation of political systems, resource redistribution, and the distribution of wealth. They will also be about the right to mobility. Not even digital creation will be able to escape this connection to processes of circulation. The demand for mobility will create deep tensions and affect the future balance of the continent as well as other of regions of the world, as the so-called migration crisis has already shown.

To fully understand the implications, we must turn our backs on neo-Malthusian discourses, which, often fueled by racist phantasmagoria, are continually regurgitated. The "rush to Europe" is, in this respect, a big myth. The fact that one in four of the world's inhabitants will soon be African does not, a priori, represent any danger to anyone. After all, of the 420 million inhabitants of Western Europe today, barely 1 percent are sub-Saharan Africans. Of the continent's 1,277,292,130 inhabitants, only 29.3 million live abroad.

Of these 29.3 million, 70 percent have not taken the path to Europe or any other part of the world. They have settled in other African countries.[31]

In fact, in addition to being relatively sparsely populated, given its thirty million square kilometers, Africans emigrate little. Compared to other continents, the movement of goods and people in Africa encounters a number of obstacles, which the times call to be torn down. Many regions are rather poorly developed. They have very few communication routes available. In many cases, goods are carried out by pack animals and, where possible, by saddle animals, when they are not on the back of a woman. Where they exist, the roads yield to all the unevenness of the landscape, with massively dense forests or overflowing rivers constituting so many internal borders.

But mere natural obstacles are not all. In a study of the political economy of road traffic in North and South Kivu (Democratic Republic of Congo), Peer Schouten, Janvier Murairi, and Said Kubuya show how heavily militarized Congolese road space is. They identify five types of barriers. Some of these barriers have the function of taxing the right of passage, whether for road users or their packages. Others are linked to the exploitation of natural resources. They allow for the taxation of both miners and their outputs. Market barriers are erected at the entrances and/or exits of localities whenever periodic markets are held. To these we must necessarily add the posts set up at the outer limits of the zones of influence of various armed actors. Individuals may pass through these posts upon payment of a simple fee. Finally, this panoply is incomplete without mentioning the borders of administrative limits between two decentralized entities.[32]

Barriers, as institutions born under colonization, were used by the colonial state as a means to impede mobility and filter the movements of those subjected to it, all for the purpose of sedentarization. Sedentarization was also an essential element in the tax system, as the control of mobility nodes was a support for the authorities in their efforts to raise taxes efficiently. Under the colonial state, mobility and circulation also followed a logic of corridors and tunnels. Where they existed, infrastructures (railroads and, rarely, paved roads) linked the extraction centers to export ports as directly as possible.[33] Their positive effects on the direct environment through which they passed were almost nil.

Priority was given to the most profitable circulation as most colonial spaces were by and large characterized by their enclavement. This tension between the fixed and the mobile would characterize the process of construction of territorial sovereignty during colonization. It would sometimes result in too many restrictions being placed on mobility and, in particular, on crossing borders, and sometimes in fluid and detached relations between the central state and its own margins.[34] The continent's enclavement remains a massive reality as the establishment of borders has outlived colonization.[35] In one way or another, their placement refers to distinct forms of value circulation. As obligatory passages, they follow the movement of people and taxable goods within economic circuits that are themselves in perpetual motion and in which distance and the modulation of speed operate as added value. It is therefore not a question here of liberating the mobile components of society, or of investing in infrastructure that generates flows and circulation, but of creating points of fixation and other bottlenecks through which to enforce taxation and predatory power.

Neither the intensification of extractive logics nor the neoliberal schemes that now determine the actions of African states have loosened Africa's excessive enclavement. On the one hand, as Hélène Blaszkiewicz explains, the outbound transport schemes that were put in place during the colonial era have been revived. But the logic behind this implementation of new infrastructures is not one of opening up remote or marginal regions. It is "a logic of speed and of the profitability of movements." Obviously, this logic "privileges mining flows, as the most profitable and most globalized of commercial flows, and the infrastructures that enable them," where priority is given to the permanent acceleration of these flows.[36] As in the colonial era, the traffic system is still characterized by its fragmentation and its effects of tunneling. Infrastructure was built to connect extraction sites to export seaports. Today, the proportion of paved roads is increasing only marginally and the railway network has advanced little. Traffic costs remain prohibitive and, with them, the price of migration.

On the other hand, the extraction economy is articulated around enclaves that are sometimes located offshore. These enclaves are characterized by the most complete possible freedom from the surrounding conditions.[37] As Nicolas Donner explains, it is a question of immunizing oneself against the potential dangers of the host environment, which is a condition for the circulation of a resource. Everything happens as if the enclaves were located in an empty and hostile environment.

As almost entirely artificial environments and space capsules, they operate as sealed zones, isolated from their immediate surroundings, protected by all sorts of gangues, walls, and selective access zones. Yet they remain connected to the rest of the distant world. Like neoliberal logics, extractive systems are not, strictly speaking, bottlenecks. They do, however, contribute to an increasing concentration of activities at certain critical points of the territory. While they undoubtedly participate in the ongoing spatial reorganization of contemporary Africa, they do not do so by facilitating people's mobility. On the contrary, they aggravate situations of isolation within African countries. In this context, it is one thing to imagine another life somewhere else. It is something entirely else to organize one's departure and actually set out. Leaving is not within everyone's reach.

As mentioned above, there are many physical and ecological constraints that continue to drastically limit the possibilities of movement. This is especially so in the forest countries. However, throughout history, African societies have, despite the constraints, by no means been isolated. They actually came to be known through the reality that consisted in what we must call their modes of circulation. Their human groups and social units were able to hold together thanks precisely to these modes. Modes of circulation did not refer only to movement, displacement, and mobility. They referred to practices of expansion as well as to practices of complementarity. In the great arid spaces, spatial relationships were made of comings and goings, of crossroads and crossings, structured as they have always been by complex polarities. When it comes down to it, the great African desert has never been an empty space. Neither from the point of view of human habitation nor from that of resources.

Contrary to a persistent myth, this desert has never been exclusively dominated by migration. There have always been nomads and sedentary people. As Denis Retaillé reminds us, the Sahara has always been populated in "distinct nuclei" supported by "oasis and urban settlements." He explains, "The nuclei of desert settlements are connected by axes running from north to south of the great desert (and partially from east to west), the trans-Saharan routes being grouped into ethnically specified clusters: the Moors in the west, the Tuareg in the center, the Toubou in the east."[38]

It is therefore important to keep in mind this distinction between migrations (legal or illegal) and circulations. By "circulations" we must understand a series of complex operations thanks to which a society invents, through movement and exchange, a vital balance with its various environments or is able to give them form and link them together. Circulation should then be taken both in the sense of social plasticity and in that of rhythm. It is a question, most of the time, of weaving networks of alliances. These networks are not necessarily territorialized. This is not to say that inequalities do not exist or that they are not institutionalized. They are indeed pervasive, as is attested by the almost permanent presence in Saharan societies of a servile population or the preeminence of warrior fractions throughout history. Most of the wars, moreover, concern the control of roads and, with them, exchange circuits. They lead to the accumulation of captives, the constitution either of a servile population or of protected populations subjected to a system of tributes. Yet it is impossible to presume any purity from the viewpoint of descent, even for slaves. Cultural assimilation is a reality. As Retaillé reminds us, there is a place not only for captives but also for clients, and even for forms of so-called contractual kinship.

Further still, circulations must be understood in their structural link with the logics of sedentarity. In truth, the former cannot exist without the latter. Control of a territory is impossible without control of a settlement nucleus. Predation itself depends on the capacity to control traces, comings and goings, crossings and linkups, in short, the organization of exchanges. For the rest, as many geographers have shown, forms of circulation or nomadism by no means eliminate the need for residency or ties, which can take the form of houses "where the elderly, some of the women and the children stay. Populations descended from slaves who have become sharecroppers of oasis farms supplying wheat and dates" also stayed there.[39]

Contraction of the World

Today, the human cost of European border control policies continues to intensify as potential migrants face heightened risks. The number of those who have died crossing no longer gets counted.[40] Each week brings its share of stories, each as scabrous as the next. These are often stories about men, women, and children who have drowned, become dehydrated, poisoned, or asphyxiated on the coasts of the Mediterranean, the Aegean, the Atlantic or, increasingly, in the Saharan desert.[41]

Violence exacted at and through borders has become one of the defining features of the contemporary condition. Little by little, the fight against so-called illegal migration is taking the form of a social war, and it is waged on a planetary scale. Directed more against classes of populations than against particular individuals, it now combines military, police, and security measures with bureaucratic-administrative means, releasing in the process, outbursts of cool violence, which, from time to time, can be no less bloody.

In this respect, it is enough to observe the vast administrative machine that allows thousands of legally settled people to be plunged into illegality every year, the string of expulsions and deportations carried out in properly appalling conditions, the progressive abolition of the right to asylum, and the criminalization of hospitality.[42] What can we say, moreover, about the deployment of colonial technologies designed to regulate migratory movements in the electronic age, together with their everyday violence, such as the endless profiling, the nonstop hunts for undocumented migrants, the many episodes of humiliation carried out in detention centers; the distraught eyes and handcuffed bodies of young blacks who are dragged through the corridors of police stations, often emerging with a black eye, a broken tooth, a broken jaw, or a disfigured face; and the crowd of migrants who, midwinter, have their last remaining clothes and blankets ripped from them, are prevented from sitting on public benches, and see potable water taps turned off when they come near?

However, this century will not only be one of obstacles to mobility, backdropped by ecological crisis and increasing speeds. It will also be characterized by a planetary reconfiguration of space, the constant acceleration of time, and a profound demographic divide. Indeed, by 2050, two continents will alone account for nearly two-thirds of the entire human population. Sub-Saharan Africa will have 2.2 billion inhabitants, or 22 percent of the world population. By 2060, it will be one of the most populous regions in the world. Humanity's demographic shift to the Afro-Asian world will be an accomplished fact. The planet will be divided into a world of old people (Europe, the United States, Japan, and parts of Latin America) and an emerging world, which will be home to the youngest and largest populations on the planet. The demographic decline of Europe and North America will continue inexorably. Migration is not going to stop. On the contrary, the Earth is on the verge of new exoduses.

The accelerated aging of the world's wealthy nations is an event of considerable impact. It is the reverse of the great upheavals caused by the demographic surpluses of the nineteenth century, which led to the European colonization of whole sections of the Earth. More than in the past, the government of human mobility will be the means by which a new partition of the globe is established. A new kind of fracture of a planetary nature will divide humanity. It will oppose those who enjoy the unconditional right to movement and its corollary, the right to speed, and those who, on essentially racial grounds, are excluded from enjoying these privileges. Those who have made off with the means of production of speed and the technologies of circulation will become the new masters of the world. They will be the only ones able to decide who can move, who should not be condemned to immobility, and who should move only under increasingly draconian conditions.

The planetary-scale government of mobility will therefore necessarily be one of the major challenges, along with the ecological crisis, of the twenty-first century. The reactivation of borders is one of the short term responses to the long-term process of repopulating the planet. Borders, however, do not solve anything. They only aggravate the contradictions resulting from the planet's contraction. Indeed, our world has become very small. In this, it differs from the world during the Age of Discovery, that is, the colonial world of explorations, conquests, and settlements. It is no longer infinitely expandable. The world is now finite and crisscrossed by all sorts of uncontrolled, indeed uncontrollable, flows of migratory movements, of capital movements linked to the extreme financialization of capitalism, and of the forces of extraction that dominate most economies, especially in the South. On top of this we must add the immaterial flows brought about by the advent of electronic and digital reason, the increase in speeds, and the disruption of regimes of time.

For a long time, the assumption was that the world we lived in had states, each of which had a corresponding population, and that each population had to reside in its own state. This assumption of residence in a given territory (the principle of sedentarity) was seen as one of the conditions for creating a habitable world.

However, the great crises we are experiencing at the beginning of this century not only challenge this principle of sedentary life. This latter is now giving way to the principle of intermingling. Many places are suffering increasing amounts of damage; whole regions are being emptied of their inhabitants; and a good many spaces have been made unlivable and been abandoned. Nowadays there are very few people who can be certain of their abode. As Isabelle Delpla rightly points out, "in view of the parts of countries that the population has almost deserted, or of countries themselves that are depopulating," many individuals "do not know any more if they happen to be inside or outside their border."[43] At the same time, between humans and nonhumans, division, parceling, and entanglement now go hand in hand. Lives and their futures now involve all sorts of links and connections.

If, in fact, there is no state in the world that does not have a population abroad, the real question is thus to know under what conditions the Earth, in its planetary dimensions, can effectively become the true cradle of all humans and the common horizon of all living beings.[44] It is, then, a question of inventing other ways of inhabiting the planet. How can we achieve this, unless by imagining political and state forms and ways of belonging that are ever more flexible, pliable, and mobile?

SEVEN
THE COMMUNITY
OF CAPTIVES

At this point in our investigation, we might usefully delve into something that has been clearly demonstrated in the preceding chapters. Indeed, the body and its living cells remain the paramount targets of the double processes of fracturing and fissuring discussed in these chapters. Contemporary forms of brutalism show this unerringly, at least, if by brutalism we understand the twofold movement of demolition and devitalization that must make it possible to refashion the existent, to grant it another face, and to prepare it to welcome other forms. The process of dematerialization, the triumph of the image, and the emergence of a nanoworld propped up by all kinds of instrumented practices were hardly enough to erase matter. On the contrary, these processes have only highlighted its controversial status. This chapter discusses two forms of "negative communities," that of captives and that of fugitives. These communities are the result of ongoing processes of fracturing, whose impasses they reproduce. The present chapter examines the impossibility that all power encounters of transcending bodily limits.

The *Spirit of Utopia* (1918) will be mentioned only indirectly.[1] Ernst Bloch's work, abundant and of a fragile beauty, is comparable to a web or an interlacing of concepts, ideas, and traces that constitute as many ropes tied in a more-or-less reticular way. It is actually a long exhortation addressed to the world and to humanity. But what kind of web did Bloch try to weave if not one of hope and, ultimately, of faith—faith put to the test of hope and hope put to the test of faith?

Why is there this desire for delusion, and why this attraction to leucotomy? "Stupidity" is not always the answer, according to Bloch. This desire and this attraction also arise, he says, because we are "born for joy," which is undoubtedly hope's firstborn daughter. Hope, he affirmed, is "grounded in the human drive for happiness." As an expectation and pursuit of a "positively visible goal," it is and always has been "too clearly a motor of history." As such, "it imprints on the sterile unfolding of time its forward movement."[2] The affect of hope, he further argued, also requires cultivation, work, and has the function of setting human beings actively on the road to a "becoming, to which they themselves belong."[3]

Hope demands not the automatic faith of flat optimism (which is, he says, a "not much less of a poison than pessimism made absolute"[4]) but that other faith in the idea that "all is certainly not yet lost" and that the future remains open. Hope for Bloch was opposed to fear and dread and also to absolute pessimism. The latter, he thought, was characterized not so much by the absence of faith as by the affirmation of a negative faith. He saw absolute pessimism as the characteristic of those who believe that "nothing is worth doing"; that "life will drag its mediocrity from century to century, that humanity will never emerge from its lethargy and that the world will always resemble a sepulchre."[5] Insofar as it is based on a sepulchral vision of the world, absolute pessimism is a corrupting factor, the motor of cynicism and nihilism.

But both mass indifference and a lack of hope in the world could ultimately be explained, for Bloch, by the "disbelief of faith in the goal." Unconditional and paralyzing pessimism, which is synonymous with resigned acceptance, is thus not opposed to some "artificially conditioned optimism"—myopia and thereby dizziness—but instead to "critical-militant optimism," which is supported by an anticipatory consciousness and oriented "entirely towards the not-yet-become, towards the viable possibilities of light." Such optimism Bloch considers impossible without faith, that is, the permanent receptiveness not to risking oneself in an abyss but to concerning oneself with "what has not yet been successful."[6]

The Desire for Delusion

The years 1920–30 were dominated by the vocabulary of blood and soil and by the theme of the "crisis of European humanity."[7] For a long time, Europe indeed lulled itself into almost uninhibited illusions. Had it not decreed that it was the only place where the truth about man could be revealed? The world, in its totality, was at its disposal. With the advent of modern times, it had convinced itself that its life and culture, unlike other civilizations, were driven by the ideal of reason as free and autonomous. Europe thought that this had enabled it to become *the* central continent in the history of humanity, an entity both *apart* and everywhere, the *universal being* and the ultimate manifestation of the Spirit. In the words of a famous critic, it knew everything, it had everything, it could do everything, and it was everything.

This myth was that of the "Enlightenment," which in truth was a theology with two bodies: one solar (the reign of reason), and the other nocturnal (indefinite production, the capture and unleashing of "force"). How else can we account for this surge of destructive energies and the persistence, over several centuries, of these rolling mills of history that were the slave trade, imperialism, colonial expansionism, and other devices of capture? Borne by a thought of excess and supremacy, the myth did not take long to crumble. The twentieth century in Europe opened with a gigantic slaughter (the 1914–18 war), followed by the Nazi seizure of power in 1933, series of atrocities, the attempt to eradicate Europe's Jews, and two atomic bombs. At this time, given this rift, the thought arose that perhaps history, an incoherent fragmentation of raw facts, no longer made sense. The greatest misfortune of humanity—the failure of reason itself—had perhaps given way to the propulsive force of the void, even to the absurd.

In fact, the dream had turned into a nightmare. Perched on its false certainties, Europe, totally bare, was henceforth unveiled to the world not under the sign of freedom, truth, and the universal, but as the archaic stage on which, as if in prefiguration, a scabrous spectacle was taking place, that of the programmed liquidation of the human species. Tired of being and of living, it was henceforth torn between two contradictory wills—on the one hand, the will to cure itself of the malaise induced by the interminable production of the world and of itself as nothingness (the *therapeutic act*) and, on the other hand, the temptation to give in to the compulsion to self-destruct, an almost irresistible desire for suicide.[8] The sun had indeed grown old, as Aimé Césaire recalls in his *Discourse on Colonialism* (1950). To ward off the desire for suicide and the will to liquidate, some again began to travel to distant lands. Hence the appearance in the field of writing and narration of the themes of "travel" (going to) and the problems of "return," whether to "origins" and "tradition" or "to one's native land." During the eighteenth century in particular, the journey to far-off places had been the prerogative of merchants, conquerors, missionaries, explorers, and some writers. There are many reasons why the theme of departure, detour, and return flourished in the nineteenth century and the first decades of the twentieth.

Great distances had been crossed. Whole sections of previously unknown territory had been torn apart. The Earth had assumed a new face. To reconfigure the field of the thinkable in general and to renew the critique of a blissful humanism, it was absolutely necessary to "leave" Europe, to turn one's back on its metaphysics (the dream of power), to claim again the world in its totality, to reconnect, if necessary, with the immensity of the universe and its flows of energy. Europe had to be "left" in order to get the proper distance from it in thought, to be able to stare at it better, to place before its eyes what it had revealed itself incapable of perceiving of itself, mired as it was in its infertility.

Perhaps the turning point we are at is no longer the same, and perhaps there can no longer be any question of leaving any place whatsoever, since every place, every corner of the Earth, is now entangled in multiple other places and points. Nevertheless, the question arises. First of all, what is our situation and what do we have the right to hope for? What about the world, humanity, all the living? In this planetary era, is there anything that belongs to all of us, that we have in common, that we are obliged to share more or less equally, and whose care falls to us collectively? Is there anything that we are obliged to *pool and share*, if only because our survival is at stake, the sustainability of this world beyond the borders that separate races (since this vile term remains our future), genders, states, peoples, nations, their territories, their languages, and their religions?

Is it true, then, that difference, and thus the border, this power of the line, is the last word for humanity? Is it true, moreover, as some claim, that we have been deceived, that we have always wanted to be deceived, that, in reality, humanity is destined to nothing, because of the very emptiness it carries within itself? In other words, has *the historical project of the human species, namely, the movement toward freedom, reached its end*? What else can be understood today by the injunction to "orient oneself in the world and in thought"? And besides, what is that thought exactly, which language is it in, from which archives does it come, and in view of what is it being deployed?

Now, if we want to project a minimum of light on the harsh and distorted space that is our world today, if we want to grasp its pulse, its breathing, and its hiccups, it can be useful to proceed by putting things into sharp relief, that is, by viewing things from places that are apparently distant and remote places, and yet in many ways so close and so intimate, places where our destiny plays out in a way *that we cannot fail to see*, or can no longer pretend to ignore, the destiny of all of us. And when I say "the destiny of all of us," I mean this "we" and this "all of us" not as a community that might already exist, beyond the heterogeneity that constitutes us, but as that which offers itself to us as a possibility "in the inexhaustible whole of the world itself."[9]

We are, as it happens, being offered the chance to summon other names, to question the nonsense of identity and difference in these paradoxical times of connection, meshing, and delinking. We have the chance to look with new eyes at *what is there, in front of us, that we cannot fail to see, but that we nevertheless find difficult to see, to pierce, to perceive.* Despite our ardent desire for blindness, however, our present is indeed populated by events that we cannot fail to see. These events are of all kinds, they are things that we thought would never happen; things that we thought would happen only to others, far away from us, and that are now approaching us, happening to us, too—amazing things, terrifying things, unheard-of things. They are things that provoke disbelief, that eat at the limits of our imagination, sometimes causing surprise, sometimes rage, sometimes commotion and panic, and sometimes astonishment and stupefaction.

Events of this sort, which happen unexpectedly, unforeseeably, without having been prepared, are happening at an increasing rate. People who have never wanted to live far away from home, who have never contemplated the possibility of leaving, wake up one morning. And the world that just yesterday had been familiar to them has almost entirely disappeared, or at least is no longer related to the one that had been there until the day before. During the middle of the night, an absolutely deafening incident has occurred. No one has been able to take the exact measure of it. But without realizing it, this something has suddenly made everyone strangers in the very place where they were born and have lived until now.

It is increasingly the case that we see these people almost every day. At the very least we hear about them—people on the run, having been forced to leave everything behind, others who have lost everything, who do not know where to go, or who, against all reason, want at all costs to go to places where they are not expected, where they will be strangers, and where, in any case, they are unwanted, a fact that will not remain hidden to them, far from it. These people know that they will not be welcomed. That they will not be given a place, that they risk being left abandoned in the street, that they risk having the little they have left ripped away from them, but they persist. They go anyway. Without any insurance. They earn their own livings.

Others can be seen dragging one or more children along by their hands, or walking with a load under their arm, bearing the little they were able to salvage from the rubble. They have walked long distances and their bodies show extreme fatigue. Their eyes distraught, they scour the debris of their lives, looking for anything that might still be of use. Others can be found under tarpaulins or in cages, camping in the rain or in the scorching sun, waiting for something, a few liters of water, some grains of rice, a piece of cloth, a look, and maybe, in the end, an official document, some papers.

Nowadays, merely by paying attention, you can also see trails of corpses that are often painful to look at—from time to time, corpses of children, women, or young people who have drowned attempting interminable crossings, or human carcasses that desert sands have buried. This is how the landscapes of our time are made. Of these hundreds of thousands of people who leave, who go away, who succumb to the flight syndrome so typical of our time, fewer and fewer arrive at their destinations. Leaving is no longer the real issue. The issue now concerns arriving and the likelihood of never reaching one's destination.

For, as mentioned in chapter 2, the majority get stuck somewhere and, captured like prey, are detained in one of the many sorts of camps with colorful names—refugee camps, displaced persons' camps, migrant camps, waiting zones for people in need, transit zones, detention centers, emergency accommodation, jungles—which, we have said, though a composite and heterogeneous landscape, can nevertheless be summed up in one term: foreigners' camps. Foreigners' camps, both in the heart of Europe and on its peripheries.

We drew attention to the fact that these are essentially places of internment, spaces of banishment, measures for segregating people considered to be intruders, unentitled, without rights, and thus devoid of dignity. And that the worlds and places from which these people flee have been made uninhabitable by a twofold predation (exogenous and endogenous), before their arrival to a place they should not have come, because they are neither invited or wanted. Their rescue is thus hardly the ultimate goal of their regrouping and exclusion. The intention of arresting them and placing them in camps is rather—after subjecting them to a state of waiting in which they are stripped of common-law status—to make them subjects able to be deported, repressed, and even destroyed. Their movement is stopped dead in its tracks.

Leaving

Many people do not remain in their place of birth, as though they might simply sit around like immobile stumps. Products of the "great dissemination" (the Atlantic slave trade), they try, each in their own way, to link their destiny to that of an entity, Africa, which they attempt to transform into a proper name, but always in memory of the world and humanity as a whole. For them, the origin becomes confused with the place from which they came and the stock from which they have been extracted, the moorings that they cut in the rise toward the open sea. Africa being, for most of them, comparable to a tree that has been cut down, they return to the foot of the tree and come closer to the trunk, or better still, to its roots, in the hope of feeding on its sap and hastening the foliation period.

There are many reasons why people may one day leave their country of origin. These reasons are rarely random. Some of them are unfathomable, proportionate to the mystery that origins themselves are. Mystery not in the Eucharistic sense of the term (the sign of something else that is constantly remembered and whose unraveling is never entirely accomplished), not in the sense of what, as secret, is suddenly the object of revelation and, possibly, causes a scandal, but in the quite singular sense of what will always remain both ordinary and enigmatic. Leaving one's country or place of birth is not always within reach for everyone. Leaving one's native country is not always a manifestation of free will. Many people, especially in our time, are pushed toward the exit door by overwhelming forces. With heavy hearts, they leave in spite of themselves, sometimes with nothing, on the roads of exodus, despite an ardent desire to stay. Indeed, there are some who, if they chose to stay, could only do so by risking their lives. So, they leave in the hope that they may one day return.

But what does it mean to leave? To leave clearly means to depart, to leave or move away from a place, to experience distance, to be absent. There is also, in the act of leaving, something that pertains to the cessation of physical, visible, immediate, and bodily presence. To leave means to run the risk of disappearance and erasure. Traces of the absent may have been left behind. Nowadays, many people leave and never arrive; they are swallowed up somewhere by solid, liquid, or barbed-wire forces, or sent away to a camp, or left abandoned in a desert. If one remains present once one has physically left, it is through memory, the memory of what one has done, who one was with others, since it is the others who, remembering us, reanimate our effigy. There is, therefore, no authentic memory except in exchange. You can, of course, remember yourself, but outside of this exchange (the other remembers me and I remember the other), the door is open to forgetting.

Yet, as has been suggested, many return only episodically, if at all. They go for good. Having removed themselves from one origin, they make their home elsewhere. But does this solve the question of origins? Indeed, one tends to confuse origins and place of birth. The belief is that one is a native of where one was born. And, accordingly, that the place of our birth determines our identity. From this comes the figure of the native. Our place of birth, however, is not the marker of all our origins and our belonging. Belonging is not an exclusively territorial matter. It is, in many ways, a matter of acceptance and recognition. It presupposes that others admit us into their midst. My certificate of belonging is always signed by someone else. Belonging only makes sense to the extent that the possibility of rejection is real. But you do not simply have to be rejected to not belong. The intruder is there, but he or she does not belong. Just like the passer-by who stays but has no calling to take up residence. You only belong from the moment you agree to make your home among others who, in return, accept you from now on as being one of them, as being part of them.

Our origins are therefore not reducible to the place where we were born. In spite of everything, however, one is always a native of somewhere, and leaving does not change anything. Being a native of somewhere hardly depends on my visible and lasting presence in the exact place where I was born. There is, in the fact that I was born in Cameroon, something that I will never be able to erase, in the sense that it is forever impossible for me to have been born elsewhere than in Cameroon. Or to have been born other than of my parents, and thus to be registered, in spite of myself, in a genealogy. We are always descendants of others, just as we are only ever born once in a single place, and this event is unrepeatable. Just like death, whether our life is taken from us or we take it from ourselves.

There is therefore something singular, indelible, and ineffaceable about origins—something that can never be gotten rid of; however, that does not make of someone's origins some destiny or fate. While you can choose to die (on such and such a date, at such and such a time, in such and such a place), you cannot choose your place of birth, nor your parents, nor your brothers and sisters, nor your relatives. To be born somewhere, of such and such a person, is fundamentally an accident, and absolutely nothing can be changed about it.

Fortunate or unfortunate, accidents are not without consequences. But they are incidental facts, at the end of the day, if we admit that everything that is or must be is never fixed or settled in advance. Origins may not be insignificant. But, as chance events, they are not essential. The essential thing is the journey, that is, the path and the crossing from one place to another, the making of a passage from one end of existence to the other, from one side of life to the other. This passage consists as much in the movement itself as in the detour of encounters.

There are encounters that are agreed upon. Others are fortuitous, unforeseen, and unexpected. Others are brutal, similar to duels, even collisions. You come out of them disfigured, as if you had finally found yourself in the presence of a malefactor, your face replaced by, or covered by, *facial profiling*. From certain encounters only hiatuses, dissonances, and even misfortunes result.

Sallies

The early twenty-first century is not exactly similar to the first decades of the twentieth. Nevertheless, there are some unmistakable similarities, and they do not mislead. There is the almost ubiquitous lifting of inhibitions. As Bloch said in his day, "Men want to be deceived."[10] This was true then, in those years of functional and systemic stupidity with their cohort of anonymous bodies, with their eyes henceforth closed, frozen, or defeated, bodies needing to breathe, of defeated humanity.[11] And it is still true today, when all sorts of limits are being crossed, one after the other, and the path is opening up, not to any miracle, but to what has all the features of a void.

Who cannot see this? Utopias of the end thrive unabated. Accumulating doubts and fears for which the drive for blood and soil constitutes the only release? In truth, these are so many warning signs and baneful omens. Some consider that history has been a huge trap and that we have now begun the countdown. In attestation are the many territories that have been abandoned to carbonization and desiccation, the oceanic immensities have been rendered toxic and emptied of their "inhabitants" in the space of a generation, diverse atmospheric disturbances, and sprawling cities of millions of people crammed in together amid unbreathable air. The Earth has allegedly entered a radioactive cycle, and at this stage of events, the survival of all species (human and nonhuman) is put at stake.[12]

It is true that manifold ill-fated stars hover constantly around us. No one is safe from being swindled, from blindness, or gullibility. No matter their social status, race, gender, or class, even the wisest among us are "taken in by what glitters; and it is not even necessary that what glitters be gold, so long as it glitters." Capitalism, observed Ernst Bloch, "has become a master in the art of handling these fireworks which do not only dazzle the eyes," but also seize bodies and colonize desires and dreams, through the pleasures of consumption.[13] We ought henceforth to include technologies of calculation, abstraction, and illumination, one of the functions of which is to manufacture manifold fictions at the same time as manifold trancelike states.

The promise of a fictive world remains one of the decisive fillips of capital's planetarization and its conquest not only of the biosphere but also of our desires and our unconscious.[14] To impose itself as a religion, capitalism must continue to appease the worries, anxieties, fears, and sufferings of those it holds in its snare. Moreover, it must continue to guarantee the functions that any religion must necessarily have, as Walter Benjamin has outlined: a permanent cult, or unremitting veneration, of the commodity form; feasts "in the dreadful sense" of displays of pomp; a saturation of the conscience resulting from the effect of guilt, including of God himself; and the celebration of a hidden and immature God.[15]

On top of this, capitalism needs organized violence—whether state violence or other, more or less private, forms of violence—without which it cannot be lastingly transformed into the mytho-symbolic organization it constantly aspires to be.[16] But, above all, it requires that there be a forgetting, or rather a selective memory, of its crimes.[17] War, for its part, remains a form of actualizing the destructive force required to consolidate markets and financial circuits.[18] Backed by silicon technologies and algorithmic reason, the new world-economy remains structured by old racial divisions, which constitute the inescapable motive of the new war being waged against races and classes of populations adjudged superfluous. Waged on a species scale, this physiological and sexual, political and economic war relies on mobilizing all sorts of pent-up drives and on channeling vile energies: racism, virilism, and state xenophobia.

The Metaphysics of "Home"

"Go home," is the message that racial or religious minorities, or migrants, refugees, and asylum seekers receive pretty much everywhere. Increasingly, for the mass of degenerate individuals who, locked in the shithox known as racism, and who now populate our present, such rallying cries spill over into blindly committed racist murders as well as into acts of utmost profanity. Many others have been put to death, sometimes the anus is torn open, or they are electrocuted, or subjected to prone restraint positions, or are the victims of gunfire issued without warning, often at the hands of the police—the rosary of the untimely dead. Today's injunction is indeed that you should return the "home" from where you are supposed to have come.

"Home," so the claim goes, is located at the place where you were born. It is, accordingly, a geographical space or a locality, a city, a village, a region, a territory, even a state made of impenetrable lines, of borders. These draw an interior to which is opposed an exterior, an interior that is constituted, essentially, by opposition to an elsewhere, by means of multiple segmentations. In its benign version, the inside refers to an almost carnal relationship that the subject is supposed to maintain with a locality and a community of which he is a full member. This community is itself rooted in a region or its soil. Community and region are, in turn, places of production of a supposedly distinct and unique history, language, collective knowledge, in short, a particular tradition. Taken together, all these elements make "home" a focus or system of dynamic interactions between a physical and biological environment and a set of both human and socio-technical factors.

In its metaphysical aspect, the "home" or locality is a subjective creation. It is held to be the privileged space for engendering the future and attesting to the past. "Home" is believed to be the place where ideals of ownership and security are realized. As a physical space and way of life, home defines the circle of irredeemable debts, those which preexist us and will survive us, starting with those that bind us to our ancestors. The community in the last instance is thought to be a community of blood ties. The nation-state is, at bottom, simply the transformation of this community of blood ties into a singular jurisdiction. This nation-state allegedly perpetuates itself through blood, that is, it generates its own time and itself. You do not truly belong unless this blood, itself subject to transmission, flows in your veins.

In the great ideologies of nativism and autochthony, however, blood, as the vector of transmission of life between generations, is not enough. It is necessary to add to blood the anchoring in what Franz Rosenzweig called the "night of the land."[19] To be established in a country, to claim it as one's own, is to make its land one's own. In fact, what distinguishes the rightful owner or the native from the foreigner, the exile, the traveler, or the temporary resident, is this anchorage in a land that, in addition to blood ties, makes it possible to take root in a soil. Only the wedding of sap, blood, and soil can be considered a real bond. Let us call all this *vitalist nationalism*, the runt par excellence of neoliberal societies.

Of all the characteristics of vitalist nationalism, two deeply mark the present. The first is the obsessive fear of duration, or of the life span of peoples, homelands, and communities; and the second is the obsessive fear of the enemy, or of imminent danger, in the form of the conqueror, the immigrant, or the individual belonging to another race, religion, or ethnic group.[20] Two factors guarantee survival and duration and protect against danger or even disappearance: blood, on the one hand, and soil, on the other—blood is that precious sap of life that flows and irrigates the soil. To remain alive, the community of blood must therefore be anchored in the "firm foundation of the Earth."[21]

For, in the spirit of vitalist nationalism, every community is first and foremost a primordial cell. Injecting foreign blood into it or joining veins or gene networks of external origin onto it results only in the disruption of its natural metabolism and the production of exotic compounds. Only the consanguineous belong, that is, inhabit the point of confluence between kinship, inheritance, and heredity. They are the only subjects with immanent rights. When it comes down to it, durable rights, including the right to protection against every outside, can only be claimed "at home."

Everyone else, coming from elsewhere, can only aspire to rights that are, by definition, revocable, never guaranteed in perpetuity. For all the others, the time is one of filtering and selection. Contemporary forms of vitalist nationalism, those that celebrate the cult of "home" and sedentariness, align with the metaphysics just briefly described. Making heterogeneous futures coexist is not their project. From this point of view, the separability and stratification of rights are the most effective means of settling the question of belonging once and for all, which is ultimately the question of selection, separation, and in the final analysis, secession.

In the postcolony, this work of fracturing and fissuring passes through "tribalism." The mobilization of ethnic or tribal identities for the purpose of private appropriation of power or common goods has indeed represented the greatest obstacle to democracy, security, and the project of freedom in formerly colonized societies. That ethnicities are merely invented ethnicities and identities, fluid, is hardly sufficient to explain the irresistible attraction of tribal consciousness in the political imagination of the formerly dominated.

More seriously still, there is no point in thinking that ethnicity will disappear one day as some consequence of economic progress, of successful national integration, or of what some people continue to call "the evolution of mentalities." Ethnic consciousness, to be sure, changes its guise according to the situation. But in reality, it is ineradicable in the same way as religion or desire. And any reflection on the possibility of a democratic organization of society must start from this postulate. But if ethnic and tribal passions can by no means be neutralized once and for all, they can perhaps be curbed. For many peoples on the planet, the last century and a half has been marked with the seal of colonial arbitrariness. To complete the picture, we must add various hybrid experiences of tyranny, with both internal and external origins. Sometimes cloaked in the mask of nationalism, anti-imperialism, or cultural sovereignty, most of these tyrannies have flourished under the cloak of decolonization.

But, almost everywhere, tyranny has needed tribalism to play out. Tribalism has not only been one of the conditions of possibility of tyrannical regimes. Tyrannical regimes have, in return, been the best incubators of tribal passions, their greatest goad. The forms of contesting tyrannies were also branded with the iron of tribalism. Nothing has predisposed people to sectarian exploitation of power as much as tribalism. Nothing, moreover, has so predisposed them to discord and even to civil war.

But what is meant by "tribe" or "tribal society"? An archaic order subject to the laws of custom? No doubt. But we must also take into account the tribe's extraordinary plasticity, its capacity for grafting, for the phagocytosis of everything that, at first sight, seems to constitute its exact antithesis. It is, clearly, a grouping within which the requirements of solidarity are based on the recognition of a common ancestry and, possibly, the possession of a territory. Further, it is a matter of blood, because, under a tribal regime, fellow citizens are not *equals*. They are, first of all, brothers and relatives, other members of the tribe. These close or distant relatives are our own, and blood obliges us to show them unfailing loyalty.

Contrary to what some have claimed, tribal consciousness is not just a colonial invention. Already present during the centuries preceding colonial conquest, the processes of "communitarization" (that is, the formation of more-or-less closed collectives based on the principle of belonging to more or less imaginary identities) intensified in the aftermath of decolonization and ended up weighing exorbitantly on the trajectories of the state and its relations with society.

As an elementary mechanism of identification, the tribe has become the language par excellence of both the desire for power and the reality of vulnerability. Wherever they have had free rein, tribalist affects have stymied the promise that political institutions in formerly colonized societies could be based not on arbitrariness but *on reason*. They have not only impeded efforts to build a civil society worthy of the name or aborted many promising mobilizations. They have also, and above all, set back ideas of equality and even notions of a "public thing" that is protected and guaranteed by the power of the same name.

Of all the forms of tribalism in the postcolony, the most corrosive has often been that which reserves priority access to all sort of "life chances" to one ethnic community over all others. In such cases, the circle of individuals who can benefit from these opportunities—whether economic opportunities or military, administrative, and civil offices—has often been limited to one ethnic group—that of the tyrant. One of the driving forces of tribalism is the struggle for extraction and predation and the appropriation and distribution of many kinds of rents. Tribalism has consisted in the appropriation, by an ethnic community and through the means of the state, of large shares of a priori common wealth, or even the unconditional alienation of property that does not belong to the tyrant privately. By abolishing republican conditions of appropriation, the path is then paved for a given ethnic community to monopolize that which, thanks to its public essence, is supposed to belong to all.

Tribalism, as it has unfolded since the end of direct forms of colonization, is therefore part of what might be called the exclusive logic of monopolistic appropriations. Under tyrannical regimes, tribalism has always aimed at transforming into ethnic property what was considered public property under the law. This is how it corrupts the republic in its principle. It institutes, for the benefit of a given community, a "power of disposal" that the community in question then seeks to convert into acquired rights, not for a given duration, but indefinitely. In this sense, tribalism is a way of monopolizing the "share of others." That is how it is fundamentally conflict-producing.

Similar to the community, neither the republic nor democracy exist a priori, as abstract and immutable essences in the name of which one would be ready to kill or, a contrario, risk one's life. Such a conception of the community, the republic, or democracy would be purely ideological. Outside of effective social struggles, the republic, the community, and democracy mean absolutely nothing. The idea of a public power to which everyone is bound is perhaps not universal. While it was not absent, nor was it shared by all African societies before colonization, the concept of "common goods" did, however, exist. Such goods were not only economic in nature but, above all, social and political. They were held to be sovereign bodies.

These goods were endowed with life. All such property, consisting of entities with lives of their own, was inalienable in the sense that it belonged to itself. These entities belonged to the community, but the community had no rights over them that exceeded those of the entities themselves. This was the case, for example, with the community's relationship to the land. There was a place for the inappropriable. There were goods that everyone was entitled to recognize as being theirs. In general, these were goods that extended beyond the individual's own body. They participated in the regeneration of the life of more than one.

Human collectives of all kinds clearly prevailed over the idea of public power or private property. The variety of forms of the "common" or "in common" was striking. Common bonds were the result either of belief or of an activity by which persons or groups of persons related to each other. Identity itself was part of the belief—language, religion, cultural traditions, physical similarities, the similarity of a habitus. The community did not have an essentialist character.

Even when it referred to shared beliefs, such as the belief in myths of origin, it was nothing more than the name of a reciprocal responsibility between generations. At the two poles of the generational arc were the ancestors on one side and the generations to come on the other. Community-making consisted in mastering the art of making the link between the two. Weaving or composing the link was a processual affair. The communities were not rigid and closed collectives in themselves but processual assemblies in permanent recomposition, capable of digesting differences by means of permanent aggregations.

Domination also took on different forms. Where it was codified, the idea of individual rights was not entirely absent. It is not certain, however, whether the content of such rights was exactly the same as that which we attribute to it in the modern sense of the term. This was very much the case with regard to the right to equality. While originality and uniqueness were promoted, this did not necessarily amount to a fundamental right to equality. Differences in status and hierarchy were codified and even assumed to be immutable. In very many circumstances, inequalities were tolerated. The lack of protection afforded to social minors was less so. This is no longer the case in states that are often states in name only.

Immobile Movement

In reality, it is a matter of countries under trusteeship, existing as crypto-colonies under the thumb of international capital and doddering bigwigs whose main job it is to manage murders and abort life. The only things, here, that seem to move the crowd are matters of organo-biological need. Day in, day out, everyone—masters and slaves, executioners and victims, rulers and subjects—takes themselves for what they are not or could not be. Groping around and staggering continually, they are threatened with confinement in an essentially sensory dungeon. Is tyranny not that which first seeks to extinguish the senses?

As the immobility repeats itself ceaselessly in apparent movement, very few seek to stay. Remaining in a country has long since given way to the desire to flee. Some leave by plane. Others leave in trucks or, if necessary, on foot. Still others leave their countries of birth with or without travel documents. Crammed together in makeshift boats, hundreds of thousands swear by the will to defect, as if all was now lost, as if there was nothing left to save in this radiant desert. Thrown on the roads of exodus, they endure long waits, multiple forms of control, arrests, detentions, and expulsions. They soon come up against Libyan prison guards. Europe finances barking dogs and hired killers, thus arranging for the migrants' death by drowning in Mediterranean waters but without seeming to do so. The remainder (the survivors) are captured only to be turned into captives to be sold at auction in the new slave markets of Tripolitania.

What name should be given to those who, seeking to get away, find themselves trapped, crammed like cattle into camps and detention centers, where they are forced to urinate in buckets, to sleep between the excrement that litters the ground, left at the mercy of an air strike? Did they really leave of their own free will, intent on rebuilding their lives? Are they "migrants" strictly speaking?

Are they not, above all, adventurers? Or, rather, *runaways* and *fugitives* in a world where there is no longer a *refuge* or, strictly speaking, a *home*? What reprehensible acts have they committed that they are forced to leave their homes and assume the status of outcasts in countries where no one expects them or, worse, wants them, and where, sooner or later, they will end up suffering many injuries?

For in contemporary conditions, spaces are divided by countless segmentations. A new partition of the world is underway. Borders are now directed both inward and outward. They have become places where the state scarcely has any need to suppress its original violence. Border lines not only distinguish between inside and outside. They screen surfaces and, above all, skin colors, of which they reveal the intrinsic vulnerability.

Taking flight is no guarantee of anything. Often, fleeing means propelling oneself headlong into pure loss. It means being caught in a Brownian movement. It means never being sure that you can return, not even to live where you were born. Fleeing has become the other name of the aspiration to live somewhere other than at home. In this, flight is a form of surrender and capitulation. As this loss creeps into each moment of a person's existence, the fugitive or runaway does not understand that a people can only liberate itself from itself, and that so much passivity endured here, calculated there, backdropped by the struggle for survival, leads only to insurmountable blockages, to unforceable locks, or that to reconquer its fate and shatter the bestiality in which brutalism tries to enclose the living, there is no other choice than to rise and *to defend oneself* hand to hand.[22]

In these laboratories of recent colonization, the damage caused by brutalism will be incalculable, starting with the vast increase in brain diseases and injuries. Wedded with tribalism, tyranny multiplies the bloated, scar-filled bodies and enfeebled minds that permanently seek to escape. Let's call it mental lobotomization, by which I mean the blunting of reason and common-sense; an anesthetizing of the senses; a confusion between desire, need, and lack; the annihilation of every desire other than sadomasochistic desire, sadistic compulsion, and—it should be noted—its charge of repetition, spontaneous obedience, and slavish imitation.[23]

How else are we to explain the existence of so many scotomized subjects, the proliferation of torture chambers, the crowd of leg- and hand-cuffed blacks, the torn and ransacked bodies, the shredded flesh of those who were electrocuted, the mutilations suffered during peaceful demonstrations, the heavy doses of tear gas being poured into people's lungs, the water trucks, the live ammunition, the lost eyes, amputated legs, preventive detentions in stinking prisons, and to top it all off, the arraignments before false courts presided over by false judges programmed to hate life?[24]

What language can describe this repeated carnage, the crushing of these individuals' lives daily, the rites of blind obedience, the habituation to humiliation and obsequiousness, the repression of singularities, the wearing of masks all day long, the absence of compassion, the reign of indifference, the extraordinary fascination for bloody sacrifices, the meting out of violent deaths to opponents, the sort of infantile regression that accompanies any process of making others savage, the weakening of entire peoples transformed into objects that are tossed about in all directions, these great and small scenes of capitulation and surrender, as if the only possible adventure would be to escape from this farce that is as grotesque as it is tragic?[25] Because here, in Africa, we live under tension, on the lookout. Permanently. We are hunters one moment, prey the next, and sometimes both at once. Crouching or kneeling, many people in Africa are effectively in the position of animals, of meat, apt for hunting, as the novelist Sony Labou Tansi describes so well.[26] Indeed, it is a matter of grabbing everything, preferably while charging right in. Brutalizing, in fact, means approaching the prey, pouncing, touching, besieging the senses, palpating, squeezing before savoring permanent contact.[27]

This may well be what fugitives and runaways want to turn their backs on—the psychiatric salons that are the French cryptocolonies of Africa in particular. They are tired of being poisoned by the range of toxins that now serve as beverages for all. The runaways want to forget tribal war, the severed hands, the racketeering at every street corner, the policemen-cum-bandits who operate in broad daylight and bleed the population dry, the predation and the corruption, the boots on the neck, the hyenas who cackle mid–torture session, the gigantic phalluses that stand as high as pylons and for which nothing is inviolable, the foul maggot-infested prisons where the innocent are stripped and from which all sorts of trumpets are made to moan—the carnival of instincts.

In any community of captives, the lot of all is to be a prisoner at one time or another. In prison is where brutalism is unveiled—man coupled with his beast, body-mass and body-meat subjected to torture and fleeing from its organs, the fatigue of living, and the desire for suicide. The prison is the primary empirical evidence of tyranny's mistaken course. Blacks are heaped up. They are turned into piles and crammed together. The fugitives no longer want to scream when faced with this odious spectacle of bloody and unpunished crimes, of turpitudes and cruelties, the deafening din of stupidity, the kind unleashed by vibrions. They do not want to die indiscriminately here and there, their hides burned, locked up in the necrotic cells of debauched and vesanic regimes.

Besides, who has not heard of these tyrants, these roughneck soldiers draped in gold and precious stones who double as tricksters in the guise of mummies? Who is not aware of the fate reserved for their opponents? Who has not heard of the atrocities, of the thousands of prisoners crammed like rogues into jails, like slaves into the holds of slave ships? What is the difference between Kondengui, Camp Boiro, Lindela and

Abu Ghraib, Guantanamo or, closer to home, Robben Island? Or between "foreign or colonial occupation" and the kind of "internal occupation or colonialism" that has succeeded foreign rule?

Who hasn't seen the images of the prey of this or that emasculated tyrant who never stops venting, deaf as he is to the clamor that rises from these violent dumpsters that official hired killers and griots continue to call "republics," as if to mask the surrounding rot? For, indeed, under the skies of the French cryptocolonies in Africa in particular, stench, tyranny, and excrement are indissociable. Tyranny is indeed the equivalent of a sewer drain, the dumping ground where the crowd of slaves and their executioners come to drink, an abyss held at arm's length by an army of small cyclops in the service of a rapacious idol.

Like a demon from down below animated by a pig-spirit, the tyrant is the interlaced figure of the ferocious beast, the snake, and the butcher as well as the transporter, the carter, the distributor of stolen and plundered goods who takes his country to auction, and the sacrificer armed with an acid-and-formalin-dipped knife who, in his megalomaniacal dreams, claims to be crushing pieces of the sun.

But we must be careful not to see tyranny as merely an African form of archaic power. In fact, contemporary brutalism—of which the postcolony is only one of many expressions—is the other name for what has been called the "becoming-black of the world." The emergence of computation as a planetary infrastructure coincides with a decisive moment in the history of wars against populations deemed superfluous. The latter are increasingly detached from the moorings of nation-states, at a moment when, as an outcome of neoliberalism, the state itself is transformed into a conglomerate of strange spaces and increasingly fragmented enclaves. The ecological crisis will only accentuate this fractionation. A new economy of partitions is being established on the Earth's surface. The immobilizing of masses deemed superfluous will go on with a vengeance. Techniques of tracking, capturing, and removing will only intensify.

EIGHT
POTENTIAL HUMANITY AND POLITICS OF THE LIVING

If, in this last chapter, we simulate a return to the shadow theaters of Western thought, it is precisely so as to gain greater distance from them. This gesture of distancing is first of all necessary in order to renew the question of the relationship between humans and manufactured objects. We must begin by getting rid of a metaphysical barrier. The objects created by humans, a result of their creative and inventive expansion, have not always had the aim of increasing automatism. Such objects are in fact often essential ingredients in the production of what should be called *binding energies*. Most African art objects fit this description. The concept of animism should perhaps be given this primary meaning. If we want to reinvest the zone of indeterminacy of which these objects are bearers and, from this position, articulate a substantial critique of contemporary materialism, this gesture of distancing then is necessary. This latter, in fact, allows us to relativize the nature-artifice polarity that has so plagued the critique of technology in the Western world. Once both the above pitfalls have been overcome, the path is open to return Africa to that of which it has been the sign throughout the centuries, namely, *potential humanity and the future object.*

Paganism and Idolatry

It is one thing to make normative and external judgments about African objects without taking into account their history, their heterogeneity, or the enigma of which they are the expression.[1] It is another thing to try to grasp, through their distinctive properties, their substance, and their functions, the ways of being and seeing of Africans; or to try to apprehend, through them, the metaphysical core that makes sense of the world of which Africans were the authors, first, in their own eyes and for themselves.[2]

Indeed, whether or not these objects were linked to the exercise of particular cults or rituals, whether or not they were mistaken for works of art, these objects, often considered disconcerting—in truth, they are all about features and traces—have always aroused all sorts of sensations, ambiguous feelings, visceral and even contradictory reactions in the West, whether obsessive fear, fascination and wonder, horror, frustration and repulsion, even abhorrence. Wherever they have appeared, they have tended to provoke effects of blindness. Originally seen as dirty, ugly, and monstrous objects, as signatures of the shadow resisting all translation, they upset existing ocular arrangements and again raised the old question of what an image is and how it differs from a simple silhouette: What is art? and What is the aesthetic experience in general? and How does this experience manifest itself in its pure truth?

Of all the ways in which these manifestations of our peoples' cultural creativity have been viewed, four in particular merit attention.

It all began in the fifteenth and sixteenth centuries when Portuguese merchants landed on the coast of what was then called Guinea. In the course of their commercial transactions with the local populations, these merchants found themselves confronted with systems of definition of value marked by structural ambiguity. The objects exchanged appeared sometimes in the material form of merchandise, and sometimes in the corporeal form of human beings, along a weft made of continuous variations, intensifications, interweavings, and constantly mutating lines.

Let us take the missionary view first, a view according to which these artifacts were essentially the stuff of a satanic imagination. This theological-pastoral gaze was already apparent during the first evangelization, which took place in the Kingdom of Kongo between 1495 and 1506, and again between the seventeenth and eighteenth centuries, and then in the Kingdom of Dahomey in the seventeenth century.[3] Clearly, the demonization of African objects from the fifteenth century onward stems from an unreflected heritage that, with a few exceptions, so many missionary figures carried.[4] Indeed, the devil had long constituted the nocturnal part of Christian culture in the West.[5]

In the course of the twelfth and thirteenth centuries, the various demons that populated the ancient imagination were reduced to one: Satan, the absolute master of Hell and God's rival on Earth. Little by little, the figure of Satan invaded many areas of imaginary and social life.[6] Satan symbolized the war of worlds and the confrontation between good and evil, madness and reason. At the same time, he bore witness to the split nature of the human figure, which he encircled and within which he hollowed out an almost insuperable void.[7] Between 1480 and 1520, and then again between 1560 and 1650, this demonic obsessive fear reached its peak, as is attested by the interminable trials, the great hunts, and the massive rise in witch burnings, when the nexus was forged between the satanic figure, on the one hand, and the body and sexuality of women, on the other.[8]

The first phase of missionary expansion in Africa bore traces of this essential tension. Thanks to the advent of the "mission," the "devil's places" moved to Africa, a part of the world believed to be governed by a chaos of life in need of order and salvation that could come only from the outside.[9] Not surprisingly, the first missionaries interpreted African objects through the paradigm of "diabolical witchcraft" that had prevailed in the West for many centuries. These objects were subjected to trials similar to those concocted, under Christianity, against needle-pierced dolls; spells cast here and there; a future that one strove to predict; the philters that one concocted; the contact that one sought with the dead; sabbaths, broomsticks, and black masses; and profaned hosts, bestial copulations, and all sorts of bloody sacrifices that, it was believed, were possible only because of the belief in Satan and his powers. Presented as material symbols of the Africans' inclination toward idolatry, the cult of the dead, and the practice of bloody sacrifices, objects of worship in particular were condemned by the missionaries.[10] For the most part, the missionaries saw in them yet another indicator of the essential difference between a savage mentality and that of civilized humanity.[11]

The same gaze asserted itself in the context of the second evangelization that began in 1822, the year of founding of the Society for the Propagation of the Faith, a complex and in many respects ambiguous missionary action aimed at converting Africans to the only worthy monotheism, that of truth, which "recognizes only one God and for whom there are no other gods."[12] In theory, it was not a question of importing into Africa the social habits of European nations but of announcing the Gospel to backward peoples whose ideas and mores had to be rectified and elevated, and who had to be delivered from the weight of superstition and led to salvation.

In reality, missionary activity was based on two pillars: the refutation of the metaphysical foundations of native cults and, wherever necessary, religious repression for the purpose of conversion.

In the logic of Christianity, the converted has to recognize his having been on a path that would have led straight to his ruin. Renouncing his life and his former ways, he has to repent and undertake an inner change, at the end of which a new subjectivity is to be achieved, including new ways of inhabiting the world, the body, and objects. In missionary theology, submission to the devil—and therefore to the principle of spiritual death and corruption of the soul—wittingly or otherwise, often had its fulcrum in objects and the relationships that the primitives entertained with them. Moreover, in its opacity, the pagan mode of existence was characterized as the domination over humans by all sorts of fetishes, which these humans ceaselessly envied or feared, constantly sought to acquire or to destroy, and onto which they transferred the strength, power, and truth due exclusively to God. In practice, conversion led to the invention of mixed religious cultures that were made up of borrowings of all kinds, games around mixing, risky reappropriations, and hybrid aesthetic practices.[13] It resulted in many misunderstandings, multiple paradoxes, and a complex process of redefinition for each of the protagonists in the encounter.[14]

This context is the one in which the *anti-pagan discourse* of the missionaries developed. More than has been recognized, this discourse influenced the conceptions that the West formed of African objects, their substance, their status, and their functions. It rested on the postulate that the Blacks lived in the night of the inmost animal. The African world was a priori bereft of any idea of a sovereign God, the supposed norm of all norms and cause of all causes. At least there was no clear consciousness of any such principle. By contrast, their world was peopled with a multitude of beings, of multiple divinities, ancestors, soothsayers, intercessors, genies of all kinds who ceaselessly vied for preeminence. With these forces and entities, primitive societies entertained relations of immediacy and immanence.[15] It was so difficult to distinguish between ritual murder, spirit worship, and that which participated in the simple worship of matter, that one could hardly speak of this multitude of beliefs as a religion as such.

Alongside these figures, an array of (mostly baleful) forces structured the universe and presided over the lives of all. Some of these forces could take on a human appearance. Others could be embodied in all sorts of elements, including the natural, organic, vegetal, and atmospheric. It was to them that cults and sacrifices were offered.[16] Cult ceremonies could take place in circumscribed places, such as temples. But, basically, it was the whole organic, vegetable, and mineral universe (river eddies, tombs, sacred woods, water, earth, air, lightning) that could be summoned and that served as a receptacle for the powers that were adored, often in the dark, through the intermediary of fetish objects of all kinds, which the missionaries likened to idols.[17] In their crudeness and excessive features, these idols constituted the objectal manifestation of the state of corruption in which the black race was mired.[18] The primitive sought to coerce and control powers through such objects, did they not? Did these objects not simultaneously manifest the fear and dependency that such peoples felt toward them? Such dependence, however, had no divine purpose. It implied nothing less than nothingness, the nothingness of man before an absolute supremacy, the presence of the horrifying.[19]

Accordingly, many of these objects were destroyed during the great religious feasts, while many others—as a result of collections, thefts, pillages, confiscations, and gifts given—found their way into the museums of the West.[20] "Do not forget to send us, at the earliest opportunity, a collection of objects from your new country," Father Augustin Planque hastened to write to the missionaries sent to Africa in 1861. "We would like to have in our museum all your gods for a start, weapons, tools, household utensils; in a word, nothing should be missing."[21] Temples were ransacked or literally desecrated.

Christianity indeed presented itself as the religion of truth and salvation. As *the* religion of radical rupture, it sought to abolish the ancient cults. Hence, vast campaigns were organized to extirpate idolatry.[22] So temples were forcibly shut, and harm was done to many fetishes—figurines made of diverse materials (hair endings, fingernails, metal nails), shells of various forms and colors, dried bugs and insects, collections of roots, marmites and pitchers filled with vegetal preparations and ointments. In their place, crosses were planted. The amulets were confiscated and rosaries and other effigies of saints distributed. Demons and sorcerers were pursued by means of public punishments and punitive spectacles.[23] The attempt was made to definitively stop all festivals and rituals; musical instruments were set upon and certain dances, as well as the supposed worship of the dead and practices of contact with the invisible, were banned.

Difference and Apocalypse

A second type of view emerged during the transition from the Enlightenment to the nineteenth century in the context of the then-fashionable theories of "universal history" and of the difference of human races. The language of race and blood was in vogue. On the one hand, the idea that God revealed himself in the Christian religion, the only true religion, remained alive. On the other hand, the thesis that the history of the world was fundamentally the history of progress toward the consciousness of freedom was consolidated.[24] This universal history, it was argued, presented itself to us as a rational process that would lead to the triumph of reason, or at least to the reconciliation of the rational and the real.[25]

But this actualization could occur, so it was supposed, only where reason entered into the great human passions (including need, force, and instincts), or where it allowed the passions to act in its stead. In other words, universal history was only possible if reason and truth consciously took the form and structure of myth.[26]

In the circumstances under discussion, the great myth of the nineteenth century was that of race.[27] It was through race, the thinking went, that the "Absolute Idea" was fulfilled. G. W. Hegel, for example, believed that in every historical epoch there was, indeed, one and only one nation, one and only one people, that truly represented the world spirit and that had "the right to rule all the others."[28] Compared to this nation, this people, or this race, "other nations [were] absolutely without rights." They "no longer count[ed] in universal history."[29] In this system, in which a given race granted itself the title of "the sole bearer of the world-spirit," and in which reason transformed into myth, race was no longer merely the name of a supposedly communal substance. It was a structuring force, a fiction with a reality of its own, capable of producing a certain reality.[30] Raciality was a biological determination (that which is of the order of blood, of hereditary transmission) as much as it was of the order of the body—the body of a people endowed with a will to power. But it was also an affective disposition that was available and that could be mobilized, if necessary, the phantasmagorical representation of a difference of an ontological nature.

African artifacts were unable to avoid this trap. The black race in particular was deemed an inferior variety of the human race. The things of which it was the author were, in principle, bereft of life. Its objects were the manifestation neither of any sovereign will, nor of its own proper energy whose ultimate aim would be freedom. In them, the very idea of the symbol found its end, yielding only to a hideous ugliness—a field for the circulation of a fundamentally arbitrary force. Because they were not made by moral subjects, the objects of blacks could arouse only contempt, horror, and disgust. Before them, one experienced a sort of impotent horror, the vertiginous feeling of danger. This is because, in this profane world of things and of bodies, man, as a living animal, had only ever been an always already alienated thing, apt for being cut up, cooked, and consumed during gory sacrifices.

During the feasts of matter, in which violence wreaked its havoc within, the body itself, like the object supposed to represent it, was no longer the substratum of any spirit.[31] The object was subjugated to the person who made and used it, just as the object-maker was subjugated to the object. Basically, a relationship of close similarity linked the two. Neither existed for its own end, but rather for an end that was alien to each. If there was bedazzlement, it could only be blind. And creation was not undertaken in the service of any lasting order. One created precisely with the aim of making the operation of sacrifice and destruction possible. And this is what these objects meant—the impossibility of escaping the limits of the thing, of returning from animal slumber, of ascending to humanity.[32]

In these works, the exorbitant and the banal came together. They attested in any case to the tragic character of an arbitrary existence, destined for nothing. If they did indeed fulfill functions, they nevertheless had no substance. Receptacles of the obscure passions of human existence, they satisfied above all desires that were either diverted from reality or not sublimated. Moreover, they were linked to repugnant bodies. The feeling of shame and a strange measure of scorn that beset these bodies got displaced onto the artifacts, as objectal metaphors of function without substance.

Finally, in their excessive crudeness, their sensual coarseness, and their thinly veiled erotic tinge, Black objects were above all sexual objects. They bore witness to an uninhibited outward thrust, an unsublimated organ life typical of primitive sexuality. In keeping with the missionary gaze, the art of the heathen, it was thought, was driven by an unintegrable violence. This is because it was seized, from its very origins, by the torment of the sexual. Here, bodily functions and genital functions were demetamorphized. If art is somehow the enactment of an unconscious, this unconscious was, among the primitives, dominated by images of archaic penetration, wild and epileptic coitus and primordial bisexuality. The individual was in truth neither man nor woman, but both animal and object, all three, only one more than the other, as Freud would say.[33]

As a result, these objects spoke above all to the predispositions of the primitives' drives. When they touched the body and the sexual, or when they made them visible, it was to open the way not to representation, and even less to sublimation, but instead to sensation and excitement. Thus, they were not about representation. They were about excitement. The drives that they triggered in those who saw them were not intended to throw any ray of light into the darkness. They aimed to awaken and reactivate a kind of link of original destructiveness that shocked as much as it attracted, fascinated, but also disturbed, generating in the end a profound castration anxiety. The affective intensity that they released was not of the order of rapture. They were capable of shocking those who encountered them, of embracing the appearances of reality while at the same time freeing themselves from it, while also giving free rein to the fundamental passions of existence that the West had wanted to keep under the yoke as a condition for the passage from the world of instinct to that of culture.

At the start of the twentieth century, a third type of gaze—at times ethnographic, at times conceptual—emerged.[34] The conceptual gaze asserted the plastic and purely formal qualities of "black objects," the sensation of depth evoked through African sculpture or, again, its way of engendering space, that, is its power of affective intensification of the image. These objects, it was deemed, liberated sculpture not only from all perspective but also from every pictorial aspect. The ethnographic gaze sought, for its part, to anchor them in their context of birth, with the aim of disclosing their social meanings. In the process, these objects were conferred a status as works of art, even if, once again, they were not really deciphered in their own terms.[35]

For Carl Einstein, for example, the art of the Black is above all shaped by religion. Sculpted works are revered just as they were by ancient peoples. The artist fashions his work as if it were divinity. Moreover, the artist creates a god, and his work is "independent, transcendent, and free of all ties." He is not commissioned to imitate nature, as in the European tradition. "The African work of art means nothing, it is not a symbol; it is the god." It collapses any distinction between the signifier and the signified.

For others, the strength of African artworks is explained by their magical charge, by their capacity to manipulate the world through magic.[36] One takes an interest in all this because it is possible to use it in the hope of overcoming the limits of Western civilization.

The idea is that Europe has forgotten something fundamental that a return to the African sign can enable it to rediscover, something pertaining to the memory of pure forms, freed from all origin and, as such, capable of opening the way to an ecstatic state, the last degree of intensity of expression and the sublime point of sensation.[37] This freeing from origin is at the same time a freeing from perspective. It is argued that in African art the psychic distance between the spectator and the image is diminished. The invisible aspects inherent in the image emerge. The possibility of absolute perception then materializes. The object is no longer contemplated only by consciousness but also by the *psyche*.

If this is so, it is because African art proposes other ways of representing space that are both symbolic and optical in nature. What it gives us to see is a mental equivalent of the image rather than the image itself. It thus gives rise to another modality of seeing. To see, there is no need to immobilize the eye. On the contrary, it is a question of freeing it, of making it active and mobile, of putting it in relation to multiple other psychological and physiological processes. Only then can it actively reconstruct reality. The eye, under these conditions, is not a dead organ. Starting from what it sees and recognizes, its work is to explore what is missing; to reconstruct, on the basis of so many traces and clues, the object depicted in the image; in short, to bring it to life.[38]

The Europe that rediscovered African objects at the beginning of the twentieth century was haunted by the twin tales of the (re)commencement and of the end. As the commencement is the starting point of a mutation toward something else, it asked the question whether art can indeed serve as such a starting point toward a future that is not a mere simple repetition of the past. As for the end, it can be inflected either in the mode of accomplishment (the living experience of meanings that would be unconditionally valid) or in that of catastrophe. There are endings that make every recommencement impossible. And there are conflagrations that prevent the advent of the end, or that envisage it only in the mode of catastrophe.

At the beginning of the twentieth century, African objects contributed to rekindling this debate in the heart of a Europe hunting for other ideas of time, the image, and truth. This Europe was a conquering Europe, whose world domination was relatively secure, but that was simultaneously beset with doubt, because, in the final analysis, this dominion over the rest of the world—colonialism in particular—rested, as Aimé Césaire would later suggest, on an apocalyptic structure.[39] It asked whether its dominion over the world was not, in the end, purely spectral; and whether it was possible to articulate a thought of time, the image, and truth that was not merely a thought of nothingness, but a veritable *thought of being and relation*.

African objects have thus fulfilled irreplaceable functions in Europe's historical trajectory. They have served not only as tokens for its chimerical (and often disastrous) quest for the unveiling and manifestation of truth in the world, or for its desperate search for a compromise between spirit, the sensible, and matter. In an almost spectral way, they will also have reminded it to what extent the appearance of spirit in matter (the very question of art) always requires a language, another language, the language of the other, the arrival of the other in language.

Today, almost everywhere in the West, the question being asked is whether or not these objects should be returned to their rightful owners. But very few are concerned with understanding what originally justified their presence in Europe and what they signified in European conscious- ness. It is important, in these circumstances, to return to the essentials. What exactly does one want to off-load? What is one trying to repatriate and why? Is the work that these objects were intended to accomplish in the history of European consciousness complete? What will it have produced in the end, and who should bear the consequences? Has Europe, after so many years of the presence of these objects within its institutions, finally learned to deal with what comes/with those who come, from outside, or from an extreme remoteness? Is it finally ready to embark on the path to those destinations that are yet to come, or is it itself no more than a pure event of cracks, this thing that is cracking in pure loss, without depth or perspective?

Millstone of Debts

Legalism and paternalism comprise the two sorts of responses generally marshaled by those who stand opposed to this project of restitution. On the one hand, some claim that, in the last instance, the law (as it happens, diverse variants of European property law) by no means authorizes the return or transfer of these artifacts to those rightfully entitled to them. Care is taken not to call into question the external origin of these artifacts and their creators. Nevertheless, the response given to the question of knowing to whom they belong is presented as if it was absolutely independent from the—supposedly prejudicial—question of knowing where they came from and who their authors were.

In other words, a cesura is introduced between the law of property and use, on the one hand, and the act of creating and the creating subject, on the other. It is notably asserted that having made something does not automatically make one the owner of that thing. Making an object is one matter. It is quite another to have the right to use, enjoy, and dispose of it exclusively and absolutely and under the restrictions of the law. And just as making is not the equivalent of owning, the origin of a work is not a sufficient condition for claiming possession or the right of possession.

It is also made to seem as if the conditions under which these objects were acquired were not at all problematic; as if, from beginning to end, it was a matter of transactions between equals on a free market where the value of the objects was determined by an objective price mechanism. The conclusion drawn is that, having undergone the market test, these objects are no longer "vacant and without masters." They are henceforth deemed "inalienable," the exclusive property either of the public authorities as such (who manage them through museum institutions), or of private individuals who, having purchased them, would be qualified, in legal terms, to enjoy them fully, without hindrance. From a legal point of view, the debate on the restitution of African objects is thus declared unfounded, as their presence in Western museums and other private institutions has nothing to do with confiscation and, in this respect, requires no judgment of a moral or political kind.

Others claim—sometimes the same individuals—that Africa does not have the necessary institutions, infrastructures, technical or financial resources, or the qualified staff or know-how to ensure that the objects in question will be protected and conserved. Returning these collections to such environments would expose them to the serious risk of destruction, or deterioration, vandalism, or despoliation. Retaining them in Western museums is thus the best way to safeguard them, even if this requires lending them to Africans from time to time for special events. Others, finally, are willing to return the objects, including in the absence of any claim from the allegedly despoiled African communities. But there can be no question of recognizing any debt whatsoever to anyone.

This way of posing the problem of restitution—insofar as it entails neither an acknowledgment of debt nor any other consequential obligation—is by no means innocent or neutral. It forms part of the strategies of obfuscation used by those who stand convinced that in a war, whether declared or not, the victor is always right and pillage is its compensation. The defeated party is always wrong; it has no choice other than to thank its executioner should the latter spare its life, and it has no automatic right to justice. In other words, might is right, and the law has no might that does not derive from the power of the victors. How can we prevent the true nature of the dispute from being obscured in this way and such an eminently political and moral cause from being reduced to a mere battle between solicitors and accountants, if not by turning our backs on such a cynical conception of law? Under the pretext that law and justice are autonomous and need no sort of supplement at all, one indeed ends up untying the law from any obligation of justice. Its function is no longer to serve justice but to sacralize existing power relations.

It is therefore necessary to distance ourselves from a purely quantifiable approach to restitution, which is thus considered only from the point of view of the institution of property and the law that ratifies it. So that the restitution of African objects is not an occasion for Europe to grant itself a good conscience at a low price, the debate must therefore be refocused on the historical, philosophical, anthropological, and political stakes of the act of restitution. We can see that any authentic policy of restitution is inseparable from a *capacity for truth*, whereby honoring the truth and repairing the world are, by the same token, the essential foundation of a new bond and a new relationship.

This is certainly not the whole of its history, but of all the regions of the Earth, ours is undoubtedly distinguished from the others by the nature, the volume, and the density of what was taken, wrested, stripped from it. Is it because the continent did not exercise an indisputable empire over the seas? Or, as the poet Aimé Césaire recalled on other occasions, because it invented neither gunpowder nor the compass?[40] Or is it because its name was never known and feared in distant lands, except perhaps for the harshness of its climate—and, according to Hegel, for the ferocity of its potentates and cannibal feasts, which is the alpha and omega of all racist phantasmagoria?

The fact remains that so many of its treasures are to be found abroad today because there is a brutal part of Africa's history comprising depredation and plunder, lacerations, continuous subtractions, and successive captures—the extraordinary difficulty of keeping its people at home and keeping the best of its labor for itself. In fact, as early as the fifteenth century, Europeans invaded the African coast. For nearly four centuries, with the active complicity of local chiefs, warriors, and traders, they maintained a lucrative armed trade in human meat, seizing millions of bodies of living, working-age men and women in the process. Then came the nineteenth century. In the course of many expeditions and other incursions, Europeans confiscated, piece by piece and despite multiple forms of resistance, everything they could get their hands on, including territories.

What they could not take away, they ransacked and often set on fire. The predation of bodies was not enough. During the colonial occupation itself, they held many inhabitants for ransom and confiscated or destroyed what they considered to be valuable. With their granaries dried up, their livestock slaughtered, and their crops burned, many lands were depopulated, subjected as they were to disease and malnutrition, forced labor, rubber extraction and other sorts of corvée, and exposed to the ecological disruption caused by colonization.[41]

Almost no area was spared—not even the ancestors and the gods. Europeans went so far as to desecrate burial places. In the whirlwind, they carried off almost everything—objects of adornment, objects for everyday use; fine fabrics; sumptuous necklaces; rings; artistically made jewelry inlaid with gold, copper, or bronze; belts; various objects filigreed with gold, including swords, shields for warriors, ornamental openwork doors; seats and thrones adorned with figures of men, women, animals, and elements of flora and fauna; magnificent fibulae; bracelets and other sequins; and thousands and thousands of "medicines" that they identified as "fetishes." What can we say about the carved wood, carved with curved lines, with interlacing? Or about the sculpted wood pieces with their finely carved curved lines and knotwork? Or about the braids and weavings of all kinds, the innumerable reliefs and bas-reliefs, the human figures in wood or bronze, combined with the heads of quadrupeds, images of birds, snakes, plants similar to the marvelous landscapes of popular tales, sounds, and multicolored fabrics? How can we forget, moreover, the thousands of skulls and the strings of human bones, most of which were piled up in the basements of universities, hospital laboratories, and the cellars of Western museums? When all is said and done, is there a single museum institution in the West that is not based, in its concept, on African bones?[42]

As several observers have noted, many ethnographic missions took on the aspect of predatory activities specific to abduction and pillaging, hunting and raiding.[43] Indeed, the adjacency of natural objects, various artifacts, and stuffed wild animals in many nineteenth-century Western museums (ethnographic and military) attests to these admixtures. The collection of material objects belonging to these "peoples of nature" was often accompanied by the collection of hunting trophies, and thus the killing and carving up of animals.[44] A museological process then ordered this set of items, transforming the totality of the spoils (including the animals) into cultural products.[45] The collection missions were therefore not limited to objects or the dismemberment of human bodies.[46] They included the capture of wild animals, "from the smallest beasts to the largest mammals."[47] This was also the case for many zoological and entomological specimens. Little wonder, then, that during mask collections the heads of the masks were separated from their costumes in a dramatic gesture of decollation. As Julien Bondaz suggests, "The vocabulary used to designate the practices of collection certainly reflects such overlaps." While it must be acknowledged that not all objects entered collections solely by means of violence, the fact remains that the modes of acquisition of these objects often obeyed practices of predation.

Loss of World

All these objects were part of a *generative economy*. Products of an open system of knowledge sharing, they expressed the marriage between the individual and singular genius and the common genius within participatory ecosystems, in which the world was not an object to be conquered but a reserve of potentials, and in which there was no pure and absolute power except that which was the source of life and fertility.

When it comes to restitution, then, we need to return to the essential point. Explaining the permanence of the removals we have suffered by the absence of scientific and technological prowess and firepower is only a veneer that hides what is most at stake. First, the history of African technical systems and their operational functions has yet to be written. Second, we have probably lost sight of the fact that the relationship that the human race has with the world, matter, and all living things is not exhausted by science and technology. Modern science and technology are only one of several mediations of the human presence in nature and existence. Science and religion are not necessarily opposed to magic, the profane is not the antithesis of the sacred, and the magical mode of existence is not necessarily pretechnical. There is no single evolutionary scale, extending along a linear trajectory, that would serve as the authoritative measure and judgment for all modes of existence.

The fact that Africa was not the originator of thermobaric bombs does not mean that it did not create technical objects or works of art, or that it was closed to borrowings or to innovation. It privileged other modes of existence in which technology in the strict sense was neither a force of rupture and diffraction, nor a force of divergence and separation, but a force of splitting and multiplication. At the heart of this dynamic, every concrete and distinct reality was always, and by definition, a symbol of something else, of another figure and structure.

In this system of permanent reflections, of mutual relations of correspondence, and multiple schemes of mediation, each object constantly enveloped, masked, disclosed, and exposed another, extended its world, and was inserted into it. Being was not opposed to nonbeing. In a tension that was as intense as it was endless, the one strove each time to incorporate the other. Becoming took the place of identity, that reality that only came about after the fact—not that which completes and consecrates, but always that which initiates, announces and prefigures; that which authorizes metamorphosis and passage (to other places, to other figures, to other moments). For this plastic humanity, inserting oneself into the world with the aim of participating in it and prolonging it was more important than mathematizing, dominating, and subjugating it.

As in the Amerindian cultures described by Carlo Severi, human beings were not the only ones to be endowed with speech, movement, and even a sex. Many artifacts were or could be as well. The same applied to animals and other living creatures. If all was begotten, all was equally subject to demise.[48] Everything had its emblem. Further still, all that exists, it was thought, was taken in a movement of constant transformation and, in singular moments, could assume the emblems and the power of another, or even of several beings at the same time. Different modes of existence could characterize any individual, "whatever its nature, animal, vegetable, human or of artifact," observed Severi.[49] Nothing translated better this idea of a potential and ceaseless transformation of all the beings than what Carl Einstein named the "drama of metamorphosis," by which we ought to understand the constant renewal of forms by their "displacement and their plural recomposition."[50]

This principle of relation expressed not by a dead identity but by a "continuous circulation" of vital energy and constant passages from one form to another did not apply only to human beings. Animals, birds, and plants could take the form of humans and vice versa.[51] This did not necessarily mean that between the person or the existent and its external double, the indistinction was complete, or that their singularity was reduced to nothingness. The same goes for the wearing of a mask. The wearer of the mask did not become the god. The masked initiator celebrated the epiphany of a *multiple* and *plastic being*, made up of multiple other beings of the world, each with their own characteristics, all united in a single body. The ability to perceive oneself as an object or as a medium did not necessarily lead to a complete fusion between subject and object.

The concept of ontological limit, therefore, never had the authority that it acquired in the trajectories taken in other regions of the world. The important thing was not to be oneself, to have been oneself, or to repeat oneself in fidelity to a primitive unity. To deny oneself, or to repeat oneself when it was necessary, was hardly an object of reprobation. *To become other*, to cross the limits, to be able to be reborn, another time, in other places, and in a multitude of other figures—an infinity of others summoned by principle to generate other flows of life. Such was the fundamental requirement, where the structure of the world was, strictly speaking, neither vertical, nor horizontal, nor oblique, but *reticular*.

If all works of art were not ritual objects, they were nevertheless brought to life through ritual acts. As it happens, the object was only ever in relation to the subject, as part of a reciprocal definition. It is through rituals, ceremonies, and these relationships of reciprocity that the attribution of subjectivity to every inanimate object took place. This is the world that we have lost, of which African objects were bearers and whose epiphany they celebrated through the plurality of their forms. This world—no one will ever be able to restore to us.

As far as the objects were concerned, they were vehicles of energy and movement. Living matter, they cooperated with life. Even when in themselves they were only utensils and devices, they had a part in life, physical life, psychic life, energetic life, the kind of life whose primary quality was circulation. This is perhaps why powers of engenderment, subversion, and masquerade were, as much as privileged markers of paganism and animism, the target of so much demonization. How can one, today, claim to restore them to us without having first de-demonized them—without having oneself "renounced the devil"?

We will thus have been, over a relatively long period of time, the world's warehouse, both its vital source of supplies and the abject subject of its extraction. Africa will have paid a heavy tribute to the world, and this is far from over. In the process, there is something colossal, uncountable, almost priceless that will have been lost for good and to which the lives of all our objects in captivity will have borne witness, as well as the lives of all our own in the prison landscape of yesterday and today.

In certain circumstances, some of these objects played a properly philosophical role within the culture. They also served as mediators between humans and the vital powers. They were used by humans as a means to think their existence in common. Behind the technical gesture of making them, a particular horizon was hidden—the mutualization of generative resources in a way that did not endanger the whole ecosystem; the unconditional refusal to turn everything into commodities; the duty to open the door and give the floor to the dynamics of partner relationships, and to the uninterrupted creation of the commons. It is thus to a real impoverishment of the symbolic world that their loss has led.

Behind each of them were also crafts, and behind each craft a fund of knowledge and skills ceaselessly learned and transmitted, a technical and aesthetic thought, figurative information, a certain charge of magic, in short, the human effort to tame the very matter of life, its assortment of substances. One of their functions was to put in relation forms and forces while symbolizing them, to activate the powers which make it possible to move the world.[52]

All that is gone. And this is the heavy tribute that Africa will have paid to Europe, that region of the world to which we are tied by an intrinsic relationship of extraction and removal. This is perhaps one of the reasons why many Africans attach to the memory of Europe a note of both fascination and infamy. Perverse fascination because of the force and raw power of lies and the almost permanent denial of responsibility. Infamy, because they are convinced that Europe does not want them, that it wants above all an obedient and docile Africa, an Africa similar to a corpse adorned with its shroud, which, although fundamentally lifeless, constantly revives and stands up in its coffin; because they are convinced that the kind of African that Europe tolerates and accepts is the African whose energies it never ceases to capture and divert, one who obeys with the docile fidelity of the animal that has recognized its master once and for all.

The Capacity for Truth

For a long time, the West has refused to acknowledge that it owes us any debt whatsoever, that it does not have that millstone of debts accumulated over the course of its conquering the planet, which it has been dragging behind it ever since. Today, most of the West's defenders claim that, on the contrary, we are indebted to it. As they put it, we owe it a debt of "civilization," insofar as some of us have, they point out, taken advantage of the wrongs committed against us, sometimes with our own complicity. Today, the West does not just want to get rid of the foreigners that we are. It also wants us to take back our objects. Without giving any account of itself, it wants to be able to finally declare: "Having caused you no harm, I owe you absolutely nothing."

By inviting us to take back our objects and free up the spaces they occupied in its museums, what is the West looking to do? To make new connections? Or, in this age of closure, to reiterate what it has always suspected, namely, that we are person-objects, disposable by definition? Will we make it easier for the West by renouncing any right to remembrance? Will we dare to go further and decline the offer of repatriation? Transforming these objects into eternal proof of the crime it has committed, but for which it does not want to acknowledge responsibility, will we ask it to live forever with what it has taken and to assume its Cain-like figure to the very end?

But suppose that we yield to the offer, and that instead of a true act of *restitution*, we satisfy ourselves with a simple *recovery of artifacts now without substance.* How can we distinguish objects and their use-values, on the one hand, from works of art sensu stricto, on the other? Or between ritual and cult objects and ordinary objects, even though very few people are sure of what each of these objects is in itself, of how it was made and how it "functioned," what energies it was the repository of, and which ones it was able to release, in what circumstances, and with what effects on the material itself as well as on humans and the living in general? When it comes down to it, all this knowledge has been lost.

As Pol Pierre Gossiaux explains, African art corresponds to an aesthetics that may be qualified as cumulative. Its objects resulted "from the assembling and accumulation of disparate elements" whose "sense and function came from the formal and semantic relations thus created by their accumulation." The object assembled in this way was qualified as "beautiful" only to the extent that it fully assumed its ritual functions. Such accumulations, Gossiaux makes clear, did not come about by chance. They demanded lengthy apprenticeships and initiations into the handling of secular knowledges that have been lost.[33] Beyond the objects as such, who will restore the acts of thought that were associated with them, the types of cognition at stake in them, the forms of memory and imagination that they mobilized and of which they were, in turn, the product?

Moreover, between what has gone and what has come back, the chasm is wide, as most of these objects have been deformed and have become unrecognizable. The objects in collections and museums have not only been isolated from the cultural contexts in which they were intended to operate.[54] Some have suffered many wounds and amputations, including physical ones, and now display significant scars.[55] Consider the masks and other artifacts used in dance ceremonies. Most of them arrived in Europe wearing headdresses, all sorts of adornments (owl, eagle, vulture, quail, or rooster feathers, or porcupine quills, even dresses made from the inner bark of pigmented papyrus). These distinctive adornments and styles, and the contexts in which they were invited to appear, made them receptacles of meaning. They were as important as the morphological qualities of the objects or, as Gossiaux puts it, the "articulation of their geometry in space." They were nevertheless systematically stripped "of all that seemed to veil their apparent structures."[56]

Supposing that, among the majority of the people who produced them, the opposition between myth and technique, and then technique and rite, was by definition fragile, how also to identify all the diverse uses between the masks, statues and reliquary-statuettes, fly swats, the vegetal debris, the human bones and amulets, animal skins, kaolin, shells and padouk powder, assegais, drums and other objects dedicated to rites of passage or initiation, those intended to honor the dead or to chase away evil spirits, and others still required for therapeutic or divinatory practices?

Who can honestly deny that what was taken were not only the objects but, with them, enormous symbolic deposits, enormous *reserves of potentials*? Who can fail to see that the monopolization of African treasures on an extended scale constituted a colossal, and practically incalculable, loss, and consequently, that this loss is not liable to purely financial compensation, since what it entailed was the *devitalization* of our capacities to give birth to worlds, other figures of our common humanity?

It is not only a question of restoring materials, styles, decorations, and functions. How will we restore the meaning? Is it lost for good? Who will compensate for the fact that we will have to live with this loss forever? Is this loss a merely compensable loss? A certain Europe does not want to bother with these questions. For it, restitution is not an obligation. Faithful to a variant of legalism inherited from its long history, it considers that an obligation arises only where there is a legal constraint. In its eyes, any restitution is, whatever one may say, one modality among others of payment. There is nothing that one must pay without there being a debt. Any restitution therefore entails the existence, avowed or not, of a debt.

Europe considers that it is not our creditor and we are not its debtors. There is therefore no debt to be honored. If there were, we would be unable to force it. It is not compellable. It considers that, in the current state of things, the means provided by the law do not allow us to compel it to return our objects. If there is an obligation of restitution, it is nonbinding. What characterizes the obligation itself is the prospect of the sanction in case of noncompliance. And if, in spite of all this, it ends up returning these objects, it will be voluntarily, in an act of generosity and liberality and not as an obligation to anyone. In this case, as in others, it is hardly a matter of doing justice but of performing a free and voluntary act. Restitution is not a matter of gratuitousness and goodness. Restitution stems from an obligation. There are obligations that cannot be fulfilled within the constraints of existing law. They are nonetheless obligations. There are others that can be fulfilled voluntarily. By duty of conscience. But we stopped believing in the effects of appeals to conscience a long time ago.

For restitution to be genuine, it must be based on an equal recognition of the seriousness of the harm suffered and the wrongs inflicted. There is strictly nothing to restitute (or to return) where one believes that one has caused no harm; that one has taken nothing that required any permission. This is how the act of restoring is inseparable from the act of repairing. To "make good" or "restore" (the other name for restitution) is not the same thing as to "repent." Moreover, the one is not the condition of the other. Similarly, any restitution without compensation (or restoration) is by definition partial. But there are irreparable losses that no compensation can ever make up for—which is not to say that one should not compensate. To have compensated does not mean to have erased the wrong. It does not result in any acquittal. To compensate, as Kwame Anthony Appiah points out, is to make an offer to repair the relationship.[57] Further, restitution is an obligation where there has been a conscious, malicious, and voluntary destruction of another's life. In precolonial systems of thought, the most damaging wrongs were those that harmed what Placide Tempels calls the "vital force."[58]

In contexts where life was fragile, where it was likely to be diminished, any attack on the integrity of being and the intensity of life, however small, deserved reparation. In its fullest sense, reparation (or restitution) implied that the damages suffered are estimated. The calculation of damages could be expressed in economic terms. But, in the last instance, damages were established according to a measure of the value of life. It was the measure of the violation of life suffered that ultimately served as the basis for assessing compensation or restitution.[59] In line with this philosophy, true restitution is therefore that which participates in the restoration of life. The law underlying it is more person-oriented than goods-and-property-oriented. There is no restitution without reparation. Nevertheless, where material damages and interest come into play, they have no meaning other than to perform this restoration of life.

Neither is there any real restitution in the absence of what we must call the *capacity for truth*. "To give back," in this perspective, pertains to an unconditional duty—the irreducible infinity that is life, all life, this form of debt from which one cannot be acquitted as a matter of principle. For

Europe, to return our objects means to stop coming to us with the attitude of one for whom only their own reality counts and is necessary. Europe cannot pretend to give us back our objects while remaining convinced that we are subjects only in the insistence on our own distinction and not in the kind of mutuality that the reticular world that ours has become requires. Each singular life counts. History is not only a matter of might; it is also a one of truth. Authority and dignity are not only a gift of strength and power. We are therefore also called to honor truth, and not only force and power.

The truth is that Europe has taken things from us that it can never give back. We will learn to live with this loss. Europe, for its part, will have to bear responsibility for its actions, this shadowy part of our common history that it seeks to get rid of. The risk is that by returning our objects to us without explaining itself, Europe concludes that it is taking away our right to remind it of the truth. No one is asking it to repent. But, for new ties to be woven, it must honor the truth, for truth is the teacher of responsibility. This debt of truth is, in principle, indelible. It will haunt us until the end of times. To honor it requires a commitment to repairing the fabric and visage of the world.

CONCLUSION

There were so many other ways available to us. We could have taken so many other paths. Nothing, indeed, condemned us to run aground on these shores.

Tomorrow, perhaps, there will be no difference between calculating machines, those we have made, and ourselves, the procreated calculating machines. The century will perhaps be the one in which humanity will finally ingest its artifacts. It will become one with these and with the outside world, which will have, by this very fact, disappeared, buried in its entrails.

In the end, we will have made an alliance with all the vehicles of the world, all the transplants, and the mysteries of the flesh will finally have been reconciled with those of the machine. The secret abolished and nothing having taken its place, the dream factory will explode and disappear in a huge cloud of smoke. This will be the sounding of humanity's death knell. The posthistorical era will finally open onto an ocean of synthetic matter and mechanical liquids.

There will be no more accidents, no more religions, no more states, no more police, no more borders, no more races, no more languages, no more erections, and no more phalluses. Everywhere there will be mechanical tube prostheses, plastic teeth, screws and chips embedded in bodies. Everywhere there will be metamorphosis, expenditure and enjoyment of waste, in the ecstasy pit that the cosmos will have become.

Transcending our bodily limits, the last frontier, has always been our dream. It will have cost us the Earth.

Now, the road leading to shock is wide open, and many people are wondering about what they call the "possibility of fascism," while liberal democracy, an empty horizon of expectation, keeps on disintegrating. It does not matter that Article 13 of the Universal Declaration of Human Rights states that every inhabitant of the Earth "has the right to freedom of movement and residence within the borders of each State." The Earth no longer belongs to everyone, and at the same time, there is scarcely any longer a "home" to which to return. Everything comes down to calculation. There are no longer any *lasting rights*. All are revocable. At the same time, computational technologies and large tentacular corporations continue to encircle us and exert an unfathomable hold on our desires and behaviors.

The era is not only strange. It is conducive to all sorts of excesses without apparent purpose.

Not so long ago, humanity was in a similar position. The question back then was how to reform vision and emerge from the crisis in a way that did not lead to nothingness.

The "possibility of nothingness" has now resurfaced and, along with it, that of the "brute beast." Since the advent of modern times, it had always been assumed that the Black was the blinding manifestation, both larval and crepuscular, of this nothingness and this "brute beast." In reality, in a formidable act of phantasmatic projection, Europe had driven its own share of darkness onto this nonexistent subject (the Black). For this reason, the debate on exiting the "crisis of European humanity" became inseparable from the Black question and, furthermore, from that of the "whole Earth."

The Black question, that is to say, the question of the "whole Earth," is one that Europe always asked itself, each time from a position of exception, of not being part of it. Now the subterranean history of Western metaphysics, of which technology is the bone, the skeleton, as much as the flesh, is underpinned by the figure of the Black, or haunted by it. The figure of the Black does not emerge from the outside, at the edge or at the confines of this Europe that arrogated to itself the title of final humanity. The Black, as the unthought of Western metaphysics, is its foundation and one of its most significant projections—the Black insofar as this is the name of the "whole Earth," or, at least, of its entrails.

This has always been so, and notably so, through the prism of what this name's supposed absence of face and name concealed, with regard to what its shapeless forms translated and, even more damningly, according to the multiple uses to which it could be put. Yesterday, in fact, "when the frenzy of gold drained the last drop of Indian blood from the market," lamented René Depestre, "they turned to the muscular river of Africa to ensure the relief of despair. Then began the rush towards the inexhaustible treasury of black flesh."[1] Flesh-body, mineral-body, metal-body, ebony-body, a people cleared out and robbed, he cried out as if to underline the drama of a humanity locked in the night of the body and, beyond, that of the "whole Earth," open in its deepest entrails, starting with Africa, its cradle and its *first native country* (Aimé Césaire).

If at the beginning of the world was Africa, Europe will nevertheless have perceived in the Black only a serious threat to man's humanity. To the only man currently taken as the standard of the human, the Black will remind him not only about what he once was and has escaped from, but also what he risked becoming again—the threat of *reversion* to a state which one supposed to have forever left behind. Did the Black not represent the subject's extinction by definition, that which would disempower the mind? Was he not fundamentally given over to loss? The "loss of the Black"—and consequently that of the "whole Earth"—was supposed to leave no trace, no mark in the groove of time and in the memory of humankind. Both the presence and loss of the Black could not be written.

When our own took hold of this hallucinatory figure in the interwar period, they set about turning it into a radical counterpoint to the myth according to which Europe was the place of the ultimate accomplishment of humanity. But perhaps we should go further today. Perhaps it will be the place where humanity finds its end, its burial site. For our predecessors, the disquieting figure of the Black served not only to pose the complex problem of the relationship between culture and race, or between history and aesthetics, in new terms. It was also a way of pondering the possibilities for emancipating the entire human race—a prerequisite, so they thought, for overcoming the contradiction between might and justice, for reinventing the Earth, and, we might say today, for repairing it.

For this is the final choice. Either repair or funeral arrangements. There will be no flight to any exoplanet. The Earth will be the oasis from which the "whole of humanity" will undertake the gigantic work of regenerating the living. Or it will be the universal tomb, its mausoleum, in keeping with the geological period of the history of the universe.

This mausoleum will not house humanity's remains but its mummy. Its funeral will not take place in great secrecy but in an absolute tumult. It will stir up a range of passions and will summon the intimate history of each person. Some will come armed with deadly memories and poisons, and others with gifts, all sorts of useless objects, trinkets, rum, cocaine and tobacco, animal skins and shotguns, a few goats and huge mirrors, worn-out fetishes, and perhaps incense. Everything will be questioned. But for a long while already the time for answers will have been definitively closed.

A new politics of reparation does not only imply a redistribution of the places that each occupies, humans, on the one hand, and everything else, on the other. It also invites other ways of negotiating and resolving the conflicts that arise from different antagonistic ways of inhabiting the world, a vast reordering of relations. Reparation requires the renunciation of exclusive forms of appropriation, the recognition that the incalculable and the inappropriable exist, and that, consequently, there can be no exclusive possession and occupation of the Earth. As a sovereign body, it belongs only to itself, and no one can enclose its reserve of germinal matter, neither in advance nor for eternity.

NOTES

Introduction

1 For one example of this techno-optimism see Christopher J. Preston, *The Synthetic Age: Outdesigning Evolution, Resurrecting Species, and Reengineering our World* (Cambridge, MA: MIT Press, 2018).

2 Mabel Gergan, Sara Smith, and Pavithra Vasudevan, "Earth beyond Repair: Race and Apocalypse in Collective Imagination," *Environment and Planning D: Society and Space*, February 7, 2018, https://doi.org/10.1177/0263775818756079.

3 Shoshana Zuboff, *The Age of Surveillance Capitalism: The Fight for a Human Future at the New Frontier of Power* (Cambridge, MA: Harvard University Press, 2018).

4 Paul Gilroy, *Postcolonial Melancholia* (New York: Columbia University Press, 2006).

5 Luiza Bialasiewicz, "Off-shoring and Out-sourcing the Borders of EUrope: Libya and EU Border Work in the Mediterranean," *Geopolitics* 17, no. 4 (2012): 843–66. See also Laia Soto Bermant, "The Mediterranean Question: Europe and Its Predicament in the Southern Peripheries," in *The Borders of Europe: Autonomy of Migration, Tactics of Bordering*, ed. Nicholas De Genova (Durham, NC: Duke University Press, 2017), 120–40.

6 For an attempt at reproblematizing the future beyond the ideology of progress, see Arjun Appadurai, *Condition de l'homme global* (Paris: Payot, 2013). In addition, readers may consult "The Futures Industry," special issue, *Paradoxa* 27 (2015). On the topic of relations between the future and the borders of life, see Juan Francisco Salazar, "Microbial Geographies at the Extreme of Life," *Environmental Humanities* 9, no. 2 (2017): 398–417.

7 Amanda H. Lynch and Siri Veland, *Urgency in the Anthropocene* (Cambridge, MA: MIT Press, 2018).

8 François Jarrige and Thomas Le Roux, *La contamination du monde: Une histoire des pollutions à l'âge industriel* (Paris: Seuil, 2017).

9 See Ian G. R. Shaw and Marv Waterstone, *Wageless Life: A Manifesto for a Future beyond Capitalism* (Minneapolis: University of Minnesota Press, 2019).

10 See Aeron Davis, "Top CEOs, Financialization and the Creation of the Super-Rich Economy," *Cultural Politics* 15, no. 1 (2019): 88–104. See also Iain Hay and Samantha Muller, "That Tiny Stratospheric Apex That Owns Most of the World," *Geographical Research* 50, no. 1 (2012): 75–88. See also Melissa Cooper, *Life as Surplus: Biotechnology and Capitalism in the Neoliberal Era* (Seattle: University of Washington Press, 2008).

11 Saskia Sassen, *Expulsions: Brutalité et complexité dans l'économie globale* (2014; Paris: Gallimard, 2016).

12 See James Tyner, *Dead Labor: Toward a Political Economy of Premature Death* (Minneapolis: University of Minnesota Press, 2019).

13 See Stefan Helmreich, *Sounding the Limits of Life: Essays in the Anthropology of Biology and Beyond* (Princeton, NJ: Princeton University Press, 2016); Istvan Praet and Juan Francisco Salazar, "Familiarizing the Extraterrestrial/Making Our Planet Alien," *Environmental Humanities* 9, no. 2 (2018): 309–24.

14 Kathryn Yusoff, *A Billion Black Anthropocenes or None* (Minneapolis: University of Minnesota Press, 2019).

15 For a case study, see Pierre Bélanger, ed., *Extraction Empire: Undermining the Systems, States, and Scales of Canada's Global Resource Empire* (Cambridge, MA: MIT Press, 2018).

16 On water we drink, see Bérengère Sim, "Poor and African American in Flint: The Water Crisis and Its Trapped Population," in *The State of Environmental Migration 2016*, ed. François Gemenne, Caroline Zickgraf, and Dina Ionesco (Liège: Presses universitaires de Liège, 2016), 75–101. On the technosphere, see Miriam L. Diamond, "Toxic Chemicals as Enablers and Poisoners of the Technosphere," *Anthropocene Review* 4, no. 2 (2017): 72–80. On the air we breathe, see Josh Berson, *The Meat Question: Animals, Humans, and the Deep History of Food* (Cambridge, MA: MIT Press, 2019).

17 Dipesh Chakrabarty, "Le climat de l'histoire: Quatre thèses," *Revue internationale des livres et des idées*, no. 15 (2010): 22–31.

18 James Lovelock, *Novacene: The Coming Age of Hyperintelligence* (Cambridge, MA: MIT Press, 2019).

19 Marcus Hall, "Chronophilia; or, Biding Time in a Solar System," *Environmental Humanities* 11, no. 2 (2019): 373–401.

20 On confinement in reserves, see Gary Fields, *Enclosure: Palestinian Landscapes in a Historical Mirror* (Berkeley: University of California Press, 2017). On carceral landscapes, see Brett Story, *Prison Land: Mapping Carceral Power across Neoliberal America* (Minneapolis: University of Minnesota Press, 2019). On colonial ravages, see Gregg Mitman, "Reflections on the Plantationocene: A Conversation with Donna Haraway and Anna Tsing," *Edge Effects*, July 18, 2019, https://edgeeffects.net/haraway-tsing-plantationocene/. On mined frontiers,

see Jason De León, *The Land of Open Graves: Living and Dying on the Migrant Trail* (Berkeley: University of California Press, 2015).

21 Mochamad Adhiraga Pratama, Minoru Yoneda, and Yosuke Yamashiki, "Future Projection of Radiocesium Flux to the Ocean from the Largest River Impacted by Fukushima Daiichi Nuclear Power Plant," *Scientific Reports* 5 (2015), https://www.ncbi.nlm.nih.gov/pmc/articles/PMC4325319/. In addition, see Sven Lütticken, "Shattered Matter, Transformed Forms: Notes on Nuclear Aesthetics, Part 1," *e-flux Journal*, no. 94 (2018), https://www.e-flux.com/journal/94/221035/shattered-matter-transformed-forms-notes-on-nuclear-aesthetics-part-1/; and "Shattered Matter, Transformed Forms: Notes on Nuclear Aesthetics, Part 2," *e-flux Journal*, no. 96 (2019), https://www.e-flux.com/journal/96/243057/shattered-matter-transformed-forms-notes-on-nuclear-aesthetics-part-2/.

22 Matthew S. Henry, "Extractive Fictions and Postextraction Futurisms: Energy and Environmental Injustice in Appalachia," *Environmental Humanities* 11, no. 2, (2019): 402–26.

23 Clive Hamilton, Christophe Bonneuil, and François Gemenne, eds., *The Anthropocene and the Global Environmental Crisis: Rethinking Modernity in a New Epoch* (London: Routledge, 2015).

24 Daniel Martinez HoSang and Joseph E. Lowndes, *Producers, Parasites, Patriots: Race and the New Right-Wing Politics of Precarity* (Minnesota University Press: Minneapolis, 2019).

25 Achille Mbembe, *Critique of Black Reason* (Durham, NC: Duke University Press, 2017).

26 Ruha Benjamin, *Race after Technology: Abolitionist Tools for the New Jim Code* (London: Polity, 2019).

27 Luciana Parisi, "Instrumentality, or the Time of Inhuman Thinking," *Technosphere Magazine*, April 15, 2017, https://technosphere-magazine.hkw.de/p/Instrumentality-or-the-Time-of-Inhuman-Thinking-5Uvwa ECXmmYev25GrmEBhX.

28 Erik Steinberg, *Afrofuturism and Black Sound Studies: Culture, Technology, and Things to Come* (London: Palgrave Macmillan, 2019).

29 Hadi Rizk, *L'activité technique et ses objets* (Paris: Vrin, 2018), 147.

30 Peter Mitchell, *African Connections: Archaeological Perspectives on Africa and the Wider World* (Walnut Creek, CA: AltaMira, 2005); Sonja Magnavita, "Initial Encounters: Seeking Traces of Ancient Trade Connections between West Africa and the Wider World," *Afriques: Débats, méthodes et terrains d'histoire*, no. 4 (2013), https://doi.org/10.4000/afriques.1145. See also the special issue of this journal (no. 6, 2015) on the networks of exchange and connection between eastern Africa and the Indian Ocean.

31 On the concept's transformations and its heuristic potentiality in the present, see Nurit Bird-David, "'Animism' Revisited: Personhood, Environment, and Relational Epistemology," *Current Anthropology* 40, Suppl. (1999): 67–91, https://doi.org/10.1086/200061; and Karl Sierek, "Image-Animism: On the

History of the Theory of a Moving Term," special issue, *Images re-vues*, no. 4 (2013), https://doi.org/10.4000/imagesrevues.2874.

32 Luciana Parisi and Tiziana Terranova, "Heat-Death: Emergence and Control in Genetic Engineering and Artificial Life," *CTheory*, May 10, 2000, https://journals.uvic.ca/index.php/ctheory/article/view/14604/0.

33 See Ian Klinke, "Vitalist Temptations: Life, Earth and the Nature of War," *Political Geography* 72 (2019): 1–9.

One   Universal Domination

1 André Leroi-Gourhan, *Gesture and Speech*, trans. Anna Bostock Berger (Cambridge, MA: MIT Press, 1993), 254.

2 See Charles Adam and Paul Tanery's edition of the *Œuvres de Descartes*, 12 vols. (Paris: Léopold Cerf, 1897–1913), in particular, the fifth part of the *Discourse on Method* (vol. 6). See also Jean-Pierre Cavaillé, *Descartes: La fable du monde* (Paris: Vrin, 1991); and Dennis Des Chenes, *Spirits and Clocks: Machine and Organisms in Descartes* (Ithaca, NY: Cornell University Press, 2001).

3 Bernadette Bensaude-Vincent and William R. Newman, eds., *The Artificial and the Natural: An Evolving Polarity* (Cambridge, MA: MIT Press, 2007).

4 See Ernst Jünger, *Storm of Steel*, trans. Michael Hofmann (London: Allen Lane, 2003); Ernst Jünger, *Fire and Blood*, trans. K. J. Elliott (N.p.: Anarch Books, 2021).

5 The concept of "technology" is used here in its most stylized sense. We might have remained satisfied with other expressions such as "the technical gesture," or even "the technological," just as we say "the political" or "the religious." On this topic, see André Leroi-Gourhan, *L'homme et la matière*, vol. 1: *Évolution et techniques*, and vol. 2: *Milieu et techniques* (Paris: Albin Michel 1945). The point here is not to grant primacy to an ontological approach to technology. We are cognizant of the fact that if a part of the technological indeed plays out in the power of matter itself, technology comes about only in the different modes of deployment of the aforementioned power, that is, in the way in which it is set in motion by situated actors, through differentiated times and social spaces.

6 Lewis Mumford, *Technics and Civilization* (San Diego: Harcourt, Brace and Company, 1934).

7 Gilbert Hottois, *Le signe et la technique: La philosophie à l'épreuve de la technique* (1984; Paris: Vrin, 2018).

8 Kostas Axelos, *Marx, penseur de la technique*, 2 vols. (1961; Paris: UGE, 1974), 1:8 and 2:82–85.

9 On the geological dimensions of technology, see Peter K. Haff, "Technology as a Geological Phenomenon: Implications for Human Well-Being," in *A Stratigraphical Basis for the Anthropocene*, ed. C. N. Waters, J. A. Zalasiewicz, M. Williams, M. A. Ellis, and A. M. Snelling (London: Geological Society, 2014), 301–9. See also Bronislaw Szerszynski, "Viewing the Technosphere in an

Interplanetary Light," *Anthropocene Review* 4, no. 2 (2016), https://doi.org/10
.1177/2053019616670676.

10 Jeffrey Herf, *Le modernisme réactionnaire: Haine de la raison et culte de la technologie aux sources du nazisme* (1984; Paris: L'Échappée, 2018).

11 Tristan Dagron, *Pensée et cliniques de l'identité* (Paris: Vrin, 2019), 41.

12 William Davies, *The Happiness Industry: How the Government and Big Business Sold Us Well-Being* (New York: Verso, 2016); Eva Illouz and Edgar Cabanas, *Manufacturing Happy Citizens: How Science and the Industry of Happiness Control Our Lives* (Cambridge, UK: Polity Press, 2019).

13 Martin Heidegger, *Pensées directrices: Sur la genèse de la métaphysique, de la science et de la technique modernes* (Paris: Seuil, 2019), 318.

14 See Michael S. Burdett, *Eschatology and the Technological Future* (London: Routledge, 2017). For two case studies, see Cecilia Calheiros, "La fabrique d'une prophétie eschatologique par la cybernétique: Le cas du projet WebBot," *Raisons politiques* 4, no. 48 (2012): 51–63; and Abou Farman, "Cryonic Suspension as Eschatological Technology in the Secular Age," in *A Companion to the Anthropology of Death*, ed. Antonius C. G. M. Robben (Hoboken, NJ: Wiley Blackwell, 2018), 307–19.

15 Pierre Musso, *La religion industrielle: Monastère, manufacture, usine; une généalogie de l'entreprise* (Paris: Fayard, 2017).

16 Baptiste Rappin, "'Esprit californien, es-tu là?' Les racines *New Age* de la société digitale," *Études digitales*, no. 5 (2018): 87–103, https://classiques-garnier.com /export/pdf/etudes-digitales-2018-1-n-5-religiosite-technologique-esprit -californien-es-tu-la.html?displaymode=full.

17 Stéphanie Chifflet, "La techno-religion du NBIC," *Études digitales*, no. 5 (2018): 71–85, https://classiques-garnier.com/export/pdf/etudes-digitales-2018-1-n-5 -religiosite-technologique-la-techno-religion-nbic.html?displaymode=full.

18 See Carlos Eduardo Souza Aguiar, "Technochamanisme et les mutations de l'imaginaire mystique contemporain," *Études digitales*, no. 5 (2018): 143–57, https://classiques-garnier.com/export/pdf/etudes-digitales-2018 -1-n-5-religiosite-technologique-technoshamanism-and-changes-in-the -contemporary-mystical-imaginary.html?displaymode=full.

19 Yuk Hui, *On the Existence of Digital Objects* (Minneapolis: University of Minnesota Press, 2016).

20 See Reyner Banham, *Le Brutalisme en architecture: Éthique ou esthétique?* (1966; Paris: Dunod, 1970). See also Laurent Stalder, "'New Brutalism,' 'Topology' and 'Image': Some Remarks on the Architectural Debates in England around 1950," *Journal of Architecture* 13, no. 3 (2008): 263–81; and Francesco Tentori, "Phoenix Brutalism," *Zodiac*, no. 18 (1968): 257–66.

21 See David T. Johnson and Jon Fernquest, "Governing through Killing: The War on Drugs in the Philippines," *Asian Journal of Law and Society* 5, no. 2 (2018): 359–90; David Garland, *Peculiar Institution: America's Death Penalty in an Age of Abolition* (Cambridge, MA: Harvard University Press, 2010).

22 Franklin E. Zimring, *When Police Kill* (Cambridge, MA: Harvard University Press, 2017).

23 George L. Mosse, *Fallen Soldiers: Reshaping the Memory of the World Wars* (New York: Oxford University Press, 1990).

24 Joanna Bourke, *An Intimate History of Killing: Face-to-Face Killing in Twentieth Century Warfare* (London: Granta, 1999).

25 See Henry De Man, *The Remaking of a Mind: A Soldier's Thoughts on War and Reconstruction* (New York: Scribner, 1919).

26 See, in particular, Georges Gaudy, *Le Chemin-des-Dames en feu (décembre 1916–décembre 1917)* (Paris: Plon, 1923); Jean Norton Cru, *Témoins* (Paris: Les Étincelles, 1929); Blaise Cendrars, *Œuvres complètes*, vol. 4 (Paris: Denoël, 1962); and Antoine Redier, *Méditations dans la tranchée* (Paris: Payot, 1916).

27 Oliver Davis, "Theorizing the Advent of Weaponized Drones as Techniques of Domestic Paramilitary Policing," *Security Dialogue* 50, no. 4 (2016): 344–60.

28 William I. Robinson, "Accumulation Crisis and Global Police State," *Critical Sociology* 45, no. 6 (2018): 848–58.

29 Edward Lawson Jr., "Police Militarization and the Use of Lethal Force," *Political Research Quarterly* 72, no. 1 (2019): 177–89, https://doi.org/10.1177/1065912918784209; Caren Kaplan and Andrea Miller, "Drones as 'Atmospheric Policing': From US Border Enforcement to the LAPD," *Public Culture* 31, no. 3 (2019): 419–45.

30 Elke Schwarz, "Prescription Drones: On the Techno-Biopolitical Regime of Contemporary 'Ethical Killing,'" *Security Dialogue* 47, no. 1 (2015): 59–75.

31 For an evaluation of these conducts in a war situation, see Antoine Prost, "Les limites de la brutalisation: Tuer sur le front occidental, 1914–1918," *Vingtième siècle*, no. 81 (2004): 5–20.

32 Daniel Pécaud, "De la banalité de la violence à la terreur: Le cas colombien," *Cultures et Conflits*, nos. 24–25 (1997): 159–93.

33 George L. Mosse, *The Image of Man: The Creation of Modern Masculinity* (Oxford: Oxford University Press, 1996). In addition, see also Mosse's *The Nationalization of the Masses: Political Symbolism and Mass Movements in Germany from the Napoleonic Wars through the Third Reich* (New York: Howard Fertig, 1975).

34 See Klaus Theweleit, *Male Fantasies*, trans. Stephen Conway (Minneapolis: University of Minnesota Press, 1987).

35 For more on this specific case, see Vasiliki Touhouliotis, "Weak Seed and a Poisoned Land: Slow Violence and the Toxic Infrastructures of War in South Lebanon," *Environmental Humanities* 10, no. 1 (2018): 86–106. More generally, see Michael Marder, "Being Dumped," *Environmental Humanities* 11, no. 1 (2019): 181–92.

36 Walter Benjamin, "Theories of German Fascism," *New German Critique*, no. 17 (1979): 120–28.

37 Friedrich Georg Jünger, *The Failure of Technology: Perfection without Purpose*, trans. Fred D. Wieck, intro. Frederick D. Wilhelmsen (Hinsdale, IL:

H. Regnery, 1949; reprint, N.p.: Der Schattige Wald, 2021), 22 (translation modified—SC).

38 Paul Virilio, *Speed and Politics*, trans. Marc Polizzotti (Los Angeles: Semiotext(e) 2006), 49. See also Eva Illouz, ed., *Emotions as Commodities: Capitalism, Consumption and Authenticity* (London: Routledge, 2018).

39 William J. Wilson, *When Work Disappears* (New York: Knopf, 1996); Ruth W. Gilmore, *The Golden Gulag* (Berkeley: University of California Press, 2007).

40 Jackie Wang, *Carceral Capitalism* (Cambridge, MA: MIT Press, 2019).

41 "Policing and Profit," *Harvard Law Review* 128, no. 6 (2005), https://harvard lawreview.org/2015/04/policing-and-profit/.

42 In more or less similar situations, see what Elsa Dorlin says about "prey." Elsa Dorlin, *Se défendre: Une philosophie de la violence* (Paris: Zones, 2017): 163–71.

43 See Leon Anderson and David A. Snow, "L'industrie du plasma," *Actes de la recherche en sciences sociales* 104 (1994): 25–33, https://www.persee.fr/doc/arss _0335-5322_1994_num_104_1_3110; Zoe Greenberg, "What Is the Blood of a Poor Person Worth?," *New York Times*, February 1, 2019. See also Harriet A. Washington, *Medical Apartheid: The Dark History of Medical Experimentation on Black Americans from Colonial Times to the Present* (New York: Doubleday, 2006).

44 Sigmund Freud, *Civilization and Its Discontents*, ed. and trans. James Strachey (New York: W. W. Norton, 2010).

45 See Scott Wark, "The subject of circulation: On the digital subject's technical individuations," *Subjectivity*, no. 12 (2019): 65–81.

46 Katerina Kolozova, "Subjectivity without Physicality: Machine, Body and the Signifying Automaton," *Subjectivity* 12 (2019): 49–64; Beverly Skeggs, "Subjects of Value and Digital Personas," *Subjectivity* 12 (2019): 82–99.

47 Frantz Fanon, *Writings on Alienation and Freedom*, trans. Steven Corcoran (London: Bloomsbury, 2018).

48 See W. E. B. Du Bois, *The Souls of Black Folk* (Chicago: A.C. McClurg, 1903).

49 Aimé Césaire, *Discourse on Colonialism* (New York: Monthly Review Press, 2000).

50 Édouard Glissant, *Poetics of Relation*, trans. Betsy Wing (Ann Arbor: University of Michigan Press, 1997).

51 See "Democracy: Its Normative Foundations and Current Crisis," special issue, *Constellations* 26, no. 3 (2019): 355–474.

52 See David Roediger, *The Wages of Whiteness: Race and the Making of the American Working Class* (New York: Verso, 1999); Theodore W. Allen, *The Invention of the White Race*, vol. 2: *The Origin of Racial Oppression in America* (New York: Verso, 1997). In the case of settler colonies, see, by way of example, Yuka Suzuki, *The Nature of Whiteness: Race, Animals, and Nation in Zimbabwe* (Seattle: University of Washington Press, 2017).

53 Immanuel Kant, *Towards Perpetual Peace and Other Writings on Politics, Peace and History*, ed. Pauline Kleingeld, trans. David L. Colclasure (1795; New Haven, CT: Yale University Press, 2006), § 62.

54 Édouard Glissant, *Une nouvelle région du monde: Esthétique 1* (Paris: Gallimard, 2006), 123 (my translation—SC).

55 Glissant, *Une nouvelle région du monde: Esthétique 1*, 161 (my translation—SC).

Two Fracturing

1 Carl Schmitt, *The Nomos of the Earth in the International Law of the* Jus Publicum Europaeum, trans. G. L. Ulmen (New York: Telos Press, 2003), 79.

2 Renée Koch Piettre, Odile Journet, and Danouta Liberski-Bagnoud, eds., *Mémoires de la terre: Études anciennes et comparées* (Grenoble: Jérôme Millon, 2019).

3 F. W. J. Schelling, *The Ages of the World*, trans. Jason M. Wirth (Albany: SUNY Press, 2000).

4 Jean-Pierre Vernant, *Mythe et pensée chez les Grecs* (Paris: Maspero, 1965).

5 Schmitt, *Nomos of the Earth*, 42.

6 Schmitt, *Nomos of the Earth*, 49.

7 Schmitt, *Nomos of the Earth*, 50.

8 Schmitt, *Nomos of the Earth*, 53.

9 Kostas Axelos, *Vers la pensée planétaire: Le devenir-pensée du monde et le devenir-monde de la pensée* (1964; Paris: Les Belles Lettres, 2019), esp. 13–54, and 339–63.

10 Schmitt, *Nomos of the Earth*, 54.

11 Schmitt, *Nomos of the Earth*, 55.

12 Nathan Wachtel, *La vision des vaincus: Les indiens du Pérou devant la conquête espagnole, 1530–1570* (Paris: Gallimard, 1971).

13 Schmitt, *Nomos of the Earth*, 54.

14 See Tanja L. Zwann, ed., *Space Law: Views of the Future* (Deventer: Kluwer, 1988); G. C. M. Reijnen and W. de Graaff, *The Pollution of Outer Space, in Particular of the Geostationary Orbit: Scientific Policy and Legal Aspects* (Dordrecht: Martinus Nijhoff, 1989).

15 On the juridical dimensions of these debates, see John P. Craven, ed., *The International Implications of Extended Maritime Jurisdiction in the Pacific: Proceedings of the 21st Annual Conference of the Law of the Sea Institute* (Honolulu: Law of the Sea Institute, 1989); Lewis M. Alexander et al., eds., *New Developments in Marine Science and Technology: Economic, Legal and Political Aspects of Change* (Honolulu: Law of the Sea Institute, 1989); John M. Van Dyke et al., eds., *International Navigation: Rocks and Shoals Ahead* (Honolulu: Law of the Sea Institute, 1988); Brian D. Smith, *State Responsibility and the Marine Environment: The Rules of Decision* (New York: Clarendon Press, 1988); John Warren Kindt, *Marine Pollution and the Law of the Sea* (Buffalo, NY: W. S. Hein, 1998).

16 Dorinda G. Dallmeyer and Louis DeVorsey Jr., *Rights to Oceanic Resources: Deciding and Drawing Maritime Boundaries* (Dordrecht: Martinus Nijhoff, 1989).

17 Barbara Kwiatkowska, *The 200-Mile Exclusive Economic Zone in the New Law of the Sea* (Dordrecht: Martinus Nijhoff, 1989); Prosper Weil, *The Law of Maritime*

Delimitation: Reflections (Cambridge: Grotius, 1989); Fillmore Earney, *Marine Mineral Resources* (London: Routledge, 1990). See also Umberto Leanza, ed., *Mediterranean Continental Shelf: Delimitations and Regimes* (Dobbs Ferry, NY: Oceana Publications, 1988).

18 Benjamin H. Bratton, *Le stack: Plateformes, logiciel et souveraineté* (Grenoble: UGA Éditions, 2019).

19 N. Katherine Hayles, *Lire et penser en milieux numériques: Attention, récits, technogenèse* (Grenoble: UGA, 2016); and Angelo Braito and Yves Citton, eds., *Technologies de l'enchantement: Pour une histoire multidisciplinaire de l'illusion* (Grenoble: UGA Éditions, 2014).

20 This second part of the chapter was first published under the title "La démondialisation," *Esprit*, no. 12 (December 2018): 86–94.

21 On these debates, see Pat O'Malley, *Risk, Uncertainty and Government* (London: Glasshouse Press, 2004); Samid Suleiman, "Global Development and Precarity: A Critical Political Analysis," *Globalization* 16, no. 4 (2019): 525–40. For a case study, see Brett Neilson, "Precarious in Piraeus: On the Making of Labour Insecurity in a Port Concession," *Globalization* 16, no. 4 (2019): 559–74.

22 On these discussions, see the informative works by Luciana Parisi, "Critical Computation, Digital Automata and General Artificial Thinking," *Theory, Culture and Society* 36, no. 2 (2019): 89–121, https://doi.org/10.1177/0263276418818889; and "Instrumental Reason, Algorithmic Capitalism, and the Incomputable," in *Alleys of Your Mind: Augmented Intelligence and Its Traumas*, ed. Matteo Pasquinelli (Lüneburg: meson press, 2015), 125–37, https://doi.org/10.14619/014.

23 Karen Jones-Mason, Kazuko Y. Behrens, and Naomi I. Gribneau Bahm, "The Psychological Consequences of Child Separation at the Border: Lessons from Research on Attachment and Emotion Regulation," *Attachment and Human Development*, November 26, 2019, https://doi.org/10.1080/14616734.2019.16 92879; see also Sarah Mares, "Fifteen Years of Detaining Children Who Seek Asylum in Australia—Evidence and Consequences," *Australasian Psychiatry*, December 8, 2015, https://doi.org/10.1177/1039856215620029.

24 Henrik Dorf Nielsen, "Migrant Deaths in the Arizona Desert: La vida no vale nada," *Journal of Borderlands Studies* 34, no. 3 (2019): 473–74; Joseph Nevins, "The Speed of Life and Death: Migrant Fatalities, Territorial Boundaries, and Energy Consumption," *Mobilities* 13, no. 1 (2018): 29–44.

25 Francesca Zampagni, "Unpacking the Schengen Visa Regime: A study on Bureaucrats and Discretion in an Italian Consulate," *Journal of Borderlands Studies* 31, no. 2 (2016): 251–66. Tamara Last et al., "Deaths at the Borders Database: Evidence of Deceased Migrants's Bodies Found along the Southern External Borders of the European Union," *Journal of Ethnic and Migration Studies* 43, no. 5 (2017): 693–712; Cédric Parizot, "Viscous Spatialities: The Spaces of the Israeli Permit Regime of Access and Movement," *South Atlantic Quarterly* 117, no. 1 (2018): 21–42.

26 See "Effets-frontières en Méditerranée: Contrôles et violences," ed. Laurence
    Pillant, Louise Tassin, Paloma Maquet, Lorenzo Gabrielli, Paolo Cuttitta, and
    Evelyne Ritaine, special issue, *Cultures et Conflits*, nos. 99–100 (2015).

27 Tamara Last, "Challenging the Anonymity of Death by Border Sea: Who Are Boat
    Migrants?" in *Boat Refugees and Migrants at Sea: A Comprehensive Approach*, ed.
    Violetta Moreno-Lax and Efthymios Papastavridis (Leiden: Brill, 2016), 79 116.

28 Catherine Lutz and Andrea Mazzarino, eds., *War and Health: The Medical Conse-
    quences of the Wars in Iraq and Afghanistan* (New York: New York University Press,
    2019); Barry S. Levy and Victor W. Sidel, "Documenting the Effects of Armed
    Conflict on Population Health," *Annual Review of Public Health* 37 (2016): 205–18.

29 Read Joseba Zulaika, *Hellfire from Paradise Ranch: On the Frontlines of Drone
    Warfare* (Berkeley: University of California Press, 2019); Katherine Chandler,
    Unmanning: How Humans, Machines, and Media Perform Drone Warfare (New
    Brunswick, NJ: Rutgers University Press, 2019). See also Jairus Victor Grove,
    Savage Ecology: War and Geopolitics at the End of the World (Durham, NC:
    Duke University Press, 2019); and Achille Mbembe, *Necropolitics*, trans. Steven
    Corcoran (Durham, NC: Duke University Press, 2019).

30 Margarida Mendes, "Molecular Colonialism," in *Matter Fictions*, ed. Margarida
    Mendes (Berlin: Stenberg Press, 2017), 125–40.

31 John R. Logan and Deirdre Oakley, "Black Lives and Policing: the Larger Con-
    text of Ghettoization," *Journal of Urban Affairs* 39, no. 8 (2017): 1031–46; Calvin
    John Smiley and David Fakunle, "From 'Brute' to 'Thug': The Demonization
    and Criminalization of the Unarmed Black Male Victims in America," *Journal
    of Human Behavior in the Social Environment* 26, nos. 3–4 (2016): 350–66.

32 Elsa Dorlin, *Se défendre: Une philosophie de la violence* (Paris: Zones, 2017).

33 Grégoire Chamayou, *Manhunts: A Philosophical History*, trans. Steven Rendall,
    (Princeton, NJ: Princeton University Press, 2012).

34 Stefan Newton, "The Excessive Use of Force against Blacks in the United States
    of America," *International Journal of Human Rights* 22, no. 8 (2018): 1067–86.

35 Louise Amoore, "Biometric Borders: Governing Mobilities in the War on Ter-
    ror," *Political Geography* 25, no. 3 (2006): 336–51; Jose Sanchez del Rio, Daniela
    Moctezuma, Cristia Conde, Isaac Martin de Diego, and Enrique Cabello, "Au-
    tomated Border Control E-Gates and Facial Recognition Systems," *Computer
    and Security* 62 (2016): 49–72. More generally, see Irma Van der Ploeg, *The
    Machine-Readable Body Essays on Biometrics and the Informatization of the Body*
    (Maastricht: Shaker Publishing, 2005).

36 Louise Amoore and Alexandra Hall, "Taking People Apart: Digitised Dissec-
    tion and the Body at the Border," *Environment and Planning D: Society and
    Space* 27 (2009): 444–64.

37 Federico Rahola, "La forme-camp: Pour une généalogie des lieux de transit et
    d'internement du présent," *Cultures et Conflits* 4, no. 68 (2007): 31–50; Michel
    Agier, "Camps, Encampments, and Occupations: from the Heterotopia to the
    Urban Subject," *Ethnos* 84, no. 1 (2019): 14–26. See, more generally, Elizabeth A.

Povinelli, "Driving Across Late Liberalism: Indigenous Ghettos, Slums and Camps," *Ethnos* 84, no. 1 (2019): 113–23.

38 Maurizio Albahari, *Crimes of Peace: Mediterranean Migrations at the World's Deadliest Border* (Philadelphia: University of Pennsylvania Press, 2015); Leanne Weber and Sharon Pickering, *Globalization and Borders: Death at the Global Frontier* (New York: Palgrave Macmillan, 2011).

39 Nick Gill, Deirdre Conion, Dominique Moran, and Andrew Burridge, "Carceral Circuitry: New Directions in Carceral Geography," *Progress in Human Geography*, November 3, 2016, https://doi. org/10.1177/0309132516671823; Alison Mountz, Kate Coddington, R. Tina Catania, and Jenna M. Loyd, "Conceptualizing Detention: Mobility, Containment, Bordering, and Exclusion," *Progress in Human Geography* 27, no. 4 (2012), https://doi .org/10.1177/0309132512460903.

40 Concerning the colonial and fascist antecedents of these forms, see Andreas Stucki, "'Frequent Deaths': The Colonial Development of Concentration Camps Reconsidered, 1868–1974," *Journal of Genocide Research* 20, no. 3 (2018): 305–26; and Javier Rodrigo, "Exploitation, Fascist Violence and Social Cleansing: a Study of Franco's Concentration Camps from a Comparative Perspective," *European Review of History* 19, no. 4 (2012): 553–73.

41 Aimé Césaire, *Discourse on Colonialism* (New York: Monthly Review Press, 2000).

42 See Hagar Kotef, *Movement and the Ordering of Freedom: On Liberal Governances of Mobility* (Durham, NC: Duke University Press, 2015).

Three Animism and Viscerality

1 Lucy Suchman, "Situational Awareness: Deadly Bioconvergence at the Boundaries of Bodies and Machines," *MediaTropes* 5, no. 1 (2015): 1–24; and Lauren Wilcox, "Embodying Algorithmic War: Gender, Race, and the Posthuman in Drone Warfare," *Security Dialogue* 48, no. 1 (2017): 11–28.

2 Thomas Lamarra, *The Anime Machine: A Media Theory of Animation* (Minneapolis: University of Minnesota Press, 2009).

3 See, for example, Stephan Scheel and Funda Ustek-Spilda, "The Politics of Expertise and Ignorance in the Field of Migration Management," *Environment and Planning D: Society and Space* 37, no. 4 (2019): 663–81, https://doi .org/10.1177/0263775819843677; or also Jutta Bakonyi, "Seeing Like Bureaucracies: Rearranging Knowledge and Ignorance in Somalia," *International Political Sociology* 12, no. 3 (2018): 256–73; and, more generally, Linsey McGoey, "Strategic Unknowns: Towards a Sociology of Ignorance," *Economy and Society* 41, no. 1 (2012): 1–16.

4 See Seb Franklin, *Control: Digitality as a Cultural Logic* (Cambridge, MA: MIT Press, 2015).

5 Matteo Pasquinelli, "Three Thousand Years of Algorithmic Rituals: the Emergence of AI from the Computation of Space," *e-flux Journal*, no. 101 (2019):

1–14. Also from Matteo Pasquinelli, "The Eye of the Algorithm: Cognitive Anthropocene and the Making of the World Brain," Academia, 2014, https://www.academia.edu/8751480/The_Eye_of_the_Algorithm_Anthropocene_and_the_Making_of_the_World_Brain; and "Machines That Morph Logic: Neural Networks and the Distorted Automation of Intelligence as Statistical Inference," *Glass Bead*, 2017, https://www.glass-bead.org/article/machines-that-morph-logic/?lang=enview.

6   Concerning this long history, see Olivier Rey, *Quand le monde s'est fait nombre* (Paris: Stock, 2016).

7   The exploration of the last continents is far from over, and that of the extraterrestrial universe and its limits has barely started. See Daniela Liggett, Bryan Storey, Yvonne Cook, and Veronika Meduna, *Exploring the Last Continent: An Introduction to Antartica* (New York: Springer, 2015); Michael J. Crowe, *The Extraterrestrial Life Debate, 1750–1900: The Idea of a Plurality of Worlds from Kant to Lowell* (Cambridge: Cambridge University Press, 1986). And Steven J. Dick, ed., *The Impact of Discovering Life beyond Earth* (Cambridge: Cambridge University Press, 2015).

8   Francis Lee and Lotta Bjorklund Larsen, "How Should We Theorize Algorithms? Five Ideal Types in Analyzing Algorithmic Normativities," *Big Data and Society* 6, no. 2 (2019), https://doi.org/10.1177/2053951719867349; Suzanne L. Thomas, Dawn Nafus, and Jamie Sherman, "Algorithms as Fetish: Faith and Possibility in Algorithmic Work," *Big Data and Society* 5, no. 1 (2018), https://doi.org/10.1177/2053951717751552.

9   For a case study, see Claire Wright, "Modèle extractiviste et pouvoirs d'exception en Amérique latine," *Cultures et conflits* 112 (2019): 93–118.

10   Friedrich Georg Jünger, *The Failure of Technology: Perfection without Purpose*, trans. Fred D. Wieck, intro. Frederick D. Wilhelmsen (Hinsdale, IL: H. Regnery, 1949; reprint, N.p.: Der Schattige Wald, 2021), 90.

11   See the contributions collected in "Algorithmic Normativities," ed. Lotta Björklund Larsen and Francis Lee, special issue, *Big Data and Society* 6, no. 2 (2019).

12   Nick Couldry and Ulises A. Mejias, "Data Colonialism: Rethinking Big Data's Relation to the Contemporary Subject," *Television and New Media* 20, no. 4 (2018): 336–49.

13   On these debates, see Rob Kitchin, "Big Data, New Epistemologies and Paradigm Shifts," *Big Data and Society* 1, no. 1 (2014), https://doi.org/10.1177/2053951714528481; Ian Lowrie, "Algorithmic Rationality: Epistemology and Efficiency in the Data Sciences," *Big Data and Society* 4, no. 1 (2017), https://doi.org/10.1177/2053951717700925.

14   Louise Amoore, "Cloud Geographies: Computing, Data, Sovereignty," *Progress in Human Geography* 42, no. 1 (2019): 4–24, https://doi.org/10.1177/0309132516662147.

15 See Scott Lash and Bogdan Dragos, "An Interview with Philip Mirowski," *Theory, Culture and Society* 33, no. 6 (2016): 123–40, https://doi.org/10.1177/0263276415623063.

16 Pierre Lévy, "Préface," in *L'être et l'écran: Comment le numérique change la perception*, by Stéphane Vial (Paris: Presses Universitaires de France, 2013), 14.

17 Edemilson Parana, *Digitalized Finance: Financial Capitalism and Informational Revolution* (London: Brill, 2018).

18 This social life unfolds in a context characterized by novel devices of mass surveillance and the rise of paranoiac behaviors. On this topic, see Dirk Helbing, ed., *Towards Digital Enlightenment: Essays on the Dark and Light Sides of the Digital Revolution* (New York: Springer, 2018); Stephen Frosh, "Relationality in a Time of Surveillance: Narcissism, Melancholia, Paranoia," *Subjectivities* 9, no. 1 (2016): 1–16.

19 Yuk Hui, *On the Existence of Digital Objects* (Minneapolis: University of Minnesota Press, 2016).

20 Lucas D. Introna and Fernando M. Ilharco, "The Ontological Screening of Contemporary Life: a Phenomenological Analysis of Screens," *Information Systems* 13, no. 3 (2004): 221–34.

21 Éric Laurent, *L'envers de la biopolitique* (Paris: Navarin, 2016), 13.

22 Maurizio Meloni, "A Postgenomic Body: Histories, Genealogy, Politics," *Body and Society* 24, no. 3 (2018): 3–38, https://doi.org/10.1177/1357034X18785445.

23 The following paragraphs take up some elements of a published interview with Bregtje van der Haak titled "Afrocomputation," *Multitudes*, no. 69 (2017): 198–204.

24 Judith Butler, *Notes Toward a Performative Theory of Assembly* (Cambridge, MA: Harvard University Press, 2015).

25 Mary Nooter Roberts, "The Inner Eye: Vision and Transcendence in African Arts," *African Arts* 50, no. 1 (2017): 60–79.

26 Babatunde Lawal, "*Aworan*: Representing the Self and Its Metaphysical Other in Yoruba Art," *Art Bulletin* 83, no. 3 (2001): 498–526.

27 Jane Guyer and Samuel M. Eno Belinga, "Wealth in People as Wealth in Knowledge: Accumulation and Composition in Equatorial Africa," *Journal of African History* 36, no. 1 (1995): 91–120.

Four Virilism

1 On this topic, see Heather Vermeulen, "Thomas Thistlewood's Libidinal Linnaean Project: Slavery, Ecology, and Knowledge Production," *Small Axe* 55, no. 1 (2018): 19–38.

2 Pascal Blanchard, Nicolas Bancel, Gilles Boetsch, Christelle Taraud, and Domi nic Richard Davis Thomas, eds., *Sexe, race et colonies* (Paris: La Découverte, 2019). In what follows, I borrow some elements from my preface to this work,

from an article published as "Si l'Autre n'est qu'un sexe . . . ," in *AOC*, August 24, 2018 (https://aoc.media/opinion/2018/08/24/lautre-nest-quun-sexe/), and from a chapter published in Gilles Boëtsch and Tiffany Roux, eds., *Sexualités, identités et corps colonisés: XVe siècle–XXIe siècle* (Paris: CNRS Éditions, 2019).

3 On this sort of questioning, see Elsa Dorlin, *La matrice de la race: Généalogie sexuelle et coloniale de la nation française* (Paris: La Découverte, 2009).

4 Wilhelm Reich, *The Function of the Orgasm: Sex-Economic Problems of Biological Energy*, trans. Vincent F. Carfagno (1927; London: Souvenir Press, 1989).

5 See Gaëtan Brulotte, *Œuvres de chair: Figures du discours érotique* (Québec: Presses de l'université Laval, 1998).

6 The following section contains elements from an interview conducted by Elsa Dorlin that appeared under title "Décoloniser les structures psychiques du pouvoir," *Mouvements*, no. 51 (2003): 142–51.

7 Edward Evan Evans-Pritchard, "L'inversion sexuelle chez les Azandé," *Politique africaine*, no. 126 (2012): 109–19, https://www.cairn.info/revue-politique -africaine-2012-2-page-109.htm.

8 Mariane Ferme, *The Underneath of Things: Violence, History, and the Everyday in Sierra Leone* (Berkeley: University of California Press, 2001).

9 James Fernandez, *Bwiti: An Ethnography of the Religious Imagination in Africa* (Princeton, NJ: Princeton University Press, 1982).

10 Arthur Bourgeois, "Yaka Masks and Sexual Imagery," *African Arts* 15, no. 2 (1982): 47–50, 87.

11 See, in particular, Sony Labou Tansi's *La vie et demie* (Paris: Seuil, 1979) and *L'état honteux* (Paris: Seuil, 1981). See also Samy Tchak, *Place des fêtes* (Paris: Gallimard, 2001).

12 Parfait Akana, "Notes sur la dénudation publique du corps féminin au Cameroun," *L'Autre* 14, no. 2 (2013): 236–43.

13 Achille Mbembe, *On the Postcolony* (Berkeley: University of California Press, 2001).

14 Hazel Carby, "On the Threshold of Woman's Era: Lynching, Empire, and Sexuality in Black Feminist Theory," *Critical Inquiry* 12, no. 1 (1985): 262–77.

15 Marnia Lazreg, *Torture and the Twilight of Empire: From Algiers to Baghdad* (Princeton, NJ: Princeton University Press, 2008).

16 Gaston Bachelard, *The Psychoanalysis of Fire*, trans. Alan C. M. Ross (New York: Beacon Press, 1987), 47.

17 On the way that contemporary art takes up the theme of masturbation, see Céline Cadaureille, "Jeux de mains . . . jeux de vilains: La masturbation dans l'œuvre de P. Meste, de V. Acconci et de P. Sorin," *Inter: Art actuel*, no. 112 (2012): 36–39, https://www.erudit.org/en/journals/inter/2012-n112-inter0343 /67683ac.pdf.

18 See, by way of example, Beatriz Preciado, *Testo Junkie: Sex, Drugs, and Biopolitics in the Pharmacopornographic Era*, trans. Bruce Benderson (New York: Feminist Press at CUNY, 2013); Paul B. Preciado, *Pornotopia: An Essay on*

Playboy's Architecture and Biopolitics (New York: Zone Books, 2014); and above all Paul B. Preciado, *Countersexual Manifesto*, trans. Kevin Gerry Dunn (New York: Columbia University Press, 2018).

19 Preciado, *Countersexual Manifesto*.

20 Here we are indeed nowhere near the sexual scenes described by Virginie Despentes, *Baise-moi*, trans. Bruce Benderson (New York: Grove Press, 2002). "As she looked down the aisle, she wondered what she would rather do there, doggy style or carnage. As the guy besotted her, she thought about the scene from the afternoon, how Nadine blew the woman against the wall, as she got destroyed by the gun. Bestial, really. Good as fuck. Unless it was the fucking she liked as the massacre." (En regardant l'allée, elle se demande ce qu'elle préfère y pratiquer, la levrette ou le carnage. Pendant que le type la besognait, elle a pensé à la scène de l'après-midi, comment Nadine a explosé la femme contre le mur, comme elle s'est fait détruire par le gun. Bestial, vraiment. Bon comme de la baise. À moins que ça soit la baise qu'elle aime comme du massacre.)

21 See Denis Sanglard, "Buto et sadomasochisme: Sade6412, un solo obscène et critique," *INTER: ART ACTUEL*, no. 112 (2012): 12, https://www.erudit.org/en /journals/inter/2012-n112-intero343/67678ac.pdf.

22 Kelly Oliver, "Women: The Secret Weapon of Modern Warfare?" *Hypatia* 23, no. 2 (2008): 1–16.

23 See Sherene Razack, "How Is White Supremacy Embodied? Sexualized Racial Violence at Abu Ghraib," *Canadian Journal of Women and the Law* 17, no. 2 (2005): 341–63.

24 See Eileen L. Zurbriggen, "Sexualized Torture and Abuse at Abu Ghraib Prison: Feminist Psychological Analyses," *Feminism and Psychology* 18, no. 3 (2008): 301–20.

25 On the topic of exploiting feminist themes as a central dimension of neoliberal policies, see Sara R. Farris, *In the Name of Women's Rights: The Rise of Femonationalism* (Durham, NC: Duke University Press, 2017); and Françoise Vergès, *Un féminisme décolonial* (Paris: La Fabrique, 2019).

26 Catherine Mavrikakis, "La virilité rasée?," review of *King Kong Théorie*, by Virginie Despentes, special issue, *Spirale*, no. 215 (July–August 2007): 28–29.

27 See Trudier Harris, *Exorcising Blackness: Historical and Literary Lynching Burying Rituals* (Bloomington: Indiana University Press, 1984).

28 Concerning the aforementioned, see the novels of Amos Tutuola, *My Life in the Bush of Ghosts* (New York: Grove Press, 1954), and *The Palm-Wine Drinkard* (New York: Grove Press, 1953).

29 See Michaël La Chance, "Vierges blanches et Vénus sanglantes: Fictions sexuelles et corps fascinés," *INTER: ART ACTUEL*, no. 112 (2012): 30–35. https:// www.erudit.org/en/journals/inter/2012-n112-intero343/67682ac.pdf.

30 La Chance, "Vierges blanches," 31–32.

31 Luciana Parisi, *Abstract Sex: Philosophy, Biotechnology and the Mutations of Desire* (London: Continuum, 2004).

32 Michaël Pécot-Kleiner, "Comment la technologie va-t-elle s'emparer de notre sexualité?," *Antidote*, October 18, 2018, https://magazineantidote.com/societe/comment-la-technologie-va-t-elle-s-emparer-de-notre-sexualite-2/.

Five **Border-Bodies**

1 Étienne Balibar, "Sur la situation des migrants dans le capitalisme absolu," *Les Possibles*, no. 19 (2019), https://france.attac.org/pdf/possibles/1777/6569.

2 Nicolas Renahy calls this "capital d'autochtonie," but he wrongly limits it to the working classes. See "Classes populaires et capital d'autochtonie: Genèse et usage d'une notion," *Regards Sociologiques*, no. 40 (2010): 9–26.

3 Reece Jones and Corey Johnson, "Border Militarization and the Re-articulation of Sovereignty," *Transactions of the Institute of British Geographers* 41, no. 2 (2016): 187–200.

4 Marcel Reinhard, "La population française au XVIIᵉ siècle," *Population* 13, no. 4 (1958): 619–30.

5 Read Paul M. Bondois, "La misère sous Louis XIV: la disette de 1662," *Revue d'histoire économique et sociale*, vol. 12, no. 1 (1924): 53–118.

6 Monique Lucenet, *Les grandes pestes en france* (Paris: Aubier, 1985).

7 François Lebrun, "Les crises démographiques en France aux XVIIᵉ et XVIIIᵉ siècles," *Annales* 35, no. 2 (1980): 205–34; Marcel Lachiver, *Les années de misère: La famine au temps du Grand Roi* (Paris: Fayard, 1991).

8 Anne-Marie Brenot, "La peste soit des Huguenots: Étude d'une logique d'exécration au xviᵉ siècle," *Histoire, Économie et Société* 11, no. 4 (1992): 553–70.

9 On these medical and biological aspects, see Jean-Noël Biraben, *Les hommes et la peste en France et dans les pays européens et méditerranéens*, 2 vols. (Paris-La Haye: Mouton-EHESS, 1975).

10 Cynthia Bouton, "Les mouvements de subsistance et le problème de l'économie morale sous l'Ancien Régime et la Révolution française," *Annales historiques de la Révolution française*, no. 1 (2000): 71–100.

11 On the topic of what are thus referred to as the "classes creuses" (hollow classes), see Jean Meuvret, "Les crises de subsistances et la démographie de la France d'Ancien Régime," *Population*, no. 4 (1946): 583–90.

12 See Jacques Véron, "Les mathématiques de la population, de Lambert à Lotka," *Mathématiques et sciences humaines*, no. 159 (2002): 43–55.

13 See, in particular, Richard Cantillon, *Essai sur la nature du commerce en général* (1755; Paris: Institut national d'études démographiques, 1952).

14 Thomas Malthus, *An Essay on the Principle of Population* (1798; London: Penguin Classics, 2015).

15 Alfred Sauvy, "Le faux problème de la population mondiale," *Population*, no. 3 (1949): 450.

16 Sauvy, "Le faux problème de la population mondiale," 453.

17 On these problems in the contemporary context, see Steve Hinchliffe, John Allen, Stéphanie Lavau, Nick Bingham, and Simon Carter, "Biosecurity and the Typologies of Infected Life: From Borderlines to Borderlands," *Transactions of the Institute of British Geographers* 38, no. 4 (2012): 532–43.

18 Arthur Young, *Travels during The Years 1787, 1788, and 1789, Undertaken more particularly with a View of ascertaining the Cultivation, Wealth, Resources, and National Prosperity of the Kingdom of France* (London: Printed for W. Richardson, Royal-Exchange, 1794), quoted in Jean Bourdon, "Remarques sur les doctrines de la population depuis deux siècles," *Population*, no. 3 (1947): 483–84.

19 See Bronislaw Geremek, *Les fils de Caïn: L'image des pauvres et des vagabonds dans la littérature européenne du XVe au XVIIe siècle* (Paris: Flammarion, 1991), and *The Margins of Society in Late Medieval Paris*, trans. Jean Birrell (Cambridge: Cambridge University Press, 2006).

20 Antony Kitts, "Mendicité, vagabondage et contrôle social du Moyen Âge au XIXe siècle: État des recherches," *Revue d'histoire de la protection sociale* 1, no. 1 (2008): 37–56.

21 Readers should consult André Gueslin, *D'ailleurs et de nulle part: Mendiants, vagabonds, clochards, SDF en France depuis le Moyen Âge* (Paris: Fayard, 2013).

22 Marc Vigie, "Justice et criminalité au XVIIe siècle: Le cas de la peine des galères," *Histoire, économie et société* 4, no. 3 (1985): 345–68.

23 Henry Reynolds, *The Other Side of the Frontier* (Townsville: James Cook University of North Queensland, 1981). See also Dirk Moses, "The Birth of Ostland out of the Spirit of Colonialism: A Postcolonial Perspective on the Nazi Policy of Conquest and Extermination," *Patterns of Prejudice* 39, no. 2 (2005): 197–219. More generally, see Hannah Arendt, *The Origins of Totalitarianism* (1951; New York: Harcourt, Brace and World, 1966). On these debates, see also Benjamin Madley, "From Africa to Auschwitz: How German South West Africa Incubated Ideas and Methods Adopted and Developed by the Nazis in Eastern Europe," *European History Quarterly* 35, no. 3 (2005), https://doi .org/10.1177/0265691405054218.

24 Cited in Bourdon, "Remarques sur les doctrines," 487.

25 Gil S. Rubin, "Vladimir Jabotinsky and Population Transfers between Eastern Europe and Palestine," *Historical Journal* 62, no. 2 (2019): 495–517.

26 Robert René Kuczynski, *Living-Space and Population Problems* (London: Clarendon Press, 1939); Imre Ferenczi, "La population blanche dans les colonies," *Annales de géographie*, no. 267 (1938): 225–36, https://www.persee.fr/doc/geo _0003-4010_1938_num_47_267_11762.

27 Robert Rochefort, "L'Europe et ses populations excédentaires," *Politique étrangère*, no. 2 (1954): 143–56.

28 See United Nations, Department of Economic and Social Affairs, *World Population Prospects 2019*, https://www.un.org/development/desa/pd/news/world -population-prospects-2019-0.

29 Sauvy, "Le faux problème de la population mondiale," 452.

30 Elsa Dorlin, "Macron, les femmes et l'Afrique: Un discours de sélection sexuelle et de triage colonial," *Le Monde Afrique*, November 30, 2017. See also Françoise Vergès, *Le ventre des femmes: Capitalisme, racialisation, féminisme* (Paris: Albin Michel, 2017).

31 On these debates in the light of the southern African experience, see Giovanni Arrighi, "Labour Supplies in Historical Perspective: A Study of the Proletarianization of the African Peasantry in Rhodesia," *Journal of Development Studies* 6, no. 3 (1970): 197–234; Harold Wolpe, "Capitalism and Cheap Labour-Power in South Africa: From Segregation to Apartheid," *Economy and Society* 1, no. 4 (1972): 425–56; Martin Legassick, "South Africa: Capital Accumulation and Violence," *Economy and Society* 3, no. 3 (1974): 253–91.

32 Read Maurizzio Lazzarato, *La Fabrique de l'homme endetté* (Paris: Éditions Amsterdam, 2011).

33 I have drawn inspiration here from Michel Feher's reflections in his "La gauche et les siens: enjeux (3/3)," *AOC*, December 11, 2019, https://aoc.media/analyse /2019/12/10/la-gauche-et-les-siens-enjeux-3-3/.

34 Simon Batterbury and Frankline Anum Ndi, "Land-Grabbing in Africa," in *The Routledge Handbook of African Development*, ed. Tony Binns, Kenneth Lynch, and E. L. Nel (New York: Routledge, 2018), 573–82; Natacha Bruna, "Land of Plenty, Land of Misery: Synergetic Resource Grabbing in Mozambique," *Land* 8, no. 8 (2019), https://doi.org/10.3390/land8080113.

35 Igor Kopytoff, ed., *The African Frontier: The Reproduction of Traditional African Societies* (Bloomington: Indiana University Press, 1989); Fred Cooper, *Africa in the World: Capitalism, Empire, Nation-State* (Cambridge, MA: Harvard University Press, 2014).

36 Yves Stourdze, "Espace, circulation, pouvoir," *L'homme et la société*, nos. 29–30 (1973): 98.

37 Dina Krichker, "'They carry the border on their backs': Atypical Commerce and Bodies' Policing in Barrio Chino, Melilla," *Area*, June 27, 2019, https://doi .org/10.1111/area.12569; and Kathryn Cassidy, "'Where can I get free?' Everyday Bordering, Everyday Incarceration," *Transactions of the Institute of British Geographers* 44, no. 1 (2018), https://doi.org/10.1111/tran.12273.

38 R. N. Ghosh, "The Colonization Controversy: R. J. Wilmot-Horton and the Classical Economists," *Economica* 31, no. 124 (1964): 385–400; Olindo De Napoli, "Race and Empire: The Legitimation of Italian Colonialism in Juridical Thought," *Journal of Modern History* 85, no. 4 (2013): 801–32.

39 André Sanson, "De l'hybridité," *Bulletins de la Société d'anthropologie de Paris*, 2nd ser., vol. 3 (1868): 730.

40 On this topic, consult Benjamin H. Bratton, *Le stack: Plateformes, logiciels et souveraineté* (Grenoble: UGA Éditions, 2019).

41 Didier Fassin, *Punir: Une passion contemporaine* (Paris: Seuil, 2017).

42 See Amnesty International, "Union Européenne. Amnesty découvre que des équipements de torture illégaux sont en vente à Paris, " November 22, 2017,

https://www.amnesty.fr/presse/union-europenne-amnesty-dcouvre-que-des
-quipements.

43 Paul Vincent, "Guerre et population," *Population* 2, no. 1 (1947): 9–30.

Six Circulations

1 Julie Peteet, "Camps and Enclaves: Palestine in the Time of Closure," *Journal of Refugee Studies* 29, no 2 (2016): 208–28.

2 Alison Mountz, "The Enforcement Archipelago: Detention, Haunting, and Asylum on Islands," *Political Geography* 30, no. 3 (2011): 118–28, https://doi .org/10.1016/j.polgeo.2011.01.005.

3 Jenna M. Lloyd and Alison Mountz, *Boats, Borders, and Bases: Race, the Cold War, and the Rise of Migration Detention in the United States* (Oakland: University of California Press, 2018).

4 From this point of view, see Eyal Weizman and Fazal Sheikh, *The Conflict Shoreline: Colonization as Climate Change in the Negev Desert* (New York: Steidl and Cabinet Books, 2015).

5 On the topic of the perpetually temporary character of these modes of existence, consult Sandi Hilal and Alessandro Petti, *Permanent Temporariness* (Stockholm: Art and Theory Publishing, 2019). On the temporality of the checkpoint, see Helga Tawil-Souri, "Checkpoint Time," *Qui Parle* 26, no. 2 (2017): 384–422.

6 Abdourahme Nasser, "Spatial Collisions and Discordant Temporalities: Everyday Life Between Camp and Checkpoint," *International Journal of Urban and Regional Research* 35, no. 2 (2016): 453–61.

7 See Adi Ophir, Michal Givoni, and Sari Hanafi, *The Power of Inclusive Exclusion: Anatomy of Israeli Rule in the Occupied Palestinian Territories* (New York: Zone Books, 2009).

8 Ruben Andersson, "Profits and Predation in the Human Bioeconomy," *Public Culture* 30, no. 3 (2018): 413–39.

9 See Pauline Maillet, Alison Mountz, and Kira Williams, "Exclusion through *Imperio*: Entanglements of Law and Geography in the Waiting Zone, Excised Territory and Search and Rescue Region," *Social and Legal Studies* 27, no. 2 (2018), https://doi.org/10.1177/0964663917746487.

10 Ruben Andersson, "The New Frontiers of America," *Race and Class* 46, no. 3 (2005): 28–38.

11 Ruben Andersson, *Illegality, Inc.: Clandestine Migration and the Business of Bordering Europe* (Oakland: University of California Press, 2014).

12 Amade M'charek, Katharina Schramm, and David Skinner, "Topologies of Race: Doing Territory, Population and Identity in Europe," *Science, Technology, and Human Values*, vol. 39, no. 4 (2014): 468–87.

13 Nicholas De Genova, "Migrant Illegality and Deportability in Everyday Life," *Annual Review of Anthropology* 31 (2002): 419–47; David Lloyd and Patrick

Wolfe, "Settler Colonial Logics and the Neoliberal Regime," *Settler Colonial Studies* 6, no. 2 (2016): 109–18.

14 See, among others, the works of Amade M'charek, "'Dead-Bodies-at-the-Border': Distributed Evidence and Emerging Forensic Infrastructure for Identification," in *Bodies as Evidence: Security, Knowledge, and Power,* ed. Mark Maguire, Ursula Rao, and Nil Zurawski (Durham, NC: Duke University Press, 2018): 89–110. Read also Tamara Last et al., "Deaths at the Borders Database: Evidence of Deceased Migrants' Bodies Found along the Southern External Borders of the European Union," *Journal of Ethnic and Migration Studies* 43, no. 5 (2017): 693–712.

15 Read Alves Jaime Amparo, *The Anti-Black City: Police Terror and Black Urban Life in Brazil* (Minnesota: University of Minnesota Press, 2018).

16 Paul Gilroy, Tony Sandset, Sindre Bangstad, and Gard Ringen Høibjerg, "A Diagnosis of Contemporary Forms of Racism, Race and Nationalism: a Conversation with Professor Paul Gilroy," *Cultural Studies* 33, no. 2 (2019): 173–97.

17 See Keller Easterling, *Extrastatecraft: The Power of Infrastructure Space* (London: Verso, 2014).

18 Bruno Latour and Camille Riquier, "Une terre sans peuple, des peuples sans Terre," *Esprit,* no. 1–2 (2018): 145–52. See also Jakob Valentin Stein Pedersen, Bruno Latour, and Nikolaj Schultz, "A Conversation with Bruno Latour and Nikolaj Schultz: Reassembling the Geo-Social," *Theory, Culture and Society* 36, nos. 7–8 (2019), https://doi.org/10.1177/0263276419867468.

19 Céline Bergeron, "Les rapports mobilité/immobilité dans le cas des situations résidentielles spécifiques: Retours et perspectives de recherche," *e-Migrinter* 11 (2003): 28–35, https://doi.org/10.4000/e-migrinter.249.

20 On the topic of multilocality and what the geographers call "polytopic dwelling" see the special issue of *Espaces et Sociétés* 120–121, nos. 2–3 (2005). See also Jean-Pierre Lévy and Françoise Dureau, eds., *L'accès à la ville: Les mobilités spatiales en questions* (Paris: L'Harmattan, 2002); and Mathis Stock, "L'habiter comme pratique des lieux géographiques," *EspacesTemps.net,* December 18, 2004, http://espacestemps.net/document1138.html.

21 See Hélène Guetat-Bernard, "Mobilités spatiales, organisation familiale et ruralités des Suds: un regard par les rapports de genre," *Géocarrefour* 88, no. 2 (2013): 91–95, https://doi.org/10.4000/geocarrefour.9070.

22 In this new context, the category of "undesirables" can hardly be limited to refugees seeking asylum. See Michel Agier, *Gérer les indésirables: Des camps de réfugiés au gouvernement humanitaire* (Paris: Flammarion, 2008); or further still, Reece Jones, *Violent Borders: Refugees and the Right to Move* (London: Verso, 2016).

23 See Michael Marder, "Being Dumped," *Environmental Humanities* 11, no. 1 (2019): 180–93, https://doi.org/10.1215/22011919-7349488; Brenda Chalfin, "'Wastelandia': Infrastructure and the Commonwealth of Waste in Urban Ghana," *Ethnos* 87, no. 4 (2017): 648–71.

24 On this subject, see the works of William Walters, "Migration, Vehicles, and Politics: Three Theses on Viapolitics," *European Journal of Social Theory* 18, no. 4 (2014), https://doi.org/10.1177/1368431014554859. See also Martina Tazzioli, "Spy, Track and Archive: The Temporality of Visibility in Eurosur and Jora," *Security Dialogue* 49, no. 4 (2018), https://doi.org/10.1177/0967010618769812.

25 For a parallel approach, see Gilbert Caluya, "Intimate Borders: Refugee Im/mobility in Australia's Border Security Regime," *Cultural Studies* 33, no. 6 (2019): 964–88.

26 See Surplus People Project, *Forced Removals in South Africa*, vol. 1 (Cape Town: Surplus People Project, 1983). See also Hilton Judin, *Blank: Architecture, Apartheid and After* (Rotterdam: NAi, 1988).

27 For a case that is seemingly rather removed, but driven by similar dynamics, see Isabelle Ohayon, "Formes et usages du territoire à la période coloniale: la sédentarisation des Kazakhs," *Cahiers d'Asie centrale*, no. 23 (2014), https://journals.openedition.org/asiecentrale/3073.

28 On this topic, see Frédéric Sandron, "L'immobilité forcée: La sédentarisation des nomades dans le Sud tunisien," *Autrepart*, no. 5 (1998): 63–77.

29 Hedi Timoumi, "La colonisation française et la sédentarisation des semi-nomades des steppes tunisiennes (Cherahil, 1905–1925)," *Cahiers de la Méditerranée*, no. 6 (1973): 95–112.

30 The following section takes up part of the text from Achille Mbembe, "Purger l'Afrique du désir d'Europe," *Le Débat*, no. 205 (2019): 100–107, https://www.cairn.info/revue-le-debat-2019-3-page-100.htm.

31 United Nations, Department of Economic and Social Affairs, Population Division, *World Population Prospects: The 2017 Revision*, https://www.un.org/en/desa/world-population-prospects-2017-revision; Marie-Laurence Flahaux and Hein De Haas, "African Migration: Trends, Patterns, Drivers," *Comparative Migration Studies* 4, no. 1 (2016), https://doi.org/10.1186/s40878-015-0015-6; Fabrizio Natale, Silvia Migali, and Rainer Münz, *Many More to Come? Migration From and within Africa* (Brussels: Joint Research Centre, European Commission, 2018).

32 The details are to be found in Peer Schouten et al., *"Tout ce qui bouge sera taxé": l'économie politique des barrières routières au Nord et Sud-Kivu* (Anvers/Copenhagen: International Peace Information Service/Danish Institute for International Studies, December 2017), https://ipisresearch.be/wp-content/uploads/2017/12/1711-DRC-roadblocks-French.pdf.

33 See H. Laurens Van der Laan, "Modern Inland Transport and the European Trading Firms in Colonial West Africa," *Cahiers d'études africaines*, no. 84 (1981): 547–75.

34 See Roland Poutier, "Le panier et la locomotive: À propos des transports terrestres en Afrique centrale," *Travaux de l'Institut de géographie de Reims*, nos. 83–84 (1993): 41–61.

35 See Peer Schouten and Soleil-Perfect Kalessopo, *The Politics of Pillage: The Political Economy of Roadblocks in the Central African Republic* (Anvers/Bangui: International Peace Information Service/Danish Institute for International Studies, November 2017), https://pure.diis.dk/ws/files/1261246/1711_CAR _roadblocks_English.pdf.

36 Hélène Blaszkiewicz, "La mise en politique des circulations commerciales transfrontalières en Zambie: Infrastructures et moment néolibéral," *Géocarrefour* 91, no. 3 (2017), https://doi.org/10.4000/geocarrefour.10342.

37 Hannah Appel, "Offshore Work: Oil, Modularity, and the How of Capitalism in Equatorial Guinea," *American Ethnologist*, vol. 39, no. 4 (2012): 692–709.

38 Denis Retaillé, "L'espace nomade," *Géocarrefour* 73, no. 1 (1998): 72.

39 Retaillé, "L'espace nomade," 74.

40 Carolina Kobelinsky, "Exister au risque de disparaître: Récits sur la mort pendant la traversée vers l'Europe," *Revue européenne des migrations internationales* 33, nos. 2–3 (2017): 115–31.

41 Charles Heller and Antoine Pécoud, "Compter les morts aux frontières: Des contre-statistiques de la société civile à la récupération (inter)gouvernementale," *Revue européenne des migrations internationales* 33, nos. 2–3 (2017): 63–90.

42 Frédérique Fogel, *Parenté sans papiers* (La Roche-sur-Yon: Dépaysage, 2019).

43 Isabelle Delpla, "Vivre au pays vide?," *Critique*, nos. 860–861 (2019): 133, https://www.cairn.info/revue-critique-2019-1-page-123.htm.

44 See Emanuele Coccia, "Gaïa ou l'anti-Léviathan," *Critique*, nos. 860–861 (2019): 32–43, https://www.cairn.info/revue-critique-2019-1-page-32.htm.

Seven **The Community of Captives**

1 In the following I have taken elements from my acceptance speech for the Ernst Bloch Prize, published under the title "Pour un droit universel à l'hospitalité," AOC, November 16, 2018, as well as from an article titled "Étrange époque," AOC, September 4, 2019.

2 Ernst Bloch, *The Principle of Hope*, trans. Neville Plaice, Stephen Plaice, and Paul Knight (Cambridge, MA: MIT Press), 443 (translation modified—SC).

3 Bloch, *Principle of Hope*, 3.

4 Bloch, *Principle of Hope*, 199.

5 Bloch, *Principle of Hope*, 445 (translation modified—SC).

6 Bloch, *Principle of Hope*, 445–46 (translation modified—SC).

7 The texts that make up Edmund Husserl's *The Crisis of European Sciences and Transcendental Phenomenology*, published posthumously in 1954, were written in 1935–36; among them is a talk called "Philosophy and the Crisis of European Humanity."

8 Sigmund Freud, *Civilization and Its Discontents* (New York: W. W. Norton, 2010).

9 Bloch, *Principle of Hope*, 284.

10 Bloch, *Principle of Hope*, 441.

11   Ernst Bloch, *Heritage of Our Times*, trans. Neville Plaice and Stephen Plaice (Los Angeles: University of California Press, 1991).

12   Hicham-Stéphane Afeissa, *La fin du monde et de l'humanité: Essai de généalogie du discours écologique* (Paris: Presses Universitaires de France, 2014).

13   Bloch, *Principle of Hope*, 522.

14   Shohana Zuboff, *The Age of Surveillance Capitalism: The Fight for a Human Future at the New Frontier of Capitalism* (Cambridge, MA: Harvard University Press, 2019); Jean Comaroff and John L. Comaroff, eds., *Millennial Capitalism and the Culture of Neoliberalism* (Durham, NC: Duke University Press, 2001).

15   Walter Benjamin, "Capitalism as Religion," in *Toward a Critique of Violence*, edited by Peter Fenves and Julia Ng (Stanford, CA: Stanford University Press, 2021), 80–82.

16   Maurizio Lazzarato, *Le capital déteste tout le monde: Fascisme ou révolution* (Paris: Éditions Amsterdam, 2019).

17   Michel-Rolph Trouillot, *Silencing the Past: Power and the Production of History* (Boston: Beacon Press, 1995).

18   Éric Alliez and Maurizio Lazzarato, *Guerres et capital* (Paris: Éditions Amsterdam, 2016).

19   Franz Rosenzweig, *The Star of Redemption*, trans. Barbara E. Galli (Madison: University of Wisconsin Press, 2005), 418.

20   Achille Mbembe, *Necropolitics*, trans. Steven Corcoran (Durham, NC: Duke University Press, 2019).

21   Rosenzweig, *The Star of Redemption*, 418.

22   Elsa Dorlin, *Se défendre: Une philosophie de la violence* (Paris: Zones, 2017).

23   Achille Mbembe, *On the Postcolony* (Berkeley: University of California Press, 2001).

24   Labou Tansi, *L'état honteux* (Paris: Seuil, 1981).

25   Yambo Ouologuem, *Le devoir de violence* (Paris: Seuil, 1968).

26   Labou Tansi, *La vie et demie* (Paris: Seuil, 1979).

27   Elias Canetti, *Masse et puissance* (Paris: Gallimard, 1966), esp. 215–26.

Eight   Potential Humanity and Politics of the Living

1   By African "objects," or "artifacts," the idea supposed is that of a general set, or again an entire population of "things" or material productions, whether these have an aesthetic function or name an investment of the same kind. On these discussions in the European context, see Jean-Marie Schaeffer, "Objets esthétiques?," *L'Homme: Revue française d'anthropologie*, no. 170 (2004): 25–45, https://doi.org/10.4000/lhomme.24782.

2   Engelbert Mveng, *L'art et l'artisanat africains* (Yaoundé: Éditions CLE, 1980); Léopold Sédar Senghor, "Standards critiques de l'art africain," *African Arts* 1, no. 1 (1967): 6–9, 52; Aimé Césaire, "Discours prononcé à Dakar le 6 avril 1966," *Gradhiva*, no. 10 (2009): 208–15, https://doi.org/10.4000/gradhiva.1604.

3   D. Lopes and F. Pigafetta, *Description du royaume de Congo et des contrées environnantes*, trans. Willy Bal (Louvain: Nauwelaerts, 1965), 81–82; J. Cuvelier, *L'ancien royaume du Congo: Fondation, découverte et première évangélisation de l'ancien royaume du Congo* (Bruges: Desclée De Brouwer, 1946); and O. Dapper, "Description de l'Afrique," in *Objets interdits*, ed. A. Van Dantzig (Paris: Fondation Dapper, 1989), 89–367. On Dahomey in the seventeenth century, see Jean Bonfils, "La mission catholique en République populaire du Benin aux XVIIe et XVIIIe siècles," *Nouvelle revue de sciences missionnaires* (1986): 161–74.

4   In the register of exceptions, read for example Martine Balard, "Les combats du père Aupiais (1877–1945), missionnaire et ethnographe du Dahomey pour la reconnaissance africaine," *Histoire et Missions Chrétiennes* 2, no. 2 (2007): 74–93.

5   See Robert Muchembled, *Une histoire du diable: XIIe–XXe siècle* (Paris: Points, 2002).

6   See "Le diable en procès: Démonologie et sorcellerie à la fin du Moyen-Âge," special issue, *Medievales*, no. 44 (2003).

7   Alain Boureau, *Satan hérétique: Naissance de la démonologie dans l'Occident médiéval (1280–1330)* (Paris: Odile Jacob, 2004).

8   Guy Bechtel, *La sorcière et l'Occident: La destruction de la sorcellerie en Europe des origines aux grands buchers* (Paris: Plon, 1997).

9   Michael McCabe, "L'évolution de la théologie de la mission dans la Société des Missions Africaines de Marion Bresillac à nos jours," *Histoire et Missions Chrétiennes*, 2, no. 2 (2007): 1–22, https://www.cairn.info/revue-histoire-monde-et-cultures-religieuses1-2007-2-page-119.htm.

10 By way of example, see Kevin Carroll, *Yoruba Religious Carving: Pagan and Christian Sculpture in Nigeria and Dahomey* (London: Geoffrey Chapman, 1967).

11 On these debates, see Lucien Lévy-Bruhl's books *Primitive Mentality* (1922; Los Angeles: HardPress Publishing, 2013); *How Natives Think*, trans. Lilian A. Claire (1927; London: Routledge, 2019); and *The 'Soul' of the Primitive* (1928; London: Routledge, 2016). On debates at the time, see O. Leroy, *La raison primitive: Essai de réfutation de la théorie du prélogisme* (Paris: Guethner, 1927); and Raoul Allier, *Les non-civilisés et nous: différence irréductible ou identité foncière* (Paris: Payot, 1927).

12 Jan Assmann, *Le monothéisme et le langage de la violence: Les débuts bibliques de la religion radicale* (Paris: Bayard, 2018), 75.

13 Cécile Fromont, *The Art of Conversion: Christian Visual Culture in the Kingdom of Kongo* (Chapel Hill: University of North Carolina Press, 2017).

14 On this topic, see Jean Comaroff and John Comaroff, *Of Revelation and Revolution*, vol. 1 (Chicago: University of Chicago Press, 1991); and, by the same authors, *The Dialectics of Modernity on a South African Frontier*, vol. 2 (Chicago: University of Chicago Press, 1997). See also Achille Mbembe, *Afriques indociles: Christianisme, pouvoir et état en société postcoloniale* (Paris: Karthala, 1988).

15 J. E. Bouche, "La religion des Nègres Africains, en particulier des Djedjis et des Nagos's," *Le Contemporain* 24 (1874): 857–75.

16 B. Salvaing, *Les missionnaires à la rencontre de l'Afrique au XIXe siècle: Cote des esclaves et pays Yoruba, 1840–1891* (Paris: L'Harmattan, 1995), 261–99.

17 Paule Brasseur, "Les missionnaires catholiques à la côte d'Afrique pendant la deuxième moitié du XIXe siècle," *Mélanges d'Ecole française de Rome, Italie et Méditerranée* 109, no. 2 (1997): 723–45, https://www.persee.fr/doc/mefr_1123 -9891_1997_num_109_2_4511.

18 Laurick Zerbini, "La construction du discours patrimonial: Les musées missionnaires à Lyon (1860–1960)," *Outre-Mers* 95, nos. 356–357 (2007): 125–38, https://www.persee.fr/doc/outre_1631-0438_2007_num_94_356_4287.

19 Pedro Descoqs, "Métaphysique et raison primitive," *Archives de philosophie* 5, no. 3 (1928): 127–65.

20 See Laurick Zerbini's chapters "Les collections africaines des Oeuvres Pontificales: L'objet africain sous le prisme du missionnaire catholique," in *Objets des terres lointaines*, ed. Essertel Yannick (Milan: Silvana Editoriale Spa, 2011), 31–51; and "L'exposition vaticane de 1925: Affirmation de la politique missionnaire de Pie XI," in *Le gouvernement pontifical sous Pie XI. Pratiques romaines et gestion de l'universel (1922–1939)*, ed. Laura Pettinaroli (Rome: Collection EFR, 2013), 649–73.

21 Cited in Michel Bonemaison, "Le Musée Africain de Lyon d'hier à aujourd'hui," *Histoire et Missions Chrétiennes* 2, no. 2 (2007): 2.

22 For a notorious case, consult Pierre Duviols, *La lutte contre les religions autochtones dans le Perou colonial: L'extirpation de l'idolatrie entre 1532 et 1660* (Toulouse: Presses Universitaires du Mirail, 2008); and Fabien Eboussi Boulaga, *Christianisme sans fétiches: Révélation et domination* (Paris: Présence africaine, 1981).

23 See, for example, José Sarzi Amade, "Trois missionnaires capucins dans le Royaume de Congo de la fin du XVIIe siècle: Cavazzi, Merolla et Zucchelli; Force et prose dans les récits de spectacles punitifs et de châtiments exemplaires," *Veritas* 139 (2018): 137–60.

24 Kant expounds on this idea in his "Idea for a Universal History with a Cosmopolitan Aim." See James Schmidt and Amélie Oksenberg Rorty, eds., *Kant's "Idea for a Universal History with a Cosmopolitan Aim": A Critical Guide* (Cambridge: Cambridge University Press, 2009).

25 G. W. Hegel's *Lectures on the Philosophy of History*, trans. Ruben Alvarado (Aalten: WordBridge Publishing, 2013); and *Philosophy of Right*, trans. S. W. Dyde (Mineola, NY: Dover Philosophical Classics, 2005).

26 Ernst Cassirer, *The Myth of the State* (New Haven, CT: Yale University Press, 2009).

27 Achille Mbembe, *Critique of Black Reason*, trans. Laurent Dubois (Durham, NC: Duke University Press, 2017).

28 Cassirer, *The Myth of the State*, 273.

29 Hegel, *Philosophy of Right*, 343.

30 Eric Voegelin, *Race and State*, trans. Ruth Hein (Colombia: University of Missouri Press, 1997).

31 Catherine Coquery-Vidrovitch, "La fête des coutumes au Dahomey: Historique et essai d'interprétation," *Annales*, no. 4 (1964): 696–716.

32 Georges Bataille, *Theory of Religion*, trans. Robert Hurley (New York: Zone Books, 1989), 52–54.

33 Sigmund Freud, *On Sexuality: Three Essays on the Theory of Sexuality and Other Works*, trans. James Strachey (London: Penguin, 1991).

34 Carl Einstein, *Negerplastik* (Leipzig: Verlag der Weissen Bucher, 1915). In this work, Einstein endeavors to study the formal qualities of "Black objects," whereas in his book *Afrikanische Plastik* (Berlin: E. Wasmuth, 1921), he is more interested in their functions and meaning within their societies of origin.

35 See Coline Bidault, "La présentation des objets africains dans documents (1929/1930), magazine illustre," *Les cahiers de l'Ecole du Louvre* 3, no. 3 (2013): 5–13.

36 André Bréton, *L'art magique* (Paris: Club français du livre, 1957).

37 Here I have reused elements of an article originally published as "À propos de la restitution des artefacts africains conservés dans les musées d'Occident," *AOC*, October 5, 2018, https://aoc.media/analyse/2018/10/05/a-propos-de-restitution-artefacts-africains-conserves-musees-doccident/.

38 I draw here in part on Carlo Severi's analysis in his *L'objet-personne: Une anthropologie de la croyance visuelle* (Paris: Editions de la Rue d'Ulm, 2017), 49–53.

39 Aimé Césaire, *Discourse on Colonialism*, trans. Joan Pinkham (1952; New York: Monthly Review Press, 2000).

40 "Those who invented neither gunpowder nor compass/those who could not ever tame steam or electricity/those who have not explored either seas or sky/but without whom the earth would not be the earth," from Aimé Césaire, *Journal of a Homecoming/Cahier d'un retour au pays natal*, trans. N. Gregson Davis (1939; Durham, NC: Duke University Press, 2017), 47.

41 By way of illustration, see *Le rapport Brazza: Mission d'enquête du Congo: rapport et documents (1905–1907)* (Neuvy-en-Champagne: Le passager clandestin, 2014).

42 Lotte Arndt, "Vestiges of Oblivion: Sammy Baloji's Works on Skulls in European Museum Collections," Darkmatter: In the Ruins of Imperial Culture, 2013, https://web.archive.org/web/20210122133433/http://www.darkmatter101.org/site/2013/11/18/vestiges-of-oblivion-sammy-baloji%E2%80%99s-works-on-skulls-in-european-museum-collections/.

43 See Julien Bondaz's articles "L'ethnograhie comme chasse: Michel leiris et le animaux de la mission Dakar-Djibouti," *Gradhiva* 13 (2011): 162–81, https://doi.org/10.4000/gradhiva.2069; and "L'ethnographie parasitée? Anthropologie et enthomologie en Afrique de l'Ouest (1928–1960)," *L'Homme: Revue française d'anthropologie*, no. 206 (2013): 121–50. See also Nancy J. Jacobs, "The Intimate

Politics of Ornithology in Colonial Africa," *Comparative Studies in Society and History* 48, no. 3 (2006): 564–603.

44 John M. MacKenzie, *The Empire of Nature: Hunting, Conservation and British Imperialism* (Manchester, UK: Manchester University Press, 1988).

45 See Nelia Dias, "L'Afrique naturalisée," *Cahiers d'études africaines* 39, nos. 155–156 (1999): 590.

46 Allen F. Roberts, *A Dance of Assassins: Performing Early Colonial Hegemony in the Congo* (Bloomington: Indiana University Press, 1998); Ricardo Roque, *Headhunting and Colonialism: Anthropology and the Circulation of Human Skulls in the Portuguese Empire, 1870–1930* (Cambridge: Cambridge University Press, 2011); and Andrew Zimmerman, *Anthropology and Antihumanism in Imperial Germany* (Chicago: University of Chicago Press, 2001).

47 Consult Julien Bondaz, "Entrer en collection: Pour une ethnographie des gestes et des techniques de collecte," *Les cahiers de l'Ecole du Louvre* 4, no. 4 (2014), https://doi.org/10.4000/cel.481.

48 Dominique Zahan, *La graine et la viande: Mythologie dogon* (Paris: Présence africaine, 1969).

49 Severi, *L'objet-personne*, 267.

50 Isabelle Kalinowski, "Les trois moments de Carl Einstein," *Gradhiva* 14 (2011): 107, https://doi.org/10.4000/gradhiva.2277.

51 Amos Tutuola, *My Life in the Bush of Ghosts* (London: Faber and Faber, 2014).

52 On this topic see Pierre Bonnafé's "Une force, un objet, un champ: Le *buti* des Kukuya au Congo," *Systèmes de pensée en Afrique noire*, no. 8 (1987): 25–67, https://doi.org/10.4000/span.1028; "Une grande fête de la vie et de la mort: Le *miyali* cérémonie funéraire d'un seigneur du Kukuya," *L'Homme* 13, nos. 1–2 (1973): 97–166, https://www.persee.fr/doc/hom_0439-4216_1973_num_13_1_367331; and *Nzo Lipfu, le lignage de la mort* (Paris: PSE, 1978).

53 Not only the making but also the conservation and restoration of objects required a host of technical knowledge about the botanical, vegetal, mineral, and organic worlds. Utilizing of wood, for example, demanded a minimum of knowledge about its components, notably about what made it moisture- and weather-resistant. Similarly for animal oils and fats, and the diverse pigments and elements such as fire, the function of which was to make objects imputrescible. On this subject, see Pol Pierre Gossiaux, "Conserver, restaurer: Écrire le temps en Afrique," *CeROArt: Conservation, exposition, restauration d'Objets d'art* 1 (2007), https://doi.org/10.4000/ceroart.253.

54 For Johannes Fabian, it is precisely this practice of "decontextualization" that is specific to ethnographic collection. See Johannes Fabian, "On Recognizing Things: The 'Ethnic Artefact' and the 'Ethnographic Object,'" *L'Homme: Revue française d'anthropologie*, no. 170 (2004): 47 60.

55 See Gaetano Speranza, "Sculpture africaine. Blessures et altérité," *CeROArt: Conservation, exposition, restauration d'Objets d'art* 2 (2008).

56 See Gossiaux, "Conserver, restaurer."

57 Kwame Anthony Appiah, "Comprendre les réparations: Réflexion prélimi-naire," *Cahiers d'études africaines* 1, nos. 173–174 (2004): 25–40.

58 Placide Tempels, *Bantu Philosophy*, trans. Colin King (Paris: Présence africaine, HBC, 1969), 80.

59 Tempels, *Bantu Philosophy*, 37.

Conclusion

1 René Depestre, *Minerai noir* (Paris: Présence africaine, 1956), 9.

INDEX